Becoming a Blessed Church

Becoming a Blessed Church

Forming a Church of Spiritual Purpose, Presence, and Power

N. Graham Standish

THE
ALBAN
INSTITUTE

Herndon, Virginia
www.alban.org

The Alban Institute
2121 Cooperative Way, Suite 100
Herndon, VA 20171-5370
www.alban.org

Cover design: Adele Robey, Phoenix Graphics

Library of Congress Cataloging-in-Publication Data

Standish, N. Graham, 1959-
  Becoming the blessed church : forming a church of spiritual purpose, presence, and power / N. Graham Standish.
      p. cm.
  Includes bibliographical references.
  ISBN 1-56699-312-1
  1. Church renewal. 2. Christian leadership. I. Title.

  BV600.3.S735 2005
  262'.001'7--dc22

                                              2004022826

12   11   10   09   08   VG   6   7   8   9   10

To the members of Calvin Presbyterian Church.
You have been such a blessing to me.

Contents

Foreword

I sat in the hospital waiting room with just one other person, a fellow waiting for a doctor to return with a prescription. Someone walking by said hello to the man, and he replied, "Have a blessed day." A short time later, I said to him, "Now that's a great phrase, 'Have a blessed day,' because it says you are trusting God to do the blessing." The man turned to me and beamed. "That's right!" he said and went on to describe the power of his experience of Christ, explaining, "Blessed means 'He will make you rise!'" After the doctor brought his prescription, this gracious man stepped into a nearby elevator, turned around, and said to me, "Have a blessed day." I waved and said, "He will make you rise!" and the man was gone. I thought, "Wow! What a marvelous way to think about being blessed. If God is going to make you rise, then God is going to bring life and love and power and presence into your life and into your church. That's blessedness!"

Years ago George Odiorne wrote about the "activity trap" in which we can get so enmeshed that we lose sight of why we are doing what we are doing. He observed that the activities become false gods or ends in themselves. In the church's own "activity trap" of people and programs, we can easily lose sight of our Lord. We lose touch with what it means to experience God's love, presence, and power. It is easy to be so consumed by what we are doing *for* God that we miss the experience of being *with* God, the experience of being blessed. Such is a common experience in mainline congregations.

With the concept of the blessed church, Graham Standish brings us back to an understanding of what it means to be the church that experiences God as well as serves God. A blessed church, Graham says, "is a glimpse of what a church can be. It is a vision, a glimpse of a healthy church uniquely grounded in a relationship with God that allows blessings to flow through it." Plainly put, the people of a blessed church experience *God* rather than merely experiencing church. They may talk about God and serve God, yet their overarching desire is actually to know and experience God in some personal and direct way.

We are experiencing a surge in thought, research, reflection, and publication about the health, dynamics, and effectiveness of the transformational congregation. Yet among the principles and patterns being offered to us, one overarching issue dominates all thinking about the transformational church. A church is alive *not* because its organization is busy. Churches are alive because God is alive. Blessed churches are in immediate touch with the living God.

We long for our congregations to pulse with life and energy, to hope that our most significant experiences of God's presence and work among us are yet to come. Most of us know intuitively that our congregations' present experience of God is not "all there is." Because it is so easy for us to be caught in the trap of "present demand," serving the program of the church while losing sight of our original purpose, we need a guide into the experience of the blessed church. Graham Standish clearly identifies the factors that have led many congregations into a lifeless functionalism and the God-given means by which our congregations may become "blessed" churches. As he says, "Becoming a blessed church means becoming awake, aware, and alive to the fact that Christ is in our midst, giving us guidance, life, and love." May God bless your journey as you become the blessed church. May God make you rise!

E. Stanley Ott
Senior Pastor
Pleasant Hills Community Presbyterian Church
Pittsburgh, Pennsylvania

Acknowledgments

———————

When my wife, Diane, and I were getting married, we hired a bagpiper for the ceremony. We've forgotten what his full name was, but in our minds he is fondly remembered as "Bagpiper Bob." We remember Bagpiper Bob not only for how well he played at our wedding, but also for his vibrant faith. When meeting him, you knew immediately that God was alive in him. He had several wonderful phrases about faith that he would weave into his conversations, and each one was a pearl of wisdom. During one conversation, he said something that I have never forgotten and that I keep at the center of my life and ministry, especially when I am down, frustrated, or confused. He said, "You know, God never sets you up to fail." I don't remember why he said that, but it was such a positive statement about God and faith that I decided then and there to hold on to that belief and never let it go.

Bagpiper Bob was right. I've discovered throughout my ministry not only that God never sets us up to fail, but also that if we are faltering and have faith, God sends all sorts of people into our lives to pick us up and make sure we don't fail. That doesn't mean that we won't go through difficult times. That God doesn't set us up to fail doesn't mean that we won't suffer, struggle, falter, or fall. It simply means that if we have faith and trust in God, God will find a way to help us. Our part is to have faith. This book is a testament to how God helps us. I've discovered through experience that when we have faith, God sets us up to receive blessings. Here I want to acknowledge such blessings and express my gratitude. I thank the following people through whom God has blessed me.

First, I thank God for allowing me the opportunity to study with Adrian van Kaam and the faculty at Duquesne University's Institute of Formative Spirituality. Even though the program no longer exists, it has blessed many of us who studied there over its 30-year history. Through my studies with van Kaam, I was introduced to a way of seeing life, faith, theology, and the church through more spiritual and mystical eyes. Much of what I write in this book has been influenced by insights I gained through my studies in spirituality. Studying with van Kaam opened me to the possibility that God can be experienced in the church if we focus on creating communities of communion rather than speculation—what a novel concept!

I thank the directors of the doctor of ministry and certificate in spirituality programs at Pittsburgh Theological Seminary, Charles Hambrick-Stowe, Jim Davison, and Mary Lee Talbot, who have allowed me to teach classes on congregational spirituality and spiritual leadership—classes that allowed me to work out and articulate the ideas that would eventually form this book. My gratitude goes also to the members of the Vineyard Guild, and especially the Vineyard Guild board of directors and my small-group cluster, who have been such a support for me. The Vineyard Guild is an organization devoted to nurturing spiritual leadership, and its members have been wonderful to me in their willingness to let me blather on about my ideas that appear in this book. They have contributed much to this book just by offering their own ideas and experiences, some of which are reflected in the stories in these pages. In addition, I thank the researchers of the Project on Congregations of Intentional Practice, Diana Butler Bass and Joseph Stewart-Sicking, who initially made the folks at Alban Institute aware of me and my interest in the subject of congregational spirituality.

I am greatly appreciative to Richard Bass and the Alban Institute for their willingness to publish this book. I am especially grateful to my project editor, Beth Gaede. She has been a true blessing. It is not often that a writer has a project editor who will go overboard to make a book better. Beth has done that. She has complimented me when my ego was fragile, challenged me when my theology and articulation were sloppy, and redirected me when I was stuck in the thickets. The editorial work on this book was a real joy. And in this I include the work I have done with my copy editor, Jean Caffey Lyles. Again, she has been wonderful in helping me articulate my thoughts more clearly. Such a blessing.

I also want to thank the staff at the Starbucks coffee shop in Cranberry Township, Pennsylvania, where I spent almost every day of a monthlong sabbatical writing this book in July 2003. I managed to write five chapters sitting at my little table, and the staff was wonderful in supplying me with endless cups of tea.

As I stated in my dedication, I am deeply indebted to the members of Calvin Presbyterian Church in Zelienople, Pennsylvania, which I serve as pastor. Recently a respected pastor I know said something I took to heart: "Graham, only one in 10 pastors ever serves in a church he or she loves. If you are in one, don't ever leave unless God hits you with a thunderbolt and says in a booming voice, 'Go forth!'" I am fortunate to be in a place I love. I cannot tell you enough how much I appreciate the members of this church because of their love, their faith, and their willingness to indulge me in all my quirks.

I want to thank my wife, Diane, and my twin daughters, Shea and Erin, for their support and love. Diane has served as the primary editor for all my books since my doctoral dissertation, and I am thankful that she has always been willing to do so. Imagine not only having to hear your husband talk all the time and spout his strange ideas, but then being willing to edit hundreds of pages of material and to read these same ideas over and over again. This willingness says a lot about Diane's love and how fortunate I am to be married to her.

Finally, I want to thank you for letting me share my ideas and experiences with you. You also are a blessing, and I hope that you will hear God's voice and sense God's presence in these pages. To prepare you as you embark on this journey, I leave you with a prayer that has been my daily prayer, the Vineyard Guild Prayer:

> Holy God, Beloved Trinity, let me always be rooted in you so that I may live in you and you in me. Bless me so that your grace may flow through me, allowing me to bear your fruit to a hungry and helpless world. As I wander, prune me of all that inhibits your growth in me. Let me do nothing apart from you so that your joy may be complete in me. In Christ's name I pray. *Amen.*

PART I

BECOMING A BLESSED CHURCH

For as long as I can remember, I have struggled with church. I think it has been one of God's holy jokes to call me to be the pastor of a church, to spend my life in the very place that I had struggled with for so long. Most of my earliest memories of church are not particularly wonderful. I remember sitting in church and being told constantly to "Quit fidgeting," "Don't sniffle," and "Be quiet." I remember being given a weekly assignment, as part of my confirmation class, to listen to the sermon and outline what it said, and then trying to cheat from my cousin's notes because I had no idea what the preacher was saying. I knew that the church was supposed to be a place of God, but I had a hard time sensing God there. Instead of being confirmed in the church, I walked away after confirmation class because I had become disillusioned with it. Looking back 25 years later, and especially on my 17-year career as a pastor, there have been times when I jokingly concluded that my being called into ministry was simply God's holy joke on me. You see, I am now the one who invokes fidgeting in young children and bewilderment in teens. Why would God call that fidgety, discontent child to become a pastor?

Regardless of how I now feel about the church, much about the Christian church turned me off as a teen. I was a turned-off teen in a tuned-out culture. The churches of my youth seemed devoid of God, and living in a culture that increasingly denigrated Christian religion helped me to tune out the church. As a youngster and a teenager, I had a tremendous spiritual hunger and a deep thirst for God that wasn't satisfied in the church of my youth. I sat through worship service after worship service, feeling little of God's presence. I don't want to give the impression that the church actually *was* devoid of God, only that I rarely sensed God's presence. There is a big difference between the two.

I was a cynical teenager in a generation of baby boomers who consistently denigrated the church at every opportunity. How was I supposed to encounter God in church when the pop icons of the early and middle 1970s were so critical of the church?

Second, I thought the church was a place of hypocrites. I couldn't get beyond the fact that I saw so many adults listening, singing, and praying on Sunday morning, but doing and saying nasty things the rest of the week. Was there anyone who didn't look like a "saint" on Sunday and act like a "sinner" on the other days? Of course there were many, but I didn't notice them. I was too focused on the "sinners" to notice the "saints."

A new pastor came to the church when I was 15, one who offered a glimmer of God's presence, but by then I was too cynical and jaded to profit from his ministry. So I walked away from the church with the intention never to return. I sought God elsewhere. Psychology became my religion. I went to college and studied to be a counselor. I developed a belief that if psychologists ran the world, the world would become a happy place. Working as a counselor in a psychiatric hospital for several years cured me of that naïve belief. The hospital was, in my experience, the most unhealthy place I had ever been, and not because of the patients. Those of us on staff didn't practice what we preached. We were unhealthy people trying to help other unhealthy people, and it didn't always work.

At this time I began to dabble in Eastern and New Age thought. I was practicing what I now call "ABC" spirituality—anything but Christianity. I read books about the psychic Edgar Cayce. I read books by a New Age guru who said he was a Tibetan lama. I read books by psychologists turned spiritual guides. And for a time all of them fed me, but it soon became apparent that they weren't offering truly nourishing food. None of them led me to encounter God. That didn't happen until I had a mystifying experience that opened me to the possibility of Christ.

The experience came through a patient I was counseling who had a mystical experience that continues to influence me to this day. A young man of 16, he had been brought to the hospital after engaging in bizarre and dangerous behavior. He was diagnosed with a bipolar affective disorder (manic-depression), and his bizarre behavior stemmed from an extreme manic state, in which psychotic episodes are not uncommon.

No improvement was evident in his first few weeks in the hospital. The treatment team decided that if he didn't improve soon, he would be sent to a long-term facility. I didn't expect him to improve much either, but he surprised me one evening when I walked into his room for one of our counseling sessions. For the first time since I had known him, he seemed clear in his thoughts. He began by saying that he wanted to tell me something, but that he was afraid I would laugh at him. I assured him I wouldn't and encouraged him to talk. So he told me his story.

A few evenings before, he had been lying on his bed when he noticed something in the window. It was Jesus. Now, being a person who didn't know what to do with the whole idea of Jesus, I didn't know what to say. So I said what all counselors are trained to say in such situations: "Ahhhhhh, go on." He told me that Jesus had been standing in the window, and behind him was a forked path. Along the left path were strewn, in his words, "bums and guys on skid row." Along the right path were strewn, in the patient's words, all sorts of successful people. I had no idea what to say. Spiritual experiences were not covered in my counseling training. In fact, I had been taught to ignore anything spiritual. But I had to deal with this one or I would lose my patient. After thinking for a long while, I asked him, "What do you think Jesus was telling you?" He thought for a while and said, "I think Jesus is telling me that I have a choice to make right now. If I keep going the way I'm going, I'm going to end up on skid row with all the bums, but if I make the choice to join Jesus, I can be successful like all the men on the other path." Not knowing what else to say, I said, "I think you'd better listen to Jesus." He did and immediately began to improve.

At a counseling session a week later he told me that he had had another experience of Jesus. This time he and Jesus were standing on the 50-yard line of a football field. A chain-link fence separated them. Looking backward, he saw that the grass was dead from the end zone to the 25-yard line, while the rest was green. Again, I asked him, "What do you think Jesus is saying?" He said, "I think Jesus is telling me that I have gone from death to life, but I still have obstacles to overcome to join him." I said, "I think you'd better listen to Jesus." And he did. He was discharged to his home within two weeks. He was a different person. His encounter with Jesus had changed him.

Now, I don't want to dismiss the impact of the medication he was receiving, but I also can't dismiss his experience of Jesus, because that experience totally changed his thinking about life. He accepted responsibility for himself and his behavior, and he became determined to get better. Jesus had used this young man's illness to show him a better way, and he took it. I saw his father a year later in a mall and asked him how his son was doing. He told me that his son was doing beautifully, he was looking at colleges, and that one would never know that he had been ill. The father then told me that we were miracle workers. I didn't know how to tell him that it wasn't me—it was Jesus.

This experience changed me because it altered my perceptions of how God works. This young man had encountered Christ, and the encounter had changed him. This is what I had been missing and what I had hungered for in my youth. I had not encountered Christ in church, but I had encountered him in a psychiatric hospital, even if it was vicariously through a patient. That experience left me questioning every assumption I had previously made about Christianity, the church, and God. It didn't immediately lead me back to church, although that process began soon afterward.

Over time the stresses of working long hours in the hospital for little pay took their toll. I burned out at age 25. I was so disillusioned with the whole field of psychology and counseling, even more than I had been with the church. I was in a crisis. I had lost my sense of purpose, and I felt isolated and alone. So I quit and moved home to live with my parents while I searched for another career.

I quit right in the middle of the recession of 1983, which left the area around Pittsburgh, Pennsylvania, where I lived, with a 12 percent unemployment rate. There were no jobs. I became more and more despondent as the months passed. Where was God? Why wasn't God helping me to find a new career? Why did it seem as though every door was closing before me? I felt as if I were drowning. A lifeline had been thrown to me a month before I quit my job as a counselor, but it took months of floundering before I could grab it. My father had told me about a program at Pittsburgh Theological Seminary. I could get a master of divinity degree there, and a master of social work from the University of Pittsburgh. I laughed. "Dad, could you actually see me as a minister?" "Sure," he replied; "I've always seen you as a minister." How ridiculous—me as a pastor. The funny thing, though, is that deep down I had that same feeling about myself. Somewhere deep inside, in a place that I really didn't have the courage to look into, I knew that I was called to be a pastor, but I was in no state to accept that knowledge. I rejected and repressed it. It took a long period of unemployment and a state of desperation finally to give me the courage to recognize that I was being called to become a pastor—to become a leader in the very body that I had tried so hard to reject and ignore. But more about that in a bit.

In the midst of my struggles I decided to join the church in January 1984. In joining the church, I became aware of something that I had refused to see before. Of course the people in the church were hypocrites. Of course the church was flawed and full of faults. I was just as aware of their faults and flaws as before, but now I recognized something even more important. I was a hypocrite, too. I was just as flawed and faulty. What better place was there for me than a church?

The choice to join the church came one evening several weeks before Christmas as I cried to God in prayer about my life. I could no longer take my loneliness, my lack of purpose, and my growing despair. I decided to make a commitment to God—to Christ. I would join the church because I needed others to join me on my journey, just as I needed to join them on their journey. The funny thing is that after making this decision, I began to experience God more tangibly in my life. Coincidences opened doors that had previously been shut. People came into my life who gave me guidance. I began to experience God all over the place. My decision to join the church was leading me to experience God tangibly, even though the church itself hadn't really changed. What changed was that I was now extremely open to God for the first time.

After making the decision to join the church, deciding to enroll in seminary was fairly easy. My intention was to go to seminary so that I could return to my career as a counselor, but this time equipped to deal with the spiritual issues that typically arise in counseling, issues that I had been discouraged from addressing in my previous work as a counselor. I went to seminary not only to be trained in theology; simultaneously I worked on a master of social work (a counseling degree) at a local university to train to become a better counselor. Through my studies I regained a sense of purpose and formed a plan to return eventually to working as a counselor, but God thwarted my plans once again. (Through experience I've discovered that God seems never to be content to let our plans be *"The Plan."* God always has deeper plans.) I thought God's plan was that I become a counselor again, but God put me back into the place that I had been trying to escape, the church. The discernment of my prayers and providential and coincidental events made it clear that God was calling me to become a pastor, to lead a church.

Still, I faced a problem. I had gone to seminary hoping to learn how to deal with the spiritual issues I had encountered in counseling others, issues that I hoped also to address as a pastor; but I never really learned to address them. I took courses in Greek and Hebrew. I took courses in pastoral care and the Bible. I took courses in ethics, Christology, theology, and the like, but I still didn't know how to deal with the spiritual issues people faced in their lives. I was no better trained to deal with the patient who saw Jesus in the window than I had been as a counselor six years before. I didn't necessarily know how to address the spiritual thirst of those in my care. I was still spiritually parched myself. How could I lead people to wells of living water when I had no map to find them myself, or even a bucket with which to draw the water? I had found God, but I didn't necessarily know how to lead others to God. I didn't really know how to pray. I didn't know how to lead a Bible study. I didn't know how to do much more than tell people to be good. Knowing how unprepared I was, I hid my deficiencies and read everything I could in the area of spirituality. I was especially drawn to the works of mystics—those who had encountered God and had written of their experiences. Eventually, I decided that I needed to study spirituality so that I could be trained to deal with the spiritual issues of those in my church, as well as my own.

I began working on a doctorate in spiritual formation at Duquesne University in Pittsburgh. It was in studying spirituality that I finally found a map that enabled me to lead others to spiritual water, and a bucket to draw it out for them. As opposed to theology, which is the study of God and life from a rational, analytical, and semiscientific perspective (using Scripture, tradition, and the insights of the Christian community throughout the ages as the material of study), the study of spirituality is the study of the lived relationship between God and us, as well as the study of the practices and perspectives that lead to a deepening of the relationship with God. The theology I had learned in seminary was important, yet it was an experience much like eating dry crackers. It could sustain me, but I couldn't completely swallow it. The study of theology seemed dry and fragmented.

In contrast, studying spirituality was like being given water to drink, allowing me finally to digest and process all the theology I had learned years before. I not only became alive; I also began to wonder why the church hadn't given me water like this years before. Why hadn't the seminary given me this kind of water? Why hadn't I been taught that theology and spirituality were partners; that spirituality was the water that gave life to theological insight? Why did it take 14 years of struggling on my own to discover this water of life?

The problem was that my seminary studies emphasized studying and speculating about God. My studies in spirituality showed me how to encounter and experience God. Unless we encounter God, speculating about God becomes nothing more than abstract conjecture and theorizing that has little impact on daily life. When we have an actual encounter with God, though, this speculation deepens us by revealing the depths of God.

After I graduated with my doctorate, it became clear to me that I was being called by God to return to the church to form a model for how to create a more spiritually vibrant church. I was being called to take the insights and practices of the growing spiritual formation movement and to find a way to bring them into the life of the local church. The vision I had was not one of simply offering retreats, classes, and small groups on spirituality. The vision was to restore to the church a clear sense of God's purpose, a transforming sense of God's presence, and an expectant sense of God's power in our midst.

I was fortunate in 1996 to be given the chance to do just that. I was called to become the pastor of Calvin Presbyterian Church in Zelienople, Pennsylvania, a place of wonderful, spiritually thirsty, and charitable people. Over the past eight years we have worked together to experiment with ways of forming a church of purpose, presence, and power. Through this book, I hope to share with you what we have discovered in our ministry together at Calvin Church: a way of doing ministry that leads to creating a church filled with God's blessings.

I have been frustrated over the years that a vast majority of the congregations in the mainstream denominations, and the denominations themselves, have adopted a functional style of church that cuts off their spiritual cores. What I mean is that too many churches focus only on function, on doing the activities of church, and not on the fact that at their heart churches are meant to be spiritual communities in which people form a relationship with and experience God. (I'll explain more in chapter 2.) In these churches there is little expectation that members will experience and encounter God, or connect what they do to God's purpose, presence, and power. The problem in many of these churches isn't so much what they do, but the spirit in which they do it. They worship, but not necessarily with an eye toward leading people to an encounter with God. They meet to do God's work, but not necessarily in ways that include prayerfully seeking God's will and way in their work. They offer prayers, but not with the expectation that the prayers will do much more than offer comfort and consolation.

Many denominations, churches, pastors, and members become mired in a series of worthless arguments in their attempt to diagnose why mainstream denominations and churches are in decline. Too many in the mainstream church think the problems have to do with theological positions, styles of worship, or availability of programs. So they say that the decline is the result of churches being too liberal or too conservative; or that the decline is due to our too-traditional worship. They say that we don't meet enough of people's needs, and we need to offer more programs.

When it comes to theological positions, I've noticed that there are many growing conservative *and* liberal churches, just as there are many declining conservative *and* liberal churches. When it comes to styles of worship, if growth is just a matter of becoming more contemporary, why do so many declining churches add a contemporary worship service but remain depleted? (Of course, many churches also remain traditional and slowly die.) Many churches continue to stagnate, even though they try to offer a multitude of programs that appeal to all. At the same time, many grow vigorously while offering little more than a caring community.

What I have consistently noticed in almost all thriving congregations, including Calvin Church, is that what makes the difference is the extent to which the community is open to God at its core. Many churches simply aren't open to God. They let the will, ego, and purpose of the dominant voices in their congregation, whether the pastor's or that of a few strong members, drive the agenda. Instead of seeking God's call and purpose, they argue over who is right and wrong. Declining churches tend not to be open to God's presence. They worship, meet, and engage in ministry and mission, but their sense is that God is in heaven, we are on earth, and all that matters is doing good deeds so that we can get into heaven. The congregants have no sense that Christ is in their midst, and that this presence of Christ can bless them and make their churches places of love. So they continue to engage in the practices of the church, but they don't expect an encounter with Christ. Finally, these churches have no awareness that God's grace and power can work in their midst. They have no awareness of the Holy Spirit. They are unaware that when we become open to God, God's Spirit flows through the church to make miracles happen.

This book is about how to open our hearts and minds to God in our communities in such a way that we become blessed in everything. It is not a book on how to turn a small church into a large church, although spiritual growth *can* lead to numerical growth. It is not about how to attract members, although that may happen because people are attracted to spiritually healthy places. It is not a book on how to become a successful pastor by the world's standards, although that may happen. Simply put, this is a guide on how to create a church that is open at its foundations to God's purpose, presence, and power. It is a book on how to create a spiritually deep congregation that becomes inwardly and outwardly healthy on every level: spiritually, psychologically, physically, and relationally. (I'll say more about this topic in chapter 2.) It is a book on how you can open your congregation to God's blessings so that these blessings flow through everything the church does, from meetings to ministry to mission.

My prayer is that as you read this book and begin to use what you discover in it, you will find your church growing in the way God is calling it to grow. Just as every pastor and layperson has a calling, so does every church. My prayer is that through this book, you will be able to discover the path God is calling your church to walk, and that as you walk it, you will discover how to open up the congregation to discover God's blessings everywhere.

Chapter 1

What Is a Blessed Church?

What exactly is a blessed church? It is a glimpse of what a church can be. It is a vision, a glimpse of a healthy church uniquely grounded in a relationship with God that allows blessings to flow through it. Unfortunately, it is a vision too few churches have today, although many are glimpsing it. There are so many factors that keep churches from becoming blessed communities that it's hard to grasp the full ramification of this vision. To understand what becoming a blessed church means, it might be helpful first to look at the factors that need to be overcome to allow a blessed church to take root and grow.

Identifying what prevents churches from becoming blessed is a kind of chicken-and-egg thing. Is the problem that pastors and church leaders no longer have the vision, faith, and skills to lead churches to blessedness? Or is it that churches have become so dry, dysfunctional, and dead that they no longer have the ability to follow pastors and church leaders into blessedness? Both seem to be true. As I look back at my training to become a pastor, I have to admit that I wasn't very well trained to lead churches into blessedness. The seminary I attended tried to prepare me to become a pastor, but like many mainline denominational seminaries, it had an overwhelming focus on all things theological that didn't prepare me to become a pastor in a church where not everything is theological. I studied theology, Christology, eschatology, teleology, ecclesiology, bibliology, and a bunch of other "ologies." I studied church history, biblical languages, pastoral care, and ethics, but I learned very little about how to lead a church. The assumption, so well articulated by a Hebrew professor, was that "you can learn how to do all that church stuff when you get out of seminary." As he said, "Seminaries are academic institutions. You have to figure out the other stuff on your own."

That's an amazing statement from someone charged with preparing pastors and church educators for ministry and church leadership.

The problem with so many mainline denominational seminaries is that their mission is often at odds with the mission of the early church, which was to bring people into a deep, spiritual, loving, saving, and healing relationship with God the Creator, Son, and Holy Spirit. Too often they see themselves primarily as academic institutions, like universities and colleges, where the focus is a rational investigation and study of theology, history, and the Bible. How does this emphasis fit with their calling to train pastors, educators, and leaders for ministry and mission? Is the main function of pastors, educators, and leaders merely to be theologians explaining the mysteries of life, or are they charged with leading others to this deep, loving relationship with the Trinity? If their calling is to train pastors, educators, or leaders, what model for ministry and the church do they use? Is it that churches should be little academic institutions where the pastors and educators act as resident theologians? Is it the corporate-culture model that assumes the church is an organization in which the pastor acts as CEO and the lay leaders act as members of the board of directors? Is it the pastoral care and counseling model that assumes the church is a counseling agency in which the pastor serves as the resident therapist? There's a lot of confusion about how to form a healthy congregation, and that confusion was imparted to me when I graduated from seminary. I wasn't sure what my role as a pastor should be or what to model to follow.

My seminary professors reflected this same confusion. Few had served as parish pastors, and even fewer had served as pastors of dynamic, growing churches. The majority were trained mainly in academia, focusing on theological study, and so their teaching focus tended to be theological, not practical. This emphasis is in direct contrast with my graduate studies in counseling, where not only had every professor been trained in the academic study of counseling, but all were still involved in private practice or as staff in a counseling agencies. I noticed the difference in my sense of competence after graduating. As a counselor, I felt prepared for most situations, and when I didn't, I knew where to get help. As a pastor, I felt unprepared. I'm not alone in feeling inadequately prepared for leadership. Many mainline pastors feel this sense of inadequacy. As one pastor confided to me, "I came out of seminary knowing how to exegete a passage, but I had no idea how to help a person struggling to find a sense of purpose or to feel God's love."

Here's an odd little statistic to reflect upon—one that demonstrates the problems with traditional seminary training. There is an inverse correlation between denominational growth and educational expectations. The more education a denomination expects of its pastors and educators, the more it shrinks. Christian Schwartz, who made a study of the qualities of growing churches, based upon a survey of 1,000 churches in 18 countries, found that seminary training has a negative correlation to both church growth and the overall quality of churches. His research found that only 42 percent of pastors in high-quality, high-growth churches had seminary training, while in low-quality, low-growth churches 85 percent had graduated from seminary.[1] Traditional mainline denominations all expect a fairly high level of education, and pastors with a Ph.D. or D.Min. are often the most respected in some denominations. In contrast, the fastest-growing movements of all are among the Pentecostals and nondenominationals, which require little advanced education at all. They still may expect the pastor to be trained, but the pastor often has on-the-job training, supplemented by workshops, seminars, and in-house training programs focused specifically on church growth and discipleship. What inhibits the formation of blessed *mainline* churches may be partly that pastors, educators, and lay leaders have been inadequately trained not only in the practicalities of church leadership, but also in the knowledge of how to tap into the power of God to guide and help them. Their training becomes so academic and intellectual that they lose the life-giving sense of God's call that initially led them into ministry and that can sustain them in ministry.

It is unfair to place the blame squarely on seminaries. Congregations present their own problems. They become so accustomed to a purely programmatic and traditional mode of operation that they don't see the possibility of creating a congregational approach that is more spiritually open, and that leads people to experience God more deeply and tangibly in their midst. In fact, some churches become so accustomed to dysfunction that they don't realize that they are dysfunctional. A seminary student who served an internship in our church said something to me once that reflects how accustomed people can be to dysfunction. After participating in our church budgeting process (which entails bringing all committees together in a time of prayer to discern what God is calling us to do, and putting aside squabbles and turf battles to seek what God wants), he said, "I didn't know it could be like this. I just thought that arguing and fighting over the budget was how it was done in all churches."

How does one lead churches like these out of the wilderness? Many pastors try. They eventually get chewed up and spit out when their congregations steadfastly resist all efforts to construct a more spiritually open approach. Some churches become so dysfunctional that their histories put one in mind of a revolving door. One pastor after another comes to the church with much fanfare; each lasts from one to three years, and leaves disillusioned by the hostility and inhospitable treatment she or he experiences while trying to lead the church out of dysfunction. In fact, many of these churches, because of their dysfunctional patterns, become adept at calling dysfunctional pastors who end up damaging the churches further because of their addictions, affairs, or embezzlements.

A final problem lies with us pastors, educators, and leaders. Many of us come to ministry with broken lives that may leave us psychologically and spiritually wounded. On the one hand, our wounds can become detrimental when they interfere with our ministry because we have denied and repressed them, refusing to do what is necessary for healing (whether that means undergoing self-examination, therapy, or spiritual direction). On the other hand, our wounds can become a source of strength if, through our self-examination, therapy, or spiritual direction, we are able to use our wounds to deepen our compassion, understanding, and care of others. Whether these wounds become a detriment or a strength depends upon the pastor's, educator's, or leader's willingness to face her or his woundedness, be healed from it, and make it a source of strength.

God seems to call broken people to ministry. I don't know why, but it's true. Read in the Bible of the people God called. Joseph, a cocky little guy hated by his brothers, was sold by them into slavery. Moses was a murderer on the run. Ruth was a widowed foreigner. King Saul was afflicted by an oversized ego and paranoia. David was the runt of his litter and eventually became an adulterer. Solomon instituted a terrible death-squad campaign upon becoming the ruler of Israel. Jeremiah was mentally ill. Many of the disciples were ignorant and selfish. Mary Magdalene had been demon-possessed. Paul was a persecutor of Christians and aided in the killing of them. Yet God called them all. God calls broken and flawed people.

But that does not mean that people called by God should remain broken and unhealed. God also calls them to seek healing. They bear responsibility for doing the best they can to live a healthy life—one that is spiritually, psychologically, physically, and relationally balanced. Becoming whole may entail going to a counselor for psychological and relational health; seeking out a spiritual director for spiritual health; engaging in a diet and exercise program for physical health—all of which many of us pastors are loathe to do. Too many pastors today don't bear enough responsibility for their own health and well-being. As a result, they become unhealthy leaders leading unhealthy congregations.

What is the path out of this wilderness? How do we lead our churches out of dysfunction and into blessing?

Rational Functionalism

To place the blame *solely* on academic seminaries, dysfunctional churches, and unhealthy pastors is not quite fair. They are all symptomatic of a far greater problem. The bigger problem is something I call "rational functionalism"—a disease that has afflicted all mainline denominations, and as a result afflicts their seminaries, churches, and pastors.

Rational functionalism is the tendency of denominations, their congregations, and their leaders to subscribe to a view of faith and church rooted in a restrictive, logic-bound theology that ignores the possibility of spiritual experiences and miraculous events, while overemphasizing a functional practice disconnected from an emphasis on leading people to a transforming experience of God. On the one hand, rational functionalism turns faith into an intellectual endeavor rooted in an excessively rational, empirical, quasi-scientific approach. This approach to faith is a by-product of the Age of Enlightenment, whose focus was on the rational and scientific pursuit of truth. Rational functionalism is rooted in the idea that we can uncover the mysteries of life and the universe mainly through rational thought and disciplined investigation. From this perspective, God is a problem to be solved through a method that mirrors the scientific method as closely as possible, and if that isn't feasible, then by restricting the inquiry to the laws of human logic and analysis.

The rational functional approach can reduce a congregation's practice to the attempt to lead people into a positivistic, logical exploration of religion and faith. The idea here is that a theological, historical, sociological, psychological, anthropological, economic, and philosophical understanding of the Christian faith will enable us to discern the laws of God and human life more clearly, and we can therefore learn to live better lives. In short, this approach reflects what a national leader in my denomination once said to me: "If we can just get people to think right theologically, then all of our problems will go away." The problem is that faith is more than just a logical, empirical inquiry into God and God's ways. It involves our minds, spirits, bodies, relationships, and beings. To address the human seeking for God from only a rational, logical, theological perspective is limiting.

One danger of rational functionalism is that it can cause pastors and leaders to become overintellectual in their approach to faith. God becomes an abstract notion, not a presence whom we can experience, form a relationship with, and love. Increasingly, these pastors and leaders endanger their faith. They don't know what to do with God. They especially don't know what to do with Jesus and the Holy Spirit. They can appreciate Jesus from a historical perspective, but what do they do with the resurrected Christ who, according to Scripture, is incarnated in the world, in relationships, and in the human heart? What do they do with the Holy Spirit, who inspires, heals, and miraculously touches life? Ultimately, they become so intellectual in their approach that they not only lose their own faith, but struggle with leading others to faith.

I am not advocating that pastors and church leaders should remain theologically and historically ignorant, or that we should blindly accept everything in the Bible as historical fact. Understanding Scripture and Christian faith from a more critical and academic point of view is a good thing because it can help us to understand the context and intent of Scripture, thus helping us hear God's voice more clearly when we read Scripture. My point is that when academic inquiry and scientific skepticism become stronger than an emphasis on forming faith and leading people to an encounter with God, the church declines because people are no longer led to form a living faith in God that can transform their lives. The church becomes little more than a social agency filled with well-meaning but spiritually dead people.

In churches caught in the grip of rational functionalism, sermons tend to become academic papers read to the people in the pews. They don't address more basic issues: How are we supposed to endure living with pain, loneliness, and turmoil? How are we supposed to find God amid life's darkness? Bible studies focus on the historical, sociological, economic, and cultural issues of the time, with the intent of uncovering what theological message the writer of a Bible passage is trying to impart. They don't address more basic issues: What is God saying to me through the Scripture about how to live my life? What is God saying to me about what God is doing in my life, especially in the face of my suffering? How is God calling me to love others and to reach out to those who are suffering, both near and throughout the world, and who are in need of God's love as well as mine?

The primary problem at the core of rational functionalism is that it fails to treat God as a tangible presence. God is treated mostly as an idea or thought, or as an entity we encounter when we die, rather than as a tangible presence in the here and now. There is no sense that God's kingdom is all around us, and that this kingdom is a spiritual reality in which we can experience God directly.

A second problem with rational functionalism is that it functionalizes the life of the church, turning everything from worship to committee meetings into routinized events with little connection to a larger purpose. In the rationally functional church, the focus is on maintaining the institution, not on creating experiences through which God can be encountered and experienced in our midst. What matters most is preaching in *the* prescribed manner, adhering to particular rituals in *the* traditional way, and singing only *the* traditional hymns. Guiding people to a tangible encounter, experience, and relationship with Christ isn't much of a concern. Teaching people how to discover the power of the Holy Spirit in their midst is never emphasized because the object of the church has been reduced to doing what we've always done, to function the way the church has always functioned simply for the sake of functioning. Guiding people to discover the Creator's call in their lives, calling them and us to live deeper, richer, and greater lives of love and service, is ignored in favor of guiding people simply to function as Christians have always functioned. In short, the message is reduced to (as someone once told me) "We should be Christians because Christianity is good and ethical, and we should be good and ethical people. The church's role is to teach us to follow the Golden Rule."

According to church-growth researcher Bill Easum, a leading writer on mainline church health and vitality, this kind of functionality (what he calls the "machine metaphor") has "made it easy for church leaders to relate to the 'church' as an institution rather than a spiritual community. It also made it easy to honor educated leaders who often ridiculed emotion and feelings. Symbols easily became the reality instead of pointing to it, . . . logic replaced passion and experience. The materialistic world was real, whereas the inner world of the soul was little more than illusion."[2] The result, according to him, is that "Institutional churches function like corporations. Pastors are CEOs. Policy manuals replace ministry. Pastors attend seminary and are referred to as 'professionals.' Denominational structures and financial needs grow faster than those of congregations. Job descriptions replace calling. Degrees are more important than proven competency. . . . In such a church, leadership is based on credentials, and faith is something to be learned. This metaphor is evident in churches that place a lot of emphasis on administration, credentials, denominationalism, meetings, and defending the faith."[3]

Ultimately, becoming a blessed church means overcoming rational functionalism. In blessed churches, people not only *expect* to experience

God; they *do* experience God. Their expectations open the door to God, who stands knocking. They *expect* to hear the Creator's voice guiding the church to what it is called to be and do. They expect to encounter and be blessed by Christ. They expect the power of God the Holy Spirit to flow through their lives and the church's, blessing them in so many ways.

The Problem of Church Growth

Becoming a blessed church does not necessarily mean becoming a growing church, at least not in numbers. Many of the large, fast-growing megachurches around the country are what I would call "blessed churches," but many are not. Numerical growth is not a defining characteristic of a blessed church, even though many think it is. In fact, the plethora of church-growth materials on the market nowadays can be a problem for many churches and their leaders who seek to grow blessed churches. Why? Because not all churches are in situations that allow them to replicate the growth of these megachurches.

The books written by megachurch pastors are filled with insights and tips on how to create a large, growing church. Many of these books have influenced my ministry and my life. The problem is that almost all these books fail to account for three primary factors that contribute to their growth—conditions that most churches can't replicate. First, most of these churches are new church developments, seeking to attract only baby boomers and generation Xers, so they don't run as forcefully into the problems inherent in turning around an established church that includes members of multiple generations. Instead, they have had the advantage of being able to create their own customs, follow new ideas, and focus much more of their energy on ministry rather than on maintaining buildings. Established churches can be difficult to turn around because their members often resist change and transformation. They cherish their customs, their hymns, and the ways they have always done things.

In addition, mainline churches are being challenged to respond to the demands of multiple generations, all seeking something different from worship and the church. Often the oldest generation, the World War II, or "GI generation," seeks to hold onto tradition. The next, the silent generation, cherishes tradition, but also supports reaching out to younger generations. Baby boomers, born between 1943 and 1960, tend to want stimulation and excitement in worship, but in a new package, which may mean contemporary worship that eliminates traditional symbols and rituals. Generation Xers are often idiosyncratic, wanting churches to tailor their efforts to their age group's varied interests and tastes (which can be almost impossible for churches to do). Finally, millennials, those born since 1982, tend to love traditional symbols and experiential rituals, while still expecting them to reflect a mixture of traditional and contemporary effects. Holding the interests of all these generations can be extremely difficult, making revitalization of a mainline church a much more daunting task than simply starting a new church that targets only one or two of these generations. Many of these megachurches have succeeded by ignoring the two oldest generations, something the mainline churches cannot do.

Turning a firmly entrenched church around to make it grow numerically takes a set of skills that many pastors don't have, either because they lack the proper training or lack the right personal attributes. It takes a special set of skills to help a struggling congregation make the transition from, as pastor and author Stan Ott says, a *traditional* church to a *transformational* church.[4]

A second factor that uniquely contributes to the growth of megachurches is that they are either planted or replanted in growing communities. There is a direct correlation between a growing community and a growing church. For instance, my own church, Calvin Presbyterian Church, has nearly doubled in size since I became its pastor. Certainly a big factor in this success is that Zelienople is a growing community near one of the faster-growing areas of the country. With the exception of Pentecostal churches, it is rare that churches grow in declining communities, and unique factors contribute to the growth of Pentecostal churches.

Third, large, growing churches tend to target and attract people who are seeking a church that does things differently. They draw members who are adaptable to change and are willing to risk, and who *don't want to be in a traditional church*, no matter how alive it is. The people in mainline churches are often the people left behind by members who have left to seek a more contemporary church. They fear risk and don't want change. They sometimes love their traditions more than they love God.

The challenge for most mainline churches is how to get church leaders, especially lay leaders, to lead a scared, resistant, and risk-averse church to grow when they are scared and resistant themselves. Many mainline churches lack a vision for change, the confidence to make changes, and the desire for change. They want stability. Their focus has slowly become fixed on themselves and their survival (and sometimes their death). Seeking what God wants is not high among their priorities.

In many ways, they become stuck. They don't want to die, but they don't know how to live. They want God to speak to them, but not if it means making changes.

Many of the pastors who lead these churches are afraid themselves. They fear leading these churches to God and transformation because of the backlash they may experience from members. They feel like failures because their churches aren't growing, and they feel like cowards for not taking more risks. I don't want to make it sound as though great pastoral leadership means changing everything. As you will see in the following chapters, I believe that change should be rooted in God's calling. Change may also mean maintaining traditional rituals and programs but adapting them ever so slightly in ways that make them fresh to new generations.

As I stated above, becoming a blessed church may not lead to church growth because the focus of a blessed church is on opening to God in our midst, not on adding members. Growth in numbers becomes a by-product of growing in a relationship with God. The focus of a blessed church is on doing what God is calling us to do, having the confidence to know that God is in our midst, and relying upon God's power to get results. This focus may not lead to numerical growth, but it does lead to health. In other words, by focusing on leading people to spiritual encounters and experiences of God, the church and its members end up forming healthier and more vibrant relationships with each other, relationships that emerge out of the deep spiritual connection with the Trinity and with each other. The more the church focuses on grounding its ministry and mission in a dynamic relationship with the Trinity, the more its members and other participants engage confidently in ministry and mission that make a difference in the local community and in the world, if only in a small way. As the church grows in its relationship with God, the members become increasingly aware of God's power in their lives. In short, becoming a blessed church means becoming a place where God is present and God is experienced. Lives are thereby healed.

If becoming a blessed church means becoming more open to God and God's power in our midst, why doesn't that automatically translate into church growth? The answer is fairly simple. Becoming a blessed church means discerning and doing what God is calling us to do, and some churches simply aren't called to grow. In fact, sometimes churches are called to die. How many of the original churches founded by Paul and the other disciples still exist? Just as people have a term of life, so do churches. Sometimes, becoming a blessed church may mean finding a way to die with faith, hope, and love. This is a hard idea to grasp in our evangelical age when success in ministry is measured by the size of a church, but sometimes churches have to die to give new life to others.

A woman told me of her experience with the death of a church that brought new life to two other churches. She served on a presbytery (the regional judicatory body of the Presbyterian Church) committee to determine what to do with the church building of a Presbyterian congregation that had shut its doors and ceased operation. The decision had been made to sell the building. Two bids came in, one from an Episcopal parish, the other from a fundamentalist Southern Baptist congregation. The Southern Baptist bid was $30,000 higher than the Episcopal, creating a dilemma. The members of the committee wanted the extra $30,000, but they didn't want a fundamentalist congregation to occupy the church building. A fight erupted within the committee. Finally, the committee leader asked the members to be quiet and to go out and pray for an hour to see what God wanted them to do rather than argue about what each wanted.

When they resumed talking, someone offered an alternate suggestion, one heard in prayer. Why not sell the building to the Southern Baptists and give the extra $30,000 to the Episcopal parish? That way, new life would be given to two churches out of the death of one Presbyterian church. The committee spent time praying about it, and all agreed. But they had one problem. How would they get the presbytery to go along with their suggestion? Wouldn't their suggestion be seen as poor stewardship, since the building was presbytery property, and the presbytery could use the $30,000? Indeed, at the next presbytery meeting a bitterly divisive argument erupted among the 120 pastors and elders. Finally, an 85-year-old woman slowly walked up the aisle and stepped to the microphone. Stamping her cane on the floor for emphasis, she said, "Can't this presbytery ever do the right thing? They heard this answer in prayer!" In that moment, everyone knew that following the committee's suggestion was what God wanted. In that moment, the presbytery became blessed, and because it did, God became ever more present to two churches of widely different theological beliefs. This kind of thing happens in a blessed church. People seek what God wants, and when they do, they discover God's unexpected blessings.

The Marks of a Blessed Church

I've spent most of this chapter discussing what a blessed church is not, and what keeps churches from becoming blessed churches. Let me now offer a vision for a blessed church.

I believe that above all, mainline churches are called to become blessed churches, to become places where God's blessings are tangibly experienced. They are called to be a healthy places where people devote their lives to God the Creator, Christ, and Holy Spirit, and where healing occurs. These are some of the marks of a blessed church.

The blessed church sees itself as the body of Christ. This is the first mark of a blessed church. To do so, the church and its members must quit considering itself to be something akin to a business, an organization, or even a family. The church has attributes that are similar to a business, an organization, and a family, but it is unique. Nothing else in the world is like a church. As Rick Warren, a leader in the church-growth movement, says, "The church is a body, not a business. It is an organism, not an organization. It is alive. . . . The task of a church leadership is to discover and remove growth-restricting diseases and barriers so that natural, normal growth can occur."[5] Blessed churches are the body of Christ, and they take that fact seriously. In 1 Corinthians 12 Paul outlines a vision of the church as a living, breathing, acting body with Christ as its head. Too few churches hold onto that vision. The blessed church is the body of Christ that follows Christ's guidance to feed, nourish, and care for itself in a way that allows it to grow and become a servant to the world.

The leaders of the body know that Christ is the head, and so they continually and prayerfully seek Christ's guidance. They move the body to act and react in certain ways, but they remain very much aware that their source has to be Christ—God's presence—in their midst. The rational, functional church forgets that Christ is in its midst. Seeking Christ's wisdom and way becomes an overwhelming passion for the blessed church, and its leaders regularly seek in prayer Christ's wisdom and way. For pastors, this means becoming people who pray, especially when they are too busy to pray. Prayer is central to the life of the blessed church. It is like the nervous system of a body. It is through prayer that the body hears what the head desires, and it is through prayer that the body communicates with the head. This emphasis on prayer must begin with pastoral leadership. If the pastor does not lead out of prayer, then the body is unlikely to pray, and without prayer the body becomes disconnected from the head. It will end up either running functionally and frenetically like a chicken with its head cut off, or it will die.

On a practical level, the meetings and matters of the blessed church are grounded in prayer as its leaders seek what God wants over what they want. Dying churches are ego driven. Blessed churches are Christ guided. Blessed churches root their ministries and mission in prayer, act confidently on what they hear, and let God take care of the results. They don't achieve these practices perfectly by any means. Faith is always sprinkled with fear and doubt in even the most faithful leaders. Still, in the end, they do their best to act in faith rather than fear.

The blessed church has a vibrant sense of faith, hope, and love. When a church lacks the faith to trust God to work in its midst, the hope to believe that good things are possible, and a basic love of God and others, it begins its slow descent toward death. Still, how does a church renew faith, hope, and love when it is struggling? So much in a church depends upon leadership—not just pastoral leadership but lay leadership as well. A church always mirrors its leaders. If the leaders are self-focused and selfish, the church will be too. If the leaders are tentative and fearful, the church will follow suit. If the leaders are afraid of God and growth, the church will also be fearful. In the same vein, if leaders have a strong sense of faith, hope, and love, then so will the church and its members. That faith, hope, and love will carry over into members' lives so that they become more faithful, hopeful, and loving with their families, in their workplaces, and in responding to the suffering of the world.

A blessed church is a church of deep faith in God and God's power. What does it mean to be a church of faith? Sadly, far too many Christians confuse faith and belief. Faith is much more than belief. It is a deep trust in God. It is an abandoning to God in which we surrender our control and power, trusting that God will act to accomplish something through, with, or among us—something wonderful and powerful that we cannot accomplish on our own. The leaders and members may be afraid of change, but in the end they always opt in faith to do what they prayerfully sense God calling them to do. They may not know with clarity what the outcome of their act of faith will be, and what they opt to do in faith may seem risky or dangerous, but when given a choice between acting fearfully to protect themselves and acting faithfully to serve God, they act in faith—though it may mean taking a path that seems uncertain and frightening.

Besides having a deep faith, the leadership has a strong sense of hope for the future, that future blessings are coming from God. This hope prevails even during bad economic times, amid troubling world and national events, and despite congregational crises. They have a strong sense that God is with them and will make good things happen, especially if they remain faithful, even if it means going through terrible times of struggle and turmoil.

Finally, the leaders have a strong sense of love for each other and the church's members, a love that leads the members eventually to reach out and love others, even those who are different. They don't react to failure and problems with anger, frustration, or impatience. They understand what it is to be afraid and to make mistakes. So they act with love. With this kind of leadership, members become people of faith, hope, and love, and this love becomes almost tangible to those visiting the church. This quality of tangible love is apparent in large blessed churches, but especially evident in small ones.

The blessed church is a church filled with God's purpose, presence, and power. I believe that we *experience* the trinitarian God as Purpose, Presence, and Power.[6] For example, one of the most tangible ways we encounter God as Creator happens as we become increasingly aware of what our *purpose* is as a church and as individuals. We encounter God in Christ when we sense Christ's *presence* in the life of the church—in worship, word, sacrament, music, drama, activities, meetings, and each other. We encounter God the Holy Spirit when we witness the *power* of God making coincidences (providences), miracles, and amazing events happen (although the Holy Spirit also works in ways that are often unseen and unencountered). Blessed churches have a relatively clear sense of what their purpose is and why God the Creator called them into existence, even if they are hundreds of years old. They tangibly sense Christ's presence. They expect the Spirit's power to work everywhere in the church, blessing the ministries, mission, and members of the church.

The blessed church embraces the sacred. The blessed church emphasizes symbols, sacraments, and rituals in a way that helps people encounter God in every dimension: spiritual, mental, emotional, subconscious, physical, and relational. Such churches emphasize rituals, sacraments, and symbols because they know that these have the power to connect people to the Trinity in sacred ways that the spoken word and music cannot.

For example, the sacraments of communion and baptism are central to their lives. Blessed churches recognize that sacraments have the power to reveal and connect a person with the divine—a power that cannot be fully explained or duplicated in any other way. So the blessed church emphasizes the power of these sacraments and places them at the center of congregational life. For instance, at Calvin Church we celebrate communion once a week in our first worship service, once a month in our second. This frequency is not typical of Presbyterian churches (typically Presbyterians celebrate communion between five times a year and once a month), but we recognize the power of communion to connect people with God's love and presence. We recognize that the sacred can be revealed through nonsacramental rituals, too. For example, we offer regular healing services as part of our worship, and we have a healing prayer ministry that reaches out to those suffering with physical, mental, and emotional illnesses, as well as other needs. Again, making healing rituals and prayers part of the worship and life of the church becomes a powerful way of connecting people to God's presence and power in their lives.

Blessed churches embrace the sacred also by placing banners, crosses, statues, and other artistic expressions of the divine throughout the sanctuary. Displaying religious and spiritual artistry runs counter to the emphasis of many contemporary churches, which often strip their worship spaces of all symbols and sacraments. The blessed church tries to create sacred spaces that reveal the Trinity through sacrament, art, architecture, and creative use of symbols and space to reveal the sacred and to connect people with the Divine.

So, one key to embracing the sacred is ensuring that rituals, symbols, sacrament, art, architecture, and space are used in ways that lead people to encounter God. The focus cannot be only on offering symbols and sacraments the way the church did 200 years ago. The sacraments and symbols can and must be transformed so that they use the language and expressions of today in a way that invites newer and younger Christians to experience the power these elements have had for Christians for over 2,000 years. When we refuse to transform the language and expression of our sacraments in meaningful ways, we make tradition and custom more important than an encounter with Christ. Transforming sacraments and symbols creates a difficult choice because it forces the church and its leaders to maintain a tension between remaining true to a tradition and creating a new tradition. In other words, we have to maintain fidelity to the intent and purpose of the sacrament or symbol while transforming it, and while resisting the temptation to create something new just for the sake of newness. The best transformation of a sacrament, symbol, or ritual happens when we understand fully its purpose and power, while transforming it in a way that touches and affects new generations. The essential point is that the blessed church appreciates deeply the power of the sacred to be revealed and experienced through much more than the spoken word or music. The blessed church recognizes that the sacred can emerge through symbols, sacraments, architecture, and art, especially when we ask God to guide us in discerning how to reveal God.

The blessed church is not afraid to serve God in its own way. It is not concerned with fitting into a mold of what church should be, nor of what its denomination expects it to be. Instead, it is concerned with responding to God's call and God's call alone. Each church has its own calling, ministry, and mission. Calvin Presbyterian Church's calling is going to be very different from that of a northern urban church; a church in Orange County, California; a church in rural Alabama; or a church in the deserts of Arizona. Our mission is not as clearly on our doorstep as it is for some churches. We don't have homeless people sleeping on our steps, nor do we have an influx of migrant workers each summer. We don't necessarily come as clearly face-to-face with our mission field. While an urban church may be called to give direct service to the poor and the homeless, or a church in Orange County, California, may be faced with reaching out to thousands of unchurched people moving into the area, much of our mission beyond evangelism is in giving money to support mission rather than engaging in a more active, hands-on mission. Some people may criticize us for that, but it's our calling. In fact, we felt that calling so clearly a few years ago that we restructured the way we give to mission. Instead of being a church that gives a huge chunk of money to the denominational mission programs, we decided to devote 30 percent of our yearly mission giving (we generally give between 19 percent and 23 percent of our yearly budget to mission) to what we call the Special Mission Fund. This fund is set up to respond to the more immediate needs of those with whom we come in contact. The fund helps a paralyzed woman purchase a voice-command control box to operate her television, telephone, and other appliances. It helps a poor woman with six children find temporary housing. It supports a faith-based organization that needs seed money. It helps an abused woman rent an apartment to start a new life. It supplements the welfare income of a man with epilepsy, and supports him in the process of receiving a house built by Habitat for Humanity volunteers. The point is that this mission fund is set up to respond to God as God is calling us to act in mission.

The ministry of a blessed church is always unique. It is a custom fit to its members and its community. I cannot stress sufficiently how important it is for blessed churches to serve in their own distinctive ways. Some Christians are always willing to tell others what they should be doing. Blessed churches resist the idea that they should do what others outside their situation demand, even if the hearts of the demanders are in the right place. The blessed church is harmonious with its own calling. It doesn't respond to people who say, "You should do this because it is what churches are supposed to do." Instead, it responds only to two questions, "God, what are you calling us to do?" and "How do we best respond to God in our own situation and context?" Bruce Smith, our music and youth director, likes to say that Calvin Church has an unofficial motto: "Calvin Church—we're not for everyone." What he is saying is that we tend to respond to God in the way we feel called to respond. If you don't want to be part of a church that responds to God in this way, there are other congregations. We want people who feel called to the same ministry and mission that we do. We want to respond to God in our own unique ways.

The "Blessed" Body of Christ

Describing the blessed church with precision is difficult because in many ways it is something experienced that cannot be outlined. There is no such thing as a perfectly blessed church because there is no perfection in the human realm. Instead, what people notice is that there is something special, something sacred and mysterious going on that leads people to encounter and experience God. Not everyone who enters a blessed church experiences this, especially if one is looking for something else. Some people who visit Calvin Presbyterian Church really are looking for a different experience. They may want a church with a particular political or social agenda, a church with less commitment or perhaps more rules, or a church that will expect less active participation. They are seeking a particular form of worship. They are looking for a church with mostly folk in their own age bracket. The mark of a blessed church is not that everyone who enters the sanctuary is "slain in the Spirit" and walks away in the conviction that this is the *only* home of God. The ultimate mark of a blessed church is that the people called to become part of it sense God's presence and power working among them, even if they can't put their finger on exactly how this presence is manifested or how the power is working.

In a blessed church, rational functionalism has been chased away. People don't discuss theology so much as they discuss life, and in the process they experience the theological teachings of the church coming alive. In a blessed church the pastor doesn't do everything. Instead, the love of the members and the leaders for one another does everything. I've experienced that activity at Calvin Church. I don't have to be the main love-giver when people go through trauma. The members of the church do it without being trained or educated to do so.

As we will see in subsequent chapters, becoming a blessed church means becoming what a church already is: the body of Christ in a particular place. It is a place in which people form a vibrant sense of faith, hope, and love that comes naturally from being part of a community of faith, hope, and love. The blessed church is a place in which people tangibly experience God as Purpose, Presence, and Power; and because they also embrace the sacred, they experience God through sacred symbols, sacraments, art, architecture, and more. Blessed churches are places where people serve God in ways that are unique to them and their context because they are trying to live in harmony with their calling. Ultimately, blessed churches are places that have discovered *the* great spiritual truth of congregational life: God wants to bless us, God wants our churches to thrive in their own way, and all we have to do is create the conditions for God to be welcome.

Reflection Questions

1. Read 1 Corinthians 12:12-21. Reflect on what specific changes would have to be made in your church to make Christ the head and to nurture health in the body.
2. Read 1 Corinthians 13. Reflect on concrete ways to make faith, hope, and especially love stronger in your church.
3. In what specific ways is your church caught in rational functionalism? How can you break its grip on your church?
4. In what ways does your church bear the marks of a blessed church:
   - as an organic incarnation of the body of Christ, rather than an organization?
   - as a place of faith, hope, and love?
   - as a place filled with God's purpose, presence, and power?
   - as a place that embraces the sacred? and
   - as a place that serves God in its own unique ways?

Chapter 2

Setting a Spiritual Foundation

What was the defining moment of the Christian church, the moment that gave it birth? It wasn't Christ's birth. His birth gave us God's revelation *in* a person rather than *through* a person (as God was revealed *through* the prophets). Jesus revealed that God is among us, and he taught us how to live in God's kingdom and presence. Still, Jesus' birth was not the defining moment of the Christian church. Nor were Jesus' death and resurrection the defining moments. They revealed that God's love is the greatest force in the universe, and they define the Christian *faith,* but not the church.

The defining moment of the Christian church was the day of Pentecost, a day too many Christians neglect. As chronicled in Acts 2:1-12, the disciples and followers of Jesus gathered to wait. They weren't sure what would happen, but Jesus had told them that they would receive the gift of the Holy Spirit after he had ascended. At their last supper together, he said, "If you love me, you will keep my commandments. And I will ask the Father, and he will give you another Advocate, to be with you forever. This is the Spirit of truth, whom the world cannot receive, because it neither sees him nor knows him. You know him because he abides with you, and he will be in you" (John 14:15-17). He also said as he ascended into heaven, "but you will receive power when the Holy Spirit has come upon you; and you will be my witnesses in Jerusalem, in all Judea and Samaria, and to the ends of the earth" (Acts 1:8).

Jesus' disciples and followers waited on the day of Pentecost, and "suddenly from heaven there came a sound like the rush of a violent wind, and it filled the entire house where they were sitting. Divided tongues, as of fire, appeared among them, and a tongue rested on each of them. All of them were filled with the Holy Spirit and began to speak in other languages, as the Spirit gave them ability" (Acts 2:1-4). Pentecost was the defining moment for the Christian church, the moment when the followers became the church—the community of Christ. They were no longer simply following the teachings of Christ, although Christ's teachings were their foundation. They were no longer simply trying to imitate Christ. The moment they became filled with the Holy Spirit was the moment the church became a living organism, just as Adam became a living being when God breathed the breath of life into him.

According to Genesis, what defined and gave life to all humans was God breathing God's breath, God's Spirit, into the first human being: "Then God formed [the human] from the dust of the ground, and breathed into his nostrils the breath [or Spirit] of life" (Genesis 2:7). From the Genesis account it is made clear that it is God's indwelling Spirit that gives us life and distinguishes us from all other life forms. The gift of the Holy Spirit makes us uniquely aware of God and the fact that we have been created by God. The same can be said about the gift of the Holy Spirit filling Jesus' followers and disciples on Pentecost. In that moment the church was given life and became a living organism. The followers no longer saw God as residing only in heaven or in the Temple of Jerusalem, but now saw themselves as the body of Christ, as Christ's presence on earth: "For in the one Spirit we were all baptized into one body—Jews or Greeks, slaves or free—and we were all made to drink of one Spirit" (1 Cor. 12:13).

The day of Pentecost was a defining moment because from that day on, the Christian church became increasingly clear each day about what it was—the community of Christ filled with the Holy Spirit. Through the power of the Holy Spirit, Christ's followers now had the living and transforming Christ alive within them, allowing them to become the living, breathing body of Christ in the world. Together and individually, they could incarnate Christ. Christ had not only ascended into heaven. Christ was still alive in the world through the community of Christians acting in the world as they shared God's healing and saving grace with the rest of the world. Without the day of Pentecost, without this "being filled" by the Holy Spirit, the Christian movement would have died. Like many fleeting movements, Christianity would have rested on a series of teachings and commandments, not on a living experience and incarnation of God.

Respiratory Failure

Despite how crucial the events of Pentecost were to the formation of the church, Pentecost isn't emphasized in many of today's mainline churches because we mainline Christians don't know what to do with the Holy Spirit. We're very comfortable with God the Father. We're relatively comfortable with Jesus, even if we can't always decide whether Jesus was God or just a great man. But the Holy Spirit seems nebulous, enigmatic, and unpredictable. We have no clear sense of who the Holy Spirit is, what the Holy Spirit does, and what will happen to us if we become open to the Spirit. We mainline Christians are an orderly bunch. We want our religion, our worship, and our experience of God to be organized, predictable, and calm—at least those of us do who have remained behind after the great exodus of members from our churches over the past 30 years.

Many of today's mainline members fear the Holy Spirit because of what they see in the Pentecostal movement, which tends to focus mostly on the Holy Spirit. Mainliners see people speaking in tongues and cover their mouths. They hear people prophesying, and shut their ears. They see dancing, swaying, and shouting, and cover their eyes. If being open to the Holy Spirit means becoming like that, they want nothing to do with it. The Holy Spirit can just fill someone else, thank you very much.

Unfortunately, too many of our churches, by ignoring and remaining closed to the Holy Spirit, have developed respiratory failure. Since we no longer breathe with the breath of the Holy Spirit, we neither *aspire* to become open to the Spirit nor allow ourselves to be *inspired* by the Holy Spirit. As a result, our churches eventually *expire*. We suffer such chronic respiratory failure—the failure to breathe in the Spirit and life—that our churches eventually take their last breath and die.

Essentially, too many mainline Christian churches—urban, suburban, and rural—are losing or have lost their spiritual core, their vibrant center. They are missing something deeply spiritual, but because they don't know what they've lost, they wheeze along desperately trying to grasp anything that promises to sustain them. They try this or that program but fail because the programs are missing the very thing that people are searching for: the breath of God in their midst, the work of the Holy Spirit that reveals Christ and leads them to live in harmony with God's plan.

Here's an example: Do you know what one of the most popular evangelizing programs has been over the past 15 years? It is the "bring-a-friend-to-church" program. Years ago, church researchers noticed that up to 85 percent of the newcomers who eventually joined growing churches had originally visited the church at the invitation of a friend who was a church member. So the creators of "Bring a Friend" tried to recreate this statistic in a functional, programmatic way by developing materials to encourage churches to designate a particular Sunday when all members would bring at least one friend.

The essential problem with this program was succinctly identified by one of my cousins. She told me that her church had a "bring-a-friend-to-church" Sunday and she didn't know what to do. She had joined the church because she wanted to expose her children to religion, but she didn't necessarily like the church. As she said, "I'm kind of embarrassed about my church. I'm not sure I want to bring a friend, because then I have to explain why my church is so dead." What good does it do to bring a friend to church if the friend can't encounter God in that church—if it is spiritually vacant?

These programs mimic the functional aspect of what takes place in growing churches, but they lose sight of what is going on spiritually—the spiritual vitality at these churches' cores. They fail to understand that growing congregations don't need to institute bring-a-friend-to-church programs because their members already want to bring their friends. The members sense that God's Spirit is alive in their church, and they want to share their experiences. They are excited about their church because they know it is a place of aspiration and inspiration. Not everyone who visits a church feels as completely inspired as its members, but many do. Their church is a place that breathes life into them.

Too many of today's mainline churches do not breathe in the breath of the Holy Spirit because they suffer respiratory failure, and they don't know how to give their church mouth-to-mouth resuscitation and instill new life. In fact, they dislike or fear the spiritual. As one pastor said to me after hearing that I had a graduate degree in spiritual formation, "Spirituality is just a fad. It will pass in time. Then we can get back to real religion." If spirituality is a fad, then so was Pentecost, and so are the power of prayer and the possibility of experiencing God. If that is the case, we are in trouble in the modern church, because according to the story of Pentecost, the body of Christ, the church, is supposed to breathe with the breath of the Spirit.

The Loss of Spiritual Vibrancy

When we breathe the breath of the Holy Spirit in our churches, we become spiritually vibrant. Unfortunately, because far too few mainline churches breathe the breath of the Spirit, there has been a loss of vitality in far too many of them. Perhaps it is simply a sign of our age. Perhaps this loss of vibrancy is evidence that the mainline Christian movement has grown old and tired, but that doesn't mean that we have to remain old and tired. If we really believe in resurrection and renewal, then new life is possible. All it takes is recapturing the vitality that exists in every lasting church at its birth. Every lasting church (and denomination, for that matter) is initially formed with a spiritually vigorous center. At its inception the original members of a church are so captured by a clear and compelling sense of spiritual life that they commit their lives to its formation and growth.

My own church, Calvin Presbyterian, was founded in 1845 by five people of Scottish descent in a town of German immigrants. They had a vital spiritual desire to gather and worship in the Scottish Presbyterian way. Once they established the church, it grew, attracting people from miles around. The founders had a real sense of spiritual vibrancy that caused them to take the extraordinary step of creating their own church so that they could encounter God in a way that captured their souls. Today, we are witnessing this same kind of vitality in the explosion of new, nondenominational churches sprouting up across the country. Becoming a part of these new churches is exhilarating, because people feel a real sense of the power of the Holy Spirit working constantly in their midst.

But all churches, no matter how vibrant, eventually lapse into a kind of *functionalism*. It happens to every church, and it will happen to these new churches, too. It doesn't happen because of anything bad or corrupt. It happens simply because humans tend towards functionality. In other words, the more we do something, the more it becomes routine and functional as we try to create systems and programs to make our churches more efficient and stable. Think about the kinds of things in your life that have become routine but that at one point were energizing and exciting.

For example, have you ever decided to go for a new look that included adopting a new hairstyle or a new fashion in clothing? If you have, you remember that at one time you were adventurous and explored various possibilities. This exploration of new looks was exciting. Then, as you settled on a look, it became more routine. You probably now have a basic fashion system that tells you what you should buy or wear. Your shopping and dressing are now more functional. Do you remember your first day on your job or as pastor of your church? It was no doubt exhilarating as you learned and developed new skills. Now it has become somewhat routine. You've developed a system. You may even have become somewhat bored with it.

Over time we slip into functional routines. We begin to do things not because of their original vitality, but because they have become just what we do. As churches slip from spiritual vibrancy to functionality, their worship, programs, and events become functionally routine. They become "the way we do things" around here. No church can avoid this fate. Becoming a blessed church is not a matter of avoiding functionality. It is a matter of recognizing when we have slipped into functionality and making choices to recapture a sense of spiritual vitality.

How do we do this? We do it by recognizing that we have lost our original sense of purpose—to guide people to ask prayerfully what the Creator's purpose is for them. We do it by recognizing that we are not encouraging people to encounter God's presence, to encounter Christ in their lives. We do it by recognizing that we are not opening people to God's power, to the power of the Holy Spirit, in their lives. We do it by recognizing that our whole approach to God has become so programmed and functional that God now seems distant, aloof, and uninvolved. God has become a theological principle we speculate about rather than a spiritual presence we encounter and experience. When we become aware of how lacking we are in spiritual animation, we then question what we are doing in the church. We look at our worship and ask, "Has our worship become routine, or does it have a sense of spiritual vibrancy at its core? Has our education program become functional, teaching kids *about* God instead of leading them to form a relationship *with* God?" We ask, "What in our church has become merely functional, and what can we do to recapture a sense of liveliness?

Not all churches are willing to ask these questions. Churches that remain unaware of this slide into functionality eventually slip from functionalism into *dysfunctionalism*. "Dysfunctional" is a psychological term used in family and marital therapy. People make the mistake of thinking it means "not functioning." It doesn't. It means "functioning in pain." When we are dysfunctional, we still function, but everything we do causes pain. Dysfunctional families still have dinner together, go to the zoo together, and take the kids to dance classes and soccer games. The difference is that all of their interactions are painful. Family members, and especially parents, argue and snipe about everything. The dinner table becomes a battleground. Rides to events become torturous. Family functions become laborious, leading all to depression and despair.

Churches that slip into dysfunctionalism do function, but they function in pain. They hold worship services, participate in committee and board meetings, make decisions, do mission work, and more, but they do so in dysfunctional ways. Sermons become berating diatribes as the pastor criticizes the congregation for failing to give enough money, to show up often enough for worship, or to volunteer enough. Church members snipe behind the pastors' backs or send them nasty letters, criticizing them for not visiting members often enough, preaching well enough, or inspiring them enough. Fights within the church erupt over budgets, plans, and more. Energy is drained from the church over every little detail. The question becomes, "What's holding this place together?"

By the time a church slips into serious dysfunctionalism, it is difficult for it to decide to move back toward spiritual vibrancy. When it does, often it does so because some catalyst sparks the movement, such as a scandal that forces the church to look at itself honestly, the intervention of denominational authorities who impose strict sanctions on the church, or the realization that the church will soon die if something isn't done. In other words, what motivates the church to recapture a sense of spiritual zest is the church's hitting rock bottom and deciding to change at its foundations. Sadly, most dysfunctional churches don't make this choice. Instead, they slip from dysfunctionalism to what I will call simple *disfunction.*

Disfunction simply means that the church stops functioning. This doesn't happen all at once. In fact, it generally happens very slowly. Oddly, when a church slips into *disfunction,* it can enter a period of relative peace as the church slowly dies. The people who argued and fought have either left, died, or accepted the inevitability of death. They don't have problems with the pastor anymore because they can't afford a pastor. Instead, they have a series of part-time interim pastors, each of whom stays for only a short time, or they find a lay pastor who will hold their hands until death comes. The ministry of the church is pretty much relegated to offering a basic worship service on Sundays, and to finding someone "pastoral" to serve as a chaplain to the dying congregation. In many ways, it is like being with a family with a loved one in long-term hospice care. Everyone knows that death is coming, and people become more caring and respectful of each other as they prepare for the inevitable. Churches that slide into *disfunction* and begin the dying process aren't going to improve no matter what happens. They don't have the capability. There's no critical mass to build upon. What remains in these kinds of churches is simply a profound sadness. They know they are dying and that death is inevitable.

Where Has All the Vibrancy Gone?

The person who made me most aware of the cause of the mainline church's loss of spiritual vibrancy was a man I studied with for more than five years while working on my doctorate in spiritual formation,

Adrian van Kaam, a Roman Catholic priest and psychologist who created Duquesne University's Institute of Formative Spirituality. He has written numerous books on spiritual formation, and he has an understanding of spirituality that goes beyond anything that I have seen in my own work or that of anyone else writing in the field of spirituality.

Van Kaam understands that the true health of an organization or person comes from being fully integrated. For him, the integration of the four primary dimensions of our lives, which he calls the transcendent, functional, vital, and sociohistoric, are what keep us healthy and energized.[1] For clarity's sake, I have altered his language slightly: In essence, he is saying that to be healthy, we need to integrate and balance the *spiritual, mental, physical,* and *relational* dimensions of life. Unfortunately, we find this kind of integration all too rarely in individuals, organizations, or churches. Without this integration there is no vitality.

Integration begins with the spiritual dimension of life, which is concerned with living in harmony with God and God's will. When we are open to the spiritual dimension, we increasingly seek God's will and begin to sense what God wants for us and from us. When our spiritual dimension is strong, we aspire to what God wants and become inspired by God. The stronger the spiritual dimension is in our lives and churches, the more God's will and ways seem to flow through our thoughts, plans, and relationships.

Whether we are talking about an individual or a church, being integrated means to live life in such a way that the spiritual, mental, physical, and relational dimensions of life all work together with a sense of consonance that brings wholeness and holiness to life. Unfortunately, we live in a culture in which these dimensions are split from each other, and in fact are often at war. They are split because at the foundations of our culture we have cut off the *spiritual dimension*, which, among other things, is also the *integrating dimension.* It is concerned with balancing life as God intended. At the foundations of our culture we have accepted a mechanistic, rationalistic, scientific view of life that either denies the existence of God, or relegates God and spiritual concerns to the margins of life. This view of life denies or ignores the spiritual dimension. The result is that we live in a fragmented world in which people think that having a perfect body, being rich, being powerful, or best, all three, will lead to happiness. Our modern view of life is very different from the ancient view of life. In the ancient world, God and the divine were considered to be part of the very fabric of life. Ancient people considered every part of life to be infused with the spiritual, and they had a sense that they were part of some divine drama. Having lost much of this ancient, integrated understanding of life, we have difficulty attending to the deeper interests of life. We are no longer concerned with our ultimate purpose or how to live a deeper, richer, more loving life. What we seem to care about is the surface of life.

Each dimension, when it is open to the spiritual dimension, has the potential to reveal deeper spiritual truths. For example, theological thinking has the power, via the mental dimension's openness to the spiritual, to reveal the wonders of God and the universe. Art and music, through the physical dimension's openness to the spiritual, reveal God's beauty and grace. Relationships, when open to the spiritual, can embody God's love. Unfortunately, when any of the dimensions are cut off from the spiritual, they lead us to become consumed with their shallow aspects.

For example, some people become dominated by concerns of the physical dimension, becoming obsessed with physical appearance, exercise, diet, sex, drugs, alcohol, pleasure seeking, and the satisfaction of urges. Others become dominated by the mental dimension, becoming obsessed with gaining and wielding power, wealth, and control. Those who are dominated by the relational dimension become obsessed with fitting in or standing out. They become slaves to fashion, custom, and conformity.

You can see the separation of the spiritual from the other dimensions in the domination of our culture by the lifestyle industry's obsession with physical beauty, sexual gratification, and the need for constant stimulation and attention. You can see it in the political and corporate realms, where politicians care only about who has power, wealth, influence, and control. You can see it in the dominance of the fashion and entertainment industries that bombard us with messages about what clothes to wear, what cars to drive, and what gadgets to acquire.

Van Kaam stresses the importance of the spiritual dimension to the life of an individual, an organization, *and* the church. He says that the spiritual dimension is the integrating dimension of life. It holds all the other dimensions in consonance. It is the dimension most concerned with living according to God's purposes. When the spiritual dimension is strong, it does not dominate the other dimensions by denying or controlling them. Instead, it guides and integrates the other dimensions so that we can live according to God's purposes in every dimension. The spiritual dimension guides us so that we can aspire to be healthier mentally, physically, and relationally, even if we live amid conflicts and struggles. Living an integrated life does not keep us from experiencing life's turmoil and pain, but it does open us to God's guidance, which enables us to live through these times in God's ways, and in the end to transcend them in a way that leads to wholeness and holiness. Churches especially need the spiritual dimension to be a strong, guiding force in members' life together. The stronger the spiritual dimension is in our churches, the more we try to live with one another according to God's purposes.

What makes the spiritual dimension the integrating force is its role as the dimension most concerned with openness to God's Spirit. When our spiritual dimension is strong, we aspire to live according to God's calling and seek the inspirations of the Spirit that teach us how to live holy, whole lives. When we aspire to live as the Creator calls us to live, and are inspired by the Spirit, the spiritual dimension guides the mental, physical, and relational aspects of our lives so that they come together in relative consonance. In short, when the spiritual dimension is strong in our lives and churches, it leads us to live healthier, holier, and more whole lives—lives grounded in God and God's love.

Respiratory Failure in the Church

Like individuals, church communities are meant to be healthy bodies whose dimensions are integrated in healthy ways. Unfortunately, because we have cut off the spiritual in many churches, they have become unhealthy places. They become dominated by the mental and relational dimensions, while simultaneously suppressing the physical dimension. You may know churches in which the mental dimension dominates. You may be a member of one. Such churches have slipped into functionalism, or worse, dysfunctionalism. Board and committee meetings often break down into ego-driven fights over who is right and who is wrong. Members of the church divide into theological and political camps as the need to be right and to wield power becomes more important than following the call of Christ to humbly love, support, and nurture each other. These churches become ruled by members and pastors who care most about achieving their ambitions, controlling the decision-making processes, and dominating the community with their positions or beliefs.

Here's an example: Early in my ministry, I served in a growing church that needed more space for its programs. The pastor had asked a member of the church, a man whose business was real estate development and construction, to draw up tentative plans to build an addition onto the church. The plans addressed the needs of the church in a well-thought-out way. The first floor would house a new classroom and an expanded choir room. The second floor would house a multi-use room with a small kitchen and fireplace. Soundproof dividers could be used to create a more intimate space around the fireplace, but the room could also be expanded to host lectures and small congregational dinners. The plans also called for adding an elevator and renovating existing rooms for new purposes. The plan was to build the expansion on the side of the church facing a large parking lot and 16 acres of wooded property.

The plans were presented at a board meeting. Questions were asked, and everyone pretty much agreed with the plans. Then one man said, "I agree with the need to build this, but I don't agree with where it is to be built. I think it should be built on the other side of the church," facing a large field and a park. An argument ensued as the board divided into two camps: those wanting the addition built on the parking lot side, and those wanting it built on the park side. For the next few meetings the discussions continued with no resolution. Both sides were adamant. To end the arguments, it was decided that a task force should be formed to refine the proposal and settle the dispute. The commission worked for eight months, and ended up being somewhat divided itself. Eventually, the senior pastor left the church, partly because of the ego-driven stalemate. Thirteen years later the addition remains unbuilt. In fact, the church has since had more conflict and has shrunk in size.

I don't write this to be critical of these people, because I think all the people involved in the dispute were good, honest people. The problem was that the spiritual dimension was just too weak in that church and its board. No one ever considered stopping the discussion and saying, "What do you think God wants?" In fact, once I led that board in an exercise designed to make board members more aware of the need to follow what God wanted. One board member said to me, "I don't like this at all. It is much easier to make a decision when you don't have to figure out what God wants. I would rather decide what I want." Making "deciding what I want" the key concern is the hallmark of a church that has cut off the spiritual dimension and is now caught in the dominating grip of the mental dimension.

Overcoming enslavement to the mental dimension is difficult. It requires training and guiding the leaders and members to put aside their own egos, ambitions, and need for control, and to seek and follow the Spirit. If the leaders remain resistant to the spiritual, then other leaders who are more open to the Spirit may have to be found. Seeking Spirit-led leaders, however, requires depending on the guidance and grace of the Holy Spirit, and may require the patience of Job to wait for God to reveal these more spiritually open leaders. The patience of Job is a particular asset in leading small churches with little growth, in which the same leaders serve on the board year after year. In their case it may be a wise step to shrink the size of the governing board, even if that means shrinking it to the bare minimum of three members. It is better to have a tiny board of faith-filled, Spirit-led leaders than a large one of functional leaders who care little about what God wants. In fact, cutting the size of boards is a good idea in churches big and small because the smaller a board is, the more it is forced to delegate and to trust in the Holy Spirit.

In some churches, where the spiritual dimension is cut off, the relational dimension dominates. You know these churches. They are the ones that become slaves to the phrase, "But we've never done it that way." They are afraid of change because of a need to conform to the church's past, to rules and customs created by people long gone who were responding to a different age. They are afraid to change because so much has changed around them. They want the church to be the one place of stability in their lives. They become mired in functionalism, doing things only because that is what we do, have done, and always have done. In seeking functional stability they slowly kill the church by sapping its spiritual vibrancy. To keep the church stable, they have to make sure that no one ever joins, no new ideas are ever implemented, and no inspirations of the Holy Spirit are ever followed. Overcoming this tendency to conform to the past can be hard. It means opening the people to the guidance of the Holy Spirit in ways that lead frightened members to feel safe. It may require that the pastor and other leaders maintain a strong and patient faith coupled with a gentle approach that enables them to listen to God while simultaneously making steady, God-inspired incremental changes. Too many pastors and leaders try to change things too fast. Even God-inspired changes take time.

The modern Christian church generally ignores the physical dimension when it comes to physical health. At the same time, the church obsesses about the physical dimension when it comes to dress, race, sexual orientation, and sex. The people of these churches become obsessed with how people are dressed, what color their skin is, what their sexual orientation is, and who is sleeping with whom. The church was more concerned with other aspects of the physical dimension in years past, especially during the Middle Ages, when the focus was on asceticism, fasting, and celibacy. Still, fixation on the physical dimension remains strong in some circles, especially in matters of sex. I'm not advocating a permissive attitude toward sex. What I am saying is that in churches where the spiritual dimension is diminished or cut off, people become obsessed with sex to the point that the church becomes divided over sexual issues and God seems absent.

Meanwhile the Christian church generally ignores other connections between the physical and the spiritual, such as the connection between prayer, healing, and health. Adherents of the New Age movement have filled the void created by the modern church's neglect of the physical by emphasizing the connection between the spiritual and the physical. With their emphasis on yoga, aromatherapy, massage, Reiki, therapeutic touch, crystals, healing, and the like, they have tried to reconnect the spiritual and the physical. Only recently have Christian churches begun to try to reconnect the two. Many churches have discovered or rediscovered the power of candles, labyrinths, incense, yoga, massage, prayer-based dieting, and more. In fact, the reconnection of the spiritual and the physical has led many churches, including nondenominational churches that have traditionally stripped their worship of Christian symbols and of sacraments other than baptism, to recognize the importance of sacraments in opening people to God's mystical presence. As a result, many are now creating new worship services that emphasize Christian sacraments and symbols. Still, most of our churches remain resistant.

The Power of the Spiritual

When the spiritual dimension is strong in a church, members are able to experience God. They discover that God isn't "out there," that God is "above all and through all and in all" (Eph. 4:6). As members become more open spiritually, they become more open to an intimate relationship with each person of God: Creator, Christ, and Holy Spirit. They have an intimate encounter with the Trinity, even if they don't necessarily describe this encounter in trinitarian terms. They come to know God more than they speculate about God. As a result, they also grow in their ability to encounter and experience God in Scripture, others, their own hearts, and the events of life.

Certain signs can reveal fairly quickly whether your church community is open to the spiritual—to the Holy Spirit—and therefore becoming integrated. The first sign of openness to the spiritual is the extent to which *Robert's Rules of Order* dominates the proceedings of the church. Standardized parliamentary procedures are good for helping a church and its committees maintain order, but they aren't designed to help us discern God's will. The more determined the church's leaders are to follow these rules to the letter, the more the spiritual is cut off. The more they are able to supplement these rules with a determined effort to discern God's guidance and voice in prayer, the more open they are to the Spirit. *Robert's Rules* has been a blessing to churches because this little book has helped churches become more orderly and less disorganized (at least when comparing church life before the creation of such procedures, when meetings were often chaotic and confusing). At the same time, strict observance of them can stifle the life of the church because over time a church can become a slave to the functionality inherent in *Robert's Rules.* Then, what matters most is following the rules, not Christ; following the will of the majority, not the will of God. What matters most is doing things in an orderly way, not in a Spirit-led way. Order and procedure become more important than seeking and serving God.

A second sign of being a spiritually integrated church is found when we ask a simple question about worship: What kind of worship is God calling us to employ so that we can reach the people God wants us to reach? Answering this question involves answering other questions: Whom are we trying to reach? What do we have the talent to accomplish? What is the calling of our church? Is it to grow in size? *Can* we grow in size? What is God's purpose in our midst? These questions cannot be answered all at once, but must be constantly asked, and the answers patiently discerned.

Churches that have cut off the spiritual aren't really as concerned about what worship God is calling them to offer, nor the question of whom they are trying to reach. Instead, "cut-off" churches tend to fight over worship styles, music, hymns, and the like. They get caught up in trying to conform to the music of the past, or in trying to force upon others the music of the present. They don't ask the fundamental question, "What worship styles, music, and hymns is God calling us to use?" I've witnessed this fight in our church. At Calvin Church, we in the leadership of the church are pretty determined to form worship styles and use music that we feel called by God to use. I suppose you could call our style "blended," but in reality we just go in the direction we feel called to go. We've kept some traditional things (wearing robes and singing some older hymns), we've adopted some contemporary things (using contemporary songs, lighting, and instruments), and even reintroduced Christian traditions long forgotten by Presbyterians such as using real wine (along with the customary grape juice) for communion, chanting, hanging symbolic banners, emphasizing the liturgical seasons. We try to create worship that is God inspired.

As in all churches that embrace change, especially change for God's sake, we have received complaints. For one particular six-month period I consistently heard complaints from two members about our worship. Both members are good people, yet both came to worship with their own beliefs about what kind of worship we should offer—their kind of worship. On most Sundays, one man in his 80s would sarcastically say on his way out, "What's the matter with the organ? Is it broken?" He was referring to the fact that we played most hymns and contemporary songs on piano, electronic keyboards, guitars, string bass, and drums. Meanwhile, a woman would complain to me that the hymns we sang were too traditional: "Contemporary worship is the wave of the future. We should be going all contemporary." It was hard for either of these worshipers to accept that we were trying to follow what God was calling us to do in our church, not what churches did 40 years ago or what "seeker" churches are doing today.

A third sign of spiritually open churches is that the preaching emphasizes teaching people how to become open to the spiritual, to the Divine, to God. In far too many of our mainline churches preaching tends to be excessively theological or speculative, rather than inspirational and applicable. Such sermons may be theologically deep, exploring the mysteries of God and the universe, but they don't necessarily help people live, or give them guidance on how to encounter God. A sign of spiritual openness is that while sermons remain theologically sound, their main focus is addressing the questions people are silently asking, instead of the questions theologians ask. We address such questions as these: How will this help me discover and hear God? How will this help me serve God in my church, home, workplace, and all other arenas of life? How will this help me discover God's presence and guidance in the grief and darkness of divorce, disease, downsizing, and death? Spiritually grounded sermons try to answer these questions in relevant, honest, and inspiring ways.

The final sign of a spiritually open church is that it integrates all the dimensions in healthy ways. For example, a healthy church is organized and has ambitions, but the leaders care most about humbly seeking God's guidance in prayer rather than pridefully attempting to achieve what they want. For a leader, being spiritually integrated may mean helping the church achieve or accomplish something that I, the pastor, don't think is right, but that other leaders have discerned in prayer. The spiritually integrated church also cares about relationships and traditions. What matters most is steeping the church in loving God with everything it has, loving others as ourselves, and not reflexively conforming to or rebelling against certain traditions and customs because of fear, anxiety, and confusion about what to do to survive. Finally, the spiritually integrated church cares about and addresses physical issues. It cares about teaching members how to develop healthy eating, drinking, sexual, and other physical habits.

Being Refilled with the Holy Spirit

How do we form a church that is spiritually vibrant and integrated? It begins with both pastoral and lay leadership. The pastor first must make a foundational decision to become spiritually open at her core. If the pastors (especially the lead or senior pastor) are closed to the Spirit, the church will be, too, no matter how many members are open to the Spirit. The pastor must become a person of prayer and discernment who seeks God's guidance in everything. The pastor must pray for the church and for the members. The pastor must pray over her sermons, asking that the sermon ring with God's voice, not her own. The pastor must pray for the board, committees, task forces, and teams of the church. The pastor must pray sincerely over his own ministry, asking whether he is God inspired and led, or ego driven and prideful. The pastor must also pray for God to reveal and bring forth other leaders who are faithfully and prayerfully open to God's Spirit. Finally, the pastor must lead the leaders to become more open to the Spirit as individuals and as a group.

Everything said about the pastor also is true of lay leaders. The lay leaders must take God seriously. They must want God to guide them in their leadership and personal lives. If lay leaders refuse to become open to God, they will end up leading the church on a path of disease. The church will slowly sicken, and perhaps even die.

Church leaders can take specific steps to encourage openness to the Holy Spirit. First, they need to make a thorough assessment of the whole church body to determine the extent to which the members are foundationally open to God. (See appendix A, "Assessing the Church's Spiritual Openness.") The point of this assessment is not for the leaders to beat up on the church, but to assess honestly the extent to which the church is open to God. The other point is for leaders to begin making concrete, prayerfully discerned, Spirit-inspired plans to open the church more fully to God.

Second, the leaders can ask questions of themselves to gain a sense of whether their leadership is open to God. For instance, do they plan their meeting agendas in ways that actually seek God's presence and guidance? Most churches that follow the traditional agendas of *Robert's Rules of Order* do not. I do not suggest jettisoning these rules and guidelines. I suggest augmenting them. For instance, in our church we made a decision to reformat our agenda to create space for God. (See appendix B, "Session Agenda.") We restructured our meeting more in the shape of a worship service, with the agenda resembling a worship bulletin. We begin by lighting a candle in a time of centering prayer, sing a hymn, pray together, and then have a time to share what is going on in our lives. We then engage in a time of study or an intensive time of prayer for the church and its ministry, depending on time constraints (studies take longer). Before acting on a committee's recommendation, and after discussing it, we spend time in prayer, discerning whether this action is one that God is calling us to take. The question asked for each vote is "All who sense this is God's will, say 'yes'; all who don't say 'no.'" The point is to emphasize that we are prayerfully seeking together what God wants, not what we want. It is amazing how just changing the question for the vote changes the emphasis. When we ask, "All in favor say 'yes'; all opposed say 'no,'" we are asking leaders to ignore what God wants in favor of what they want. We are saying that we don't care what God wants, and assuming that God's will always rests with the majority. By pointedly asking people to discern whether something is God's will, we are saying that we care most about seeking what God wants.

At the end of the meeting, we take another time for prayer, say the Lord's Prayer, and sing the Doxology. Then I say a benediction as the candle is extinguished. Many good resources are available for helping leaders decide how to restructure meetings in a more spiritually vital, integrated way. Among the best are Danny Morris and Charles Olsen's *Discerning God's Will Together,* or Roy Oswald and Robert Friedrich's *Discerning Your Congregation's Future.*[2] One note of caution, though. While these books can open us to becoming more spiritually available in the work of the church, even these programs can be too orderly. Remember that the original church did not have *Robert's Rules.* Instead, people simply tried to root themselves in discerning the will of Christ. It is more important to create a culture or ethos of spiritual openness than to follow a program of spiritual openness. I tend to believe that the simplest approach is best. (I will discuss this topic in more detail in chapter 3.)

Other practices can help the church leadership become spiritually centered. For instance, leadership boards can regularly engage in studies designed to deepen and open them spiritually. Our session makes the study and discussion of spiritual writings part of our monthly meetings. Retreats should be held to train leaders in prayer, discernment, and spiritual openness.

It is also helpful for church leaders to share the leadership. Leadership boards should be willing to delegate and decentralize so that decisions can be made by committees, task forces, and teams without micromanagement by the leaders. This willingness is a huge part of being spiritually centered. We have to trust the Spirit to take care of the cracks in the church. In a healthy, growing, spiritually vital church, the leaders don't always know everything that is going on. I know that in my church I don't have a handle on everything. I can't. I ask the leaders to let me know the things they think I need to know, but for the most part I have to be willing to trust the leaders. More than that, I have to be willing to trust the Spirit to take care of things I don't see or don't know about. This doesn't mean that I abdicate my responsibilities. All it means is that if I try to be in control, I push out the Spirit. My role is to share control with the other leaders and the Spirit so that the Spirit has room to work as it will, not as I will.

The amazing thing that I've experienced is that whenever I trust in God, great things happen. I've never been disappointed. If I prayerfully sense that a new program or approach should be instituted, but we have no one to run it, I will pray about it and try to wait patiently. It is amazing how often something does happen after I have given the matter to God in prayer. A new member joins the church who can run the program, or someone else comes forward to do it. It may take a while for this to happen, but it always does if I pray and have patience. For example, when we needed to create a Web site and had no clue how to do it, a new member came forward and said, "I've always wanted to create a Web site. I'm not working for the first time in 20 years, and this will give me a something fun and creative to do." She created the site from scratch and did an excellent job. When we needed a new treasurer, one came forward to take the position and revolutionized our bookkeeping process. When we needed to buy property to expand our program, a house next door to the church came up for sale as if on mystical cue. Also, because we were in the middle of a capital campaign at the time, we had the money on hand to buy it outright without going into debt. What I've noticed is that every time the leaders of the church pray together, seek God's will, and trust in God, miraculous coincidences happen *all the time.*

Ultimately, becoming a spiritually vibrant, blessed church means becoming a church that cares deeply about being centered in God's will in everything, so that God's blessings flow through meetings, worship, program, mission, and every other part of the church's life. It means becoming a church that is prepared to be blessed by God to do what God is blessing.

Reflection Questions

1. How have your denomination and congregation suffered from respiratory failure by being resistant to the Holy Spirit's work?
2. How has your church lost its spiritual vibrancy? Is it immersed in functionalism or dysfunctionalism?
3. In what ways is your church unintegrated? In other words, how has the spiritual dimension been unintentionally cut off, and what dimensions are now vying for control of the soul of your church?
4. What steps can your church, and especially your leaders, take to become more open to and guided by the spiritual dimension and so recapture a sense of spiritual vibrancy?

PART II

FORMING A CHURCH OF
PURPOSE, PRESENCE, AND POWER

If I were to pinpoint the biggest problem in the mainline church today, it would be that the modern church has succumbed to treating God as a theological ideal, as an abstract concept, rather than as an experience, an encounter, an embrace of One with whom we can have a deep and transforming relationship. Too many churches never emphasize the encounter with God that leads to an experience of God, but instead emphasize a knowledge of God that leads to—well, where does it lead? Because we too seldom ground our understanding *of* God in a relationship *with* God, we don't truly understand the teachings of the Christian faith. The odd thing about Christian beliefs and doctrines is that they don't really make sense until we experience their truth through an encounter with God.

Most of the essential beliefs of Christianity—the incarnation of God in Christ, the virgin birth, Jesus' death and resurrection, the coming of the Holy Spirit, and many more—become real only when we tangibly experience their truth through an encounter with God. For example, while we can cognitively understand the doctrine of the Trinity with our minds by studying the theology of the Trinity, it is not until we spiritually encounter and experience God as Trinity that we are able to begin to understand God as triune. The simple fact is that most modern mainline Christians don't know what to do with the Trinity because it has been treated predominantly as a doctrine throughout the centuries, rather than as an experience. These Christians believe in God. They believe in the Creator. They believe in Jesus. They believe in the Holy Spirit. But they don't know how God can be one and three at the same time.

To witness how much mainline Christians struggle with the concept of the Trinity, all it takes is engaging them in a discussion about the Trinity and what they think of it. You will find that they hold a vast variety of opinions and beliefs. Many mainline Christians, in their more candid moments, confide that they don't understand the Trinity. "Why not just call God 'Father' and get on with it?" they think privately. When they pray they tend to pray to "Father," "Mother," "Father-God," "Creator," or "Creator-God." While they may say they are trinitarian, in practice they focus mainly on God as Father, Creator, or even Mother. They have experienced God as being one God, similar to the Jewish or Muslim concept of God as the Source, the Creator, the Master of the Universe, who completely transcends this world. The problem is that because they experience God as one God, they don't know what to do with Jesus or the Holy Spirit. They haven't experienced God as Christ or Spirit, and so they may consider themselves to be Christian, but their faith is mostly Father, Creator, or Mother focused. As one person who joined our church said, "I consider myself to be Christian. I pray every day; in fact I pray all the time. You wouldn't believe how much I pray. And I experience God all the time, but I don't know what to do with Jesus."

In contrast to this focus on God the Father, evangelical Christians talk mostly about Jesus. They talk about the importance of being "Christ-centered" and being saved only by a "personal relationship with Christ." They suggest that those who don't focus mainly on Jesus aren't really Christian. They believe in God, but to them Christ is the most important person of the Trinity. Their experiences are centered on Christ Jesus.

Charismatics and Pentecostals emphasize the Holy Spirit. They emphasize praying in the Spirit, being baptized in the Spirit, being filled with the Spirit. They believe in Jesus and pray to the Father, but it is the Holy Spirit who consumes their thoughts because the Holy Spirit is the person of God they truly encounter and experience tangibly.

For the many Christians who don't really experience God as three persons, the Trinity remains a theological and doctrinal idea they say they ascribe to, but that they don't fully believe. They recite the creeds but don't understand them. For example, what does the Apostles' Creed mean when it says that we believe in "God the Father Almighty," and "in Jesus Christ his only Son our Lord"? Does this mean that the Father is the only person of the Trinity who is really God, while Jesus, being the Son, is something like the vice-president of earth in charge of salvation? What does it mean that Jesus is Lord? Does that make him merely a man imbued with divine powers? Does that make him a prophet with mystical powers? Does that make him something like God but not really God?

Is Jesus God? If Jesus is the Savior, then what do the Father and the Holy Spirit do? Do they save, too?

And what is the Holy Spirit's role in our life? Is the Holy Spirit just the spirit of God, kind of like an emanation from God, or is the Holy Spirit God?

All these are questions that people in our pews ask privately but are much too polite, timid, or embarrassed to ask publicly. Few would ever consider asking the pastor, "Can you explain the Trinity to me?—because I have absolutely no idea what it's all about." A lot of pastors, if asked, would squirm in response, reluctant and embarrassed to admit they too are baffled. Most people just say what a friend of mine once said: "What difference does the Trinity make? It's just a concept, a thought. As long as you believe in God, it doesn't matter." It's hard to argue the point, because to disagree is to come close to making our relationship with God come down to getting God's name right. From a practical standpoint, my friend may be right. Does God get upset when we don't call God "Father?" Does God get upset when we don't call God "Jesus"? I've met Christians who seem to think the latter. An evangelical pastor once criticized me because I kept talking about God rather than Jesus. Isn't Jesus God? If Jesus is God, why does it matter if we call God "God" and not "Jesus?" Will God deny us our salvation if we don't call God "Jesus"?

Ultimately, most mainline Christians simply don't know what to do with the Trinity. Is this a problem? From a purely practical perspective, it may not matter much. I've noticed that God seems to be willing to bless churches whether they are truly trinitarian or not. God has blessed many mainline churches that are almost solely Father, Mother, or Creator focused; evangelical churches that are almost solely Jesus focused; and charismatic churches that are mainly Spirit focused. God seems to want a relationship with us regardless of what we call God.

While it may not matter much whether we are trinitarian from a functional perspective, it does seem to matter from a "blessing" perspective. What I mean is that if we are in a church that feels called to become a blessed church, the more intentionally trinitarian we become, the more we open avenues to God's blessings in our midst. My belief is that the way to forming a deeply blessed church lies precisely in leading our congregations as a whole, and our members as individuals, into a deeper encounter and experience with God as all three persons: Creator, Christ, and Holy Spirit.

How do we go about creating a more intentionally trinitarian community? I think it begins with recognizing that above all, the concept of the Trinity is a paradox. The Trinity makes no rational sense. How can God be one and three at the same time? If we really believe we are mono-theistic, then how can we say God is three? From a purely logical per-spective, God can't be. Almost all the major beliefs of Christianity are paradoxes.[1] Does it make sense that God would become human in Jesus Christ? Does it make sense that God, as a human, died? Does it make sense that God, who is dead, would be able to resurrect God? We don't believe these things because they appeal to human rules of logic. We believe them because we have spiritually grappled with them, and over time our experiences of God have led us to believe in our hearts, whether or not we understand in our heads. In other words, we believe in the Trinity because we've experienced it, not merely because someone taught us that it is true.

The Trinity is a paradox we come to experience as true when we form a relationship with God as Creator, Christ, and Holy Spirit. When we engage our congregations in these same paradoxical experiences, they come alive.

I believe that our churches need to be mindful of being trinitarian if they are to become truly blessed churches. We need to be people who are (1) grounded in the purpose that God the Creator created us for; (2) alive to the presence of God in Christ in our midst; and (3) open to the miraculous power of God the Holy Spirit flowing through everything we do. We need to create communities that are grounded in God's Pur-pose, alive to God's Presence, and open to God's Power.

To become truly blessed, our churches need to become trinitarian both in faith and practice, not just in doctrine and belief. We need to form churches that prepare people to encounter and experience God as Creator, Christ, and Holy Spirit throughout their lives. I ask readers in the next three chapters to focus on the Trinity as an *experience of, and an encounter with, God as Purpose, Presence, and Power.* I offer an approach to forming a church that is grounded in God's purpose, presence, and power. I believe that if you use this approach in your congregation, it will unleash God's blessings more strongly in your midst.[2] In chapter 3, I will focus on ways to form churches that are steeped in the work of the first person of God, God the Creator—God the *Eternal Purpose.* In chap-ter 4 we will discuss how to form churches that are alive to Christ, God as *Incarnational Presence.* Finally, in chapter 5 we will examine ways to become open to the Holy Spirit, God as *Inspiring Power.*

Chapter 3

Grounded in God's Purpose

Many of today's mainline churches are wandering aimlessly in the desert, wondering what to do to inject new life into their congregations. I've talked to many pastors and leaders of these churches in my work in retreats, at conferences, and as a spiritual director. They struggle painfully as they try to find the right approach, the right program, the right system to get their church moving and growing. They go to conferences and workshops that promise them a fast-growing, healthy church if only they do this or that. They return from the conference or workshop armed with new ideas and renewed energy, only to find three months later that they are back where they were before—demoralized and drained of energy.

Why? Why are so many pastors, church leaders, and churches wandering in the wilderness? They're wandering for the same reason the Israelites wandered in the wilderness for 40 years: they weren't grounded in God's purpose. The Israelites were called by God to serve God. Unfortunately, during their years in Egypt they forgot their calling. They became a timid and oppressed people, crying in their misery but unwilling or unable truly to follow God's call. They believed in and worshiped God, but they weren't truly grounded in God's call and purpose, and so they became disconnected from their purpose—to be a people of God who lived according to God's law and grace.

Moses was the first Israelite to discover God in the wilderness, and to rediscover God's purpose for the Israelites. In the wilderness, God called Moses to lead the Israelites out of captivity and into the Promised Land. By means of that leadership, Moses rerooted them in their purpose: to be God's chosen people and to live by faith in God. Being God's chosen people had been the Israelites' purpose from the moment God said to Abraham, "Go from your country and your kindred and your father's house to the land I will show you. I will make of you a great nation, and I will bless you, and make your name great, so that you will be a blessing" (Gen. 12:1-2). Abraham's purpose was to be the father of God's chosen people, a people who would reveal God to the world. As both Abraham and Moses became grounded in God's purpose, they were filled with the life and grace of God. In other words, both became *alive* to God's presence and *open* to God's power, which inspired and empowered their service to God.

Focusing specifically on the Israelites and how they rediscovered a sense of purpose through Moses' leadership, we can examine their struggles to embrace their purpose as they embarked on their journey, on what was initially to be a fairly short journey. At first, their journey was amazing. As long as they were grounded in God's purpose, wonderful miracles led and sustained them. They followed God, who appeared as a pillar of cloud by day and a pillar of fire by night. When they hungered, God provided manna and quail from heaven. When they thirsted, God provided water. As long as they remained true to God's purpose, blessings flowed, but when Moses left the Israelites to meet God on Mount Sinai and to discern even more clearly God's purpose, the people became afraid. Lacking a leader grounded in God's purpose, they desperately sought anyone who could offer them a purpose, even a false purpose. They built a golden calf, hoping that this false idol would give them a new sense of purpose. It didn't. Their subsequent 40 years of wandering were a time of becoming grounded more solidly in their purpose: to be a people prepared for the Promised Land.

As the Israelites demonstrated in the desert, fear grows when purpose is lacking, and this same fear afflicts churches. Too many of our modern churches don't know their purpose. They don't know what they were created for. Having lost a sense of connection with God as Purpose, they wander aimlessly. In reaction to this loss, they run about trying this or that program, this or that worship style, this or that approach to ministry and mission. Sometimes such efforts lead to temporary growth and rejuvenation, but more often they simply lead to confusion, conflict, chaos, and decline.

For churches to become blessed churches, the first thing they must do is to become grounded in God's purpose by reconnecting with God the Creator, God the Eternal Purpose. They must become more aware of who they are and why they exist. The more firmly grounded in its purpose a church is, the more it opens conduits of grace that allow God's blessings to flow. For a church truly to become a blessed church, it must become grounded in a deep experience of and relationship with God as Purpose.

Planting a Garden for God

Churches are like gardens in that they grow best when planted and cultivated according to a clear plan and purpose. In fact, certain types of gardens resemble specific kinds of churches.

For instance, the old English garden is a carefully planned plot of flowers, shrubs, walkways, fountains, and walls. Typically, a whole slew of professional gardeners meticulously maintain it. Its purpose is to provide a beautiful and inspiring landscape to awe and inspire visitors. As a result, it is most impressive when seen from afar. It is highly ordered and organized, so one must be careful not to handle anything too much. Its purpose is to induce awe and inspiration, not interaction. Traditional, cathedral-inspired churches are somewhat like these gardens. They are beautiful, magnificent, well-organized places. They have awe-inspiring stained-glass windows and expensive pipe organs. They are meticulously maintained by a large staff. Their purpose is to provide a space where people are inspired to worship the transcendent God in holy space. Like the old English garden, the structure and architecture of this majestic church dwarf us as we worship God from afar, a God who seems so distant, transcendent, and otherworldly. Among members there isn't much sense of a relationship. People of these churches come to worship to be awed, inspired, and transported into a mystical, sacred world.

The cottage garden is built around a home or cottage using a variety of plants. It provides beauty, shade, screening from nosy neighbors, inspiration, and comfort. It takes only a few people to maintain it. This is a garden to be enjoyed at close proximity, not witnessed from afar. When we sit on the patio of the cottage garden, our senses come alive with textures, smells, sights, sounds—and sometimes tastes, even if they are faint. Some churches are like cottage gardens. I believe that my own Calvin Presbyterian Church is like a cottage garden. Its purpose is to provide shade for those scorched by life's heat, small-scale beauty for those needing respite from life's ugliness, inspiration for those seeking God's Spirit, and comfort for those suffering pain. In these churches much more interaction connects the members. These are not awe-inspiring churches in architecture and program, but churches that cause people to feel at home, comfortable, and part of a beautiful nook in an otherwise busy world.

Then there is the vegetable garden. Its purpose is to feed others. Many churches are like vegetable gardens. They are mission-focused churches, often in the inner city, whose purpose is to feed others physically, mentally, and spiritually. Sometimes they ship their food (their mission and missionaries) off to other places to feed people they don't know. More often they simply offer food to those in their midst. Like those working in a vegetable garden to grow food, they focus on feeding those who hunger for love and God.

The herb garden's purpose is to provide spice and healing. Many of the herbs are medicinal, while others add flavor to food. Some churches are places of healing for those who are broken and hurting, salving their wounds and helping them discover God's love. They also provide flavor to the lives of people whose existence has become bland and flavorless. Healing services, as well as inspirational songs and messages, figure prominently in these churches.

Another garden to consider is the wilderness garden. Planted on a large tract of land, it has some organization, but the gardeners also have a propensity to let plants and flowers grow wild. These gardens offer delightful experiences but have dead patches as well. They can be places of inspiration, but also mazes where people get lost and confused. The closest parallel to this garden in the religious world may be the New Age movement. Much in the New Age movement is inspiring and nourishing, but other aspects are deadly and misleading. Discerning which is which can be difficult.

Finally, there is the conservatory. A conservatory is a large structure containing many kinds of gardens. Upon entering, you are immediately immersed in a leafy jungle. Turning to the left you find a manicured flower garden. Soon you come to a room with a small pond and fountains. To the right is a small English-style garden, appropriate for weddings. The conservatory also has Japanese, butterfly, desert, tropical, and country gardens. Each room of the conservatory offers a contrast. Visitors are invited to spend as much time as they want in each garden, or to walk through all. Some churches are like conservatories, especially the large nondenominational churches that present a range of experiences. They offer a wide variety of Bible studies and small groups, as well as all sorts of worship, mission, ministry, Christian education, and spiritual experiences. They try to offer a bit of everything.

Why this comparison of churches to gardens? Because just as there are many kinds of gardens in the world, there are many kinds of churches. Unfortunately, we live in a cookie-cutter McWorld and would prefer to find the *one* model that fits all churches. But like gardens, churches are meant to be unique. The point is that when planting a garden, gardeners have to be true to their purpose. It makes no sense to treat a vegetable garden like an old English garden because heavily pruned vegetable plants will produce nothing. It makes no sense to treat an herb garden like a wilderness garden because weeds will grow and choke the herbs. To plant and cultivate a healthy garden, we have to be as clear as possible that we are being true to the garden's purpose. Otherwise the garden becomes chaotic. Weeds proliferate and choke the life out of some plants, while other plants die from too little or too much water and fertilizer. A particular church should be treated like a different church only when it becomes clear that it has a new purpose, that it is called to become a new kind of church. When a congregation intentionally follows a new purpose, a time of crisis and difficulty will follow, but because God is calling the church to transformation, the transformation will succeed in the end.

Rick Warren has said that the church is alive, that it is an organism rather than an organization, and that the focus of leadership is to nurture the church so that it can grow in a healthy way. He says that the task of church leadership is to discover diseases and barriers to growth, but there is more to leadership than that. Just as gardeners have to be sure what kind of garden they are growing, church leaders have to be clear about what kind of church they are growing.

A model for the kind of organic church growth that we have been discussing comes from John 15, where Jesus says that he is the vine, we are the branches, and the first person of the Trinity, "the Father," is the vinegrower. The Vinegrower, God the Creator and Purpose, plants the vineyard for a purpose: to bear fruit that feeds and nourishes others. When we fail to live according to God's purpose, our fruit withers on the vine and eventually is pruned. For the church to become truly blessed with God's grace and bear fruit, it must live and grow according to the purpose it was created for. Church leaders need to be clear about God's purpose for the church, rather than trying to graft on an unsuitable purpose. Nothing is more frustrating for pastors and members than wandering aimlessly with no guiding purpose, or worse, aggressively following a purpose for which the church is unsuited. Unfortunately, this is happening all over as denominations and their local churches try to follow models created for nondenominational contemporary churches. Some will thrive by doing so, but many more will simply experience frustration and conflict.

When churches are unclear about their purpose—what God created them to be—they begin to look like my garden. I am not a very good gardener. I have been guilty again and again of choosing plants that I thought would look good around my house but that weren't right for our soil, the amount of sun they received, or the lack of attention I would give them (my garden could be called an absentee-landlord garden: I plant and neglect). I've killed more than my share of trees and shrubs by planting the wrong plants in the wrong places.

Many churches are guilty of my gardening sins. They try to plant just anything, and then wonder why the garden keeps dying. They create a contemporary service, but fail because they don't have the talent or charisma to pull it off. They follow an evangelization program designed for a large, suburban church, and wonder why it won't work in their small, rural church. They try to get an older, suburban congregation excited about inner-city mission, and wonder why no one will sign up to help. They never ask, "God, what is your calling for us?"

What Is Our Purpose?

All churches are started for a purpose. All churches are started in response to God's call, whether it is the calling of a pastor planting a new church, or of a group of immigrants coming together to worship God according to their traditional languages, beliefs, and practices. Looking at the history of any church reveals that it originally had a strong sense of purpose. Perhaps it was to reach out to farmers. Perhaps it was to reach out to people in the inner city. Perhaps it was to reach out to people in a new suburb. Perhaps it was to be a place to raise families. Perhaps it was to reach out to boomers or generation Xers. Whatever the purpose, these churches were once clear about their calling. But over time churches forget. They forget that God created them for a specific reason. When churches forget, they lose their sense of connection with God.

Whenever we lose a sense of connection with our purpose as a church body, we lose our connection with God as Purpose. We can try all we want to be a place of Christ and the Holy Spirit, but if we have lost our purpose, we drift and suffer. Many churches are adrift because they have no real sense of what God is calling them to do or be. This is not just a contemporary phenomenon. Even the first Christian churches lost their purpose. In the book of Revelation, we find a clear example of churches that have lost their sense of purpose.

In Revelation 1:17–3:22, God's angels deliver messages to seven churches. Five of them are sharply criticized, two are praised. The five are criticized for one simple reason: they abandoned their purpose, their calling. The church at Ephesus was criticized for abandoning its original call to love (Rev. 2:2-4). The church at Pergamum was criticized for promiscuity and for mixing other faiths with their Christian faith (2:14). The church at Thyatira was criticized for letting a false prophetess lead the people to promiscuity and false practices (2:18-20). The church at Sardis was criticized for being dead (3:1). The church at Laodicea was criticized for being lukewarm (3:15). Two churches were praised, the ones in Smyrna and Philadelphia. They were praised because they remained faithful to their calling, even though they suffered all sorts of afflictions, especially the slanderous accusations of some of the Jewish residents who saw this Christian movement as a threat.

To begin the process of becoming a blessed church, we must communally ask a basic question that lies at the heart of the life, ministry, and mission of a church: "God, what is your call for us?" Rick Warren underlines this idea: "If you want to build a healthy, strong, and growing church you *must* spend time laying a solid foundation. This is done by clarifying in the minds of everyone involved exactly why the church exists and what it is supposed to do."[1] He goes on to say, "A clear purpose not only defines what we do, it defines what we do not do." Bill Easum, in his book *Leadership on the Other Side*, echoes this emphasis by saying that every church has DNA, a kind of genetic code created by God, at its core. Every church is a living, breathing organism that lives according to its DNA: "When churches know their DNA and individuals use their genes to enhance the DNA, growth *just happens*. Just like grass grows and fish swim, organic churches grow."[2] He goes on to say that the church's DNA "defines who we are without making us all exactly the same. It allows each part of the Body of Christ to be different while focusing on the same God-given mission." To come alive, a church must live according to its DNA, its purpose, its call. It is in actively seeking God's call for us that we form a deep and guiding relationship with God who created our cosmos, universe, galaxy, solar system, world, nation, community, and church with a specific purpose in mind—a purpose in harmony with God's eternal plan for everything.

The more we ask, "God, what is your call for us?" and patiently listen for the answer, the more we become a blessed church. The less we ask this question, the more God's blessings are dammed up. Prayerfully seeking God's will is like divining and drilling for living water. We have to make sure that we are drilling where the water is—not where we want it to be. Here's an example: A friend of mine discovered how powerful living according to God's purpose can be when he was the executive presbyter of a presbytery (a regional Presbyterian governing body) in Northeastern Ohio. He was asked by a small congregation to help it prayerfully discern its future. This struggling church was slowly dying, so he spent a weekend with the leaders, helping them discern what God was calling them to do. Surprisingly, at the end of the weekend they clearly sensed that God was calling them to start a new church. You could hear the objections that would eventually be, and were, shouted by other members of the presbytery: "How could they possibly start a new church? They don't even know how to grow their own church. This is crazy!" In essence, my friend's response was "Are you saying that in all their prayer they couldn't possibly have heard God?"

The church decided to follow God's calling, and an amazing thing happened. The members started a new church, it grew, and miraculously so did their own congregation. Ironically, they had reconnected with God's original purpose for them. Part of their mission 70 years earlier had been to plant other churches in the area. In their discernment they had rediscovered God's purpose for them, and in the process they became blessed by God. They had reconnected with God as Purpose, and in the process had become a blessed church.

Prayerful Discernment of Our Purpose

Many churches desperately seek ways to ground their ministry and mission in God's purpose and call but aren't sure how to do it. Too often the models they use come from the secular world—not necessarily a bad thing. The secular world, especially the corporate business world, has developed some remarkable processes for determining an organization's purpose. These processes are designed to define a purpose succinctly for the creation of vision and mission statements, as well as strategic and tactical plans.

Many churches follow these secular models for good reason: they are effective. Still, the processes they use aren't rooted in *discerning God's purpose for the church.* They are rooted in *determining what the members want the purpose of the church to be.* There is a huge discrepancy between the two. One is grounded in God and the guidance of Proverbs 3:5-6: "Trust in the Lord with all your heart, and do not rely on your own insight. In all your ways acknowledge God, and he will make straight your paths." The other is grounded in us—our goals, desires, and egos. I'm not suggesting that we avoid secular models and programs, but that whatever process or model we use, we make sure that its objective is seeking God's purpose, not our own purpose masquerading as God's.

I once took part in a process, as a consultant, to help a church discern the purpose of a new ministry—a process adapted from the corporate world. The church had been given a large grant to create a spirituality center focused on deepening the faith and spirituality of members, friends, and visitors of this large, urban church.

Almost 50 people gathered one weekend to identify the purpose of the program. Much energy was devoted to the process as people talked about their hopes for the program, brainstormed possibilities, and targeted areas of focus. In the end, the result was somewhat confusing because there was too much: too many ideas, too many different focuses. The problem inherent in the process was that it used all of the most modern techniques, but never asked the crucial question, "What is God calling us to do?"

Over the years I have kept an eye on this center from a distance. I have noticed that it struggled for a time to gain an identity. The center has done wonderful work, but it was difficult for those involved to discern what to do and what not to do. At times they tried to do too much, and at others not enough. In the end, I'm not sure that the program fully discerned its purpose. Too many people were involved, including me. I'm not sure I should have been invited, nor should have the rest of the consultants. Probably it would have been much more effective had those feeling a call to this ministry sat together in simple discernment and listened for God's voice in their midst. They might have gathered interested people and invited them to meet over several months, together reading Scripture and relevant contemporary writings (writings that help people grow spiritually). They then might have spent time in prayerful discussion, trying to gather a sense of what God was calling them to do, and how to implement these ideas concretely. Today the program really does bless many people's lives. It is following its purpose, but I'm convinced that it could have had a much more powerful start had it been clearer about trying to discern God's purpose.

I believe that the simpler the approach, the better. The key to discerning and articulating God's purpose lies in seeking a simple process for discernment. So how do we go about choosing or creating a simple process for discerning God's purpose? I offer a process in appendix C, "Discerning God's Purpose for the Church," but other processes are available. I also encourage you to develop your own process, one that is compatible with the needs of your own church. The key is choosing or creating one that is rooted in prayerful discernment and the leadership group's temperament (for example, if the group is mostly filled with extroverts, spending 20 minutes in silent discernment will probably not work). Still, several elements are important in forming a prayerful discernment process:

- Choose or create a discernment process that emphasizes prayerfully seeking God's will and call;
- Invite into the discernment only those leaders who are deeply interested in God's will rather than their own;

- Allow time for prayerful discernment, with an emphasis on listening for God's voice;
- Formulate a succinct statement that captures the essence of the discerned call.

The first element of discerning God's purpose entails *choosing or creating a discernment process that emphasizes prayerfully seeking God's will and call.* Many processes created by organizational experts can help organizations and companies figure out their vision and mission. These processes are great for secular groups, but they are not right for churches. The main focus of any church is prayerfully seeking what Christ, the head of the church, wants for the church. To discern the purpose of the church requires a process that emphasizes prayerful listening. It requires spending time with relevant Scripture that sheds light on how to hear God. For example, the following Scripture passages open people to ways of hearing God: Proverbs 3:5-8; 1 Corinthians 12:4-31; Ephesians 3:14-21; John 15:1-17; Ephesians 4:1-16; John 13:1-20; 2 Timothy 2:14-19; and James 4:1-10.

Any good discernment process also invites people to discuss the present situation of the church, as well as possibilities for the church. It allows for brainstorming, but always with an emphasis on what God may be calling us to do. Finally, it invites people into the hard but fruitful work of prayerfully sifting through all possibilities to center in on those that most strongly seem to come from God.

For help in better understanding group discernment, several resources are available—for example, *Listening Hearts* by Suzanne Farnham, Joseph Gill, Taylor McLean, and Susan Ward; and *Discerning Your Congregation's Future* by Roy M. Oswald and Robert E. Friedrich.[3] Another possibility is Rick Warren's *The Purpose-Driven Church,* although I do offer one caveat. I think Warren's book is a wonderful resource, and it is clear that he has grounded his ministry in spiritual discernment. It has helped me tremendously in my own leadership and ministry, yet the processes Warren advocates often are not clearly connected to discerning God's will. He pushes the idea that the leaders and the church need to be clear about their purpose, but he isn't as clear that the purpose must be discerned from God. His process is often more functional than spiritual, but it can be modified to be made more prayerful and spiritual.

Whatever process is chosen or developed, expect people to resist it. Unfortunately, most members of modern mainline churches aren't particularly mature spiritually. The reason is that our churches haven't emphasized spiritual growth. We don't necessarily expect our members to be biblically literate. Our Christian education tends to emphasize imparting religious and theological information rather than nurturing spiritual formation. Most of the spiritual nurturing that people get comes through worship. Unfortunately, the typical worship service does not require the kind of self-examination, study, and practice that leads a person to grow spiritually. Combine all of these factors, and they suggest that our members are not very mature spiritually.

In fact, too many of our church leaders aren't spiritually mature; it is important to train them in spiritual discernment. Unfortunately, too many church leaders are chosen for their functional abilities to organize and get projects done, not for their spiritual maturity. They may be good problem solvers in their work and in other facets of their lives, but this doesn't necessarily mean they will be people of faith committed to discerning God's will, instead of problem solving. People who are used to problem-solving analysis don't like doing discernment. Earlier I quoted a leader in the first church I served who said, after participating in an exercise designed to help the leaders listen for God's will, "I don't like this 'trying to hear what God wants' business. It's too hard. It's much easier for me just to decide to do what I want." He recognized the importance of listening to God, but also his own resistance. Resistance to discerning God's will cannot be overcome through pushing and shoving people. It is overcome by gently helping people to identify the source of their resistance, and then patiently encouraging them to try something new and God centered. We need to help people recognize that although discernment is scary—after all, we are stepping boldly into what God wants, not what we want—we can trust God to continue caring for us throughout our seeking.

Discernment is also not a one-time process. It requires that we constantly refine our discernment. Even when we have discerned what God is calling us to do, we have to return to discernment again and again to discover what new and wonderful things God may be calling us to do. Discernment is a lifelong commitment for the blessed church and its members.

The next step is *inviting into the discernment process only those leaders who are deeply interested in God's will rather than their own.* There is no way to overemphasize this point. Too often the people we ask to determine and articulate a church's vision are more interested in what they want than in what God wants. Whenever that is the case, the resulting purpose statement ends up reflecting the members' will rather than God's. Seeking what members want rather than what God wants is a major problem in the modern church. For that reason I am not a big fan of church surveys that care mostly about what the people in the pews want.

This does not mean that church surveys aren't valid and should never be used. I just think that we need to be aware that when we base our decisions on surveys about what people want, we may be missing what God wants. Most declining and dying churches are declining and dying precisely because they have focused too much on what their members want rather than on what God wants.

Spiritual leaders point and motivate people to go where God is going, not where the people want to go. The best leaders encourage people to want what God wants. What God wants and what members want are not necessarily the same, and we need to recognize that church members are not mere consumers. I became very clear on that point when I was an associate pastor serving in my first church. The personnel committee used an evaluation process taken from the committee chair's employer, a large corporation. The group didn't change the evaluation form much, other than to change the name at the top from the company name to the name of our church, as well as to change the name of the corporate position to "associate pastor." The questions asked in the evaluation weren't particularly suited to evaluating a pastor. For example, the form asked: "How well does the associate pastor respond to *the consumer?*" The implication was clear. As associate pastor my responsibility was to please the consumers—the members of the church—not God. I wasn't evaluated on whether or not I prayed, helped people connect with God, or did what God was calling me to do. Secular models focus too much on what members (consumers) want and not on what God wants.

What do members usually want? Most members want stability. They want the church to respond to *their* needs and desires. If new members join, old members want new members to bring their wallets and energy, but not necessarily their ideas, needs, and desires. They don't want too much change. Unfortunately, surveys never ask the question "OK, enough about what you want. What do you sense *God* wants?" What if God wants the church to change? What if God wants the church to grow? What if God wants the church to engage in a new mission or ministry? What if God wants the church to reach out to the new people moving into the area? What if God wants the church to move or die? (I do believe that sometimes God calls churches to die.)

I am not suggesting that leaders ignore what members want. Certainly God can speak to us through the voices of our members, and often God does. Still, good leaders also have to have the wisdom to distinguish God's voice coming through the members from the members' voices drowning out God. Perhaps a way around this tendency to seek what the people want rather than what God wants is to design surveys that invite people to engage in a time of prayer and to write down what they sense God wants for the church.

The third step in discerning God's purpose is *allowing time for prayerful discernment, with an emphasis on listening for God's voice.* The process of discernment is very different from the way most of us have learned to determine a course of action. Most of us have been trained in analysis rather than discernment. Analysis is the process of dissecting a problem to figure out its root. It literally means to "loosen throughout" or "tear apart" something to figure it out, and then we offer solutions based on human logic. In scientific and technological fields we analyze something by tearing apart a machine, a substance, or a molecule to find the problem, and then we apply human logic to determine how to fix it. When we analyze a problem in business or politics, we break everything down and determine the weakness of an approach or argument, and then use rational projections to apply a solution. Too often we apply these same methods of analysis in the operation of our churches. When addressing a situation or a problem, we analyze rather than discern, and in the process we can end up with an elegant human solution that moves in a completely different direction from what God wants. At times what God wants doesn't make human sense, yet it is what God wants that God blesses. If all we do is analysis, we can end up missing what God is ready to do in our midst. Discernment discovers what God is doing.

Discernment is more like sifting or panning for gold. We slowly sort through all the junk and false answers to discover God's answer at the center—the nugget of gold in the midst of worthless pebbles. Discernment requires faith, prayer, and patience. It calls individuals and groups to sit and wait for God's answer, even if it takes months to discern. Discernment is not a quick process, and its slowness can frustrate those for whom haste is a constant imperative. God can take a while to provide an answer. It can take us a long time to sift through all the noise of the world and finally hear God's whisper. It requires letting go of not only the voices of convention, security, and stability, but also the voices of pride and fear that can scream out from within all of us. (For help in discerning a particular issue, see appendix D, "Discerning Direction for a Particular Issue.")

The final step of discernment is *formulating a short, succinct statement that captures the essence of the call.* Too often churches create elaborate vision and mission statements that no one follows because they are too long and involved. It is difficult to distill our discernments into a short, succinct statement of purpose, but when we do, the statement can guide everything we do in a church. For instance, Calvin Presbyterian Church's purpose statement describes the congregation as "a spiritual family sharing the gospel of Jesus Christ and discerning God's purpose and will through sincere commitment, prayer, fellowship, teaching, and mission." I think our purpose statement is almost too long, but within it lie two phrases that articulate our purpose and guide me in my role as a spiritual leader. These two phrases are *a spiritual family sharing the gospel of Christ* and *sincerely committed to discerning God's purpose and will.* I can't think of anything more expressive of our purpose.

The phrase "spiritual family" was coined by a member during our discernment process. We were trying to express what our foundation is, and she expressed it perfectly: "I'm not sure what else we are, but this is my spiritual family. It's my home. No matter what is happening in my life, no matter how bad things get, I always know I can come here and people will care about me." Over the years, we have worked hard to nurture this identity as a spiritual family that shares the gospel of Christ. We are spiritual in that we know that it is not our biology but our faith in Christ's love and presence that binds us. We are also family in that we are trying to create a place that accepts all people to the best of our abilities, while also nurturing them to mature spiritually. Our church is a place where all people, regardless of how hurt or broken they are, will find love from others. And sometimes we are like the family of the prodigal son. We are willing to let frustrated people go, and to celebrate when they return. We are not very good in our church at stressing purity or righteousness. Some churches in our area call us the "church of sinners"—a description that we take as a good thing, even though it isn't meant that way. People who come here know that they aren't going to be judged. As one woman said, "I like Calvin Church because it is the one church where I am allowed to be divorced. People don't hold it against me, and they care about me." In the process of being a spiritual family, we try to be a healthy family. Certainly some dysfunctional people are in our church. We try to be compassionate with them without becoming ineffectual. In other words, we care about people, but we do not let their personal issues cause us to form detrimental patterns of relating with each other. It is our hope that by taking this approach we can nurture them to health.

The downside of being a spiritual family is that we are not as strong in some aspects of church life as we could be. We are not as strong in mission or evangelism as some churches are—perhaps because our commitment to prayerfulness prompts us to give God responsibility for leading us in mission and evangelism. In other words, we allow God to bring us mission opportunities to which we respond, and we let God be our evangelism program, calling people to become part of our community.

The result has been that our mission giving makes up 20 percent of our budget, and over the past eight years we have been able to triple the number of dollars we give to mission. Also, despite *not* having a structured evangelism program, we have managed to double our membership, and more than double our weekly attendance over the course of eight years. I believe that all these elements are part of becoming a blessed church. When we are centered in trying to do what God is calling us to do, God gives us opportunities to bless others through mission, and God brings people to the church who will bless us and whom we can bless. I believe that because we are trying to be centered in God's purpose, God blesses us by allowing amazing things to happen in our midst—miraculous and inspiring blessings—and they don't happen by our own hands or efforts. They come as gifts from God.

In addition to focusing on our call to be a spiritual family, we also stress "discerning God's purpose and will." We emphasize this aim in meetings of our governing board, committees, and congregation by grounding our work in one central question: God, what are you calling us to do? In personal counseling sessions I stress that people should seek God's will. Ultimately, becoming a church or a person of purpose originates in spending time in prayer, discerning God's will for us.

Creating a Culture of Discernment

It is not enough simply to discern a purpose for the church. We also need to create an ethos or a culture of discernment that permeates everything we do. We need to make discernment part of the overall life of the church. For example, in our board and committee meetings, do we operate in a way that is open to God's call and voice? Are we open to God as Purpose in our midst? If we are guided by *Robert's Rules of Order*, can we modify the procedures in a way that allows for discernment?[4]

At Calvin Presbyterian Church we include several elements in our session meetings to encourage discernment. First, we create a spiritual atmosphere by modestly decorating the room where we meet with spiritual symbols, and by placing a candle in the middle of the table. We light the candle at the beginning of the meeting and extinguish it at the end, just as we do in our worship service. As I mentioned earlier, we design the agenda for our session meetings so that it follows a worship agenda and looks like a worship bulletin, including time for music, prayer, study, discernment, and reflection. When we are making a decision, I ask people to spend time in silent prayer, putting aside their own desires to listen for God's call and voice. When I ask them to vote, I say,

"All who sense this may be God's will say 'aye.' All who don't say 'no.'" If we fail to reach a consensus, I take this outcome as a sign that we have not listened carefully enough to God, so I generally ask the members to postpone the decision so that they can pray over it for a month and, we hope, discern more clearly God's will. I call this action "postponing in prayer." Then we take up the matter in the next meeting. If the elders still cannot reach a decision, I will continue to postpone in prayer. We usually move forward only when we have reached either *unanimity* (we agree unanimously) or *unity* (some still disagree, but they believe it is best to move forward together and support the decision because they aren't sure or convicted of God's will.)

It isn't only in meetings that we are called to seek God's purpose. In every operation of the church we have to look for ways to seek God's will. For instance, at Calvin Church we try to bring listening to God into our budgeting and stewardship programs. For the budgeting process, we ask each committee in September to spend time in prayer asking what God is calling it to do in the next year. (See an agenda for these meetings in appendix E, "A Prayerful Process for Discerning Committee Budgets.") Then in October, we bring all the committees together to discern the overall budget. (See an agenda for this meeting in appendix F, "All-Committee Budgeting Process.") We ask all the committee members to put aside their commitment to their own committee budgets and to become part of the body as a whole, seeking what God wants for the whole church.

Each committee presents its budget while others pray for that group's work and mission. Then we discuss and provisionally decide what the overall budget total should be. Afterward, all pray for God's continued guidance and blessings. Then we communicate to the members our plans for the following year, and in our stewardship program we ask them to pray about what God is calling them to give. (See appendix G, "Guiding Members to Give," for information on how to create a prayer-based stewardship program, and appendix H, "Sample Stewardship Materials," for the pieces used to communicate with the congregation.) Since we instituted this process, we have consistently and significantly increased our budget each year, yet we have continued to end each year with a surplus. I am convinced it has to do with our grounding ourselves in God's purpose, which connects us with God's blessings.

Another area where God's purpose has to be emphasized is in preaching and teaching. To be a church grounded in God as Purpose, we need to preach consistently to people in a way that teaches them how to discern God's will in their personal lives. The more a church discerns as a body of individuals, the more a church can discern as a community. Classes, retreats, and programs for childhood through adulthood must be offered that teach discernment (of course, without becoming obsessive about it).

Finally, our outreach, both local and global, must be grounded in God's purpose. One reason so many churches struggle in outreach is that they try to do what they think they ought to do, rather than what God is calling them to do. Every church has its own unique missional call that reflects its situation. We cannot follow the call of another church. We have to be true to God's call to us. A sure-fire way to ensure that a mission program will fail is to try either to do too much without ever asking "Is all of this true to our purpose?" or to engage in mission that is not our discerned purpose at all. We are called to reach out to others for Christ, and we are called to stretch ourselves, but we still need to be mindful that what we are doing is according to God's will.

Leading with Purpose

It is not easy to get a church to be centered in Purpose. As stated earlier, people will resist the process because it is new and uncomfortable, and because we are naturally, sinfully more interested in our own desires than God's. Still, good leadership finds a way to ground people in Purpose despite their discomfort. Blessed leaders, leaders who are relatively clear about what God's calling is for them and the church, understand that members will be anxious and uncertain because they are not used to seeking God's purpose for themselves or the church. So blessed leaders must work hard to forge a strong faith in God as Purpose so that those with a weaker faith can lean on them. These leaders must be firm but gentle in their determination to follow God's purpose. They must lovingly and prayerfully encourage people to be grounded in Purpose. They cannot coerce and force people. They must be patient, understanding that being grounded in God's purpose is something new and takes time.

Blessed leaders also must make sure that the church continues to seek God's purpose, because over time the functional tendencies of people will always pull the church back to a more functional style. They must make discerning God's purpose one of the bedrock norms of the church. How do leaders know when the congregation has become blessed? They know it when an issue comes up and the members remind the leaders to discern God's purpose. I've had this happen to me many times when I've been anxious about something, and an elder or other church member has simply said to me, "Don't worry, Graham. Just try to listen to what God wants and it will all work out." That says to me that we are a church grounded in God's purpose, and that I have done a good job of being a spiritual leader.

It is important to realize that even though becoming grounded in God's purpose will breathe new life into the church, this does not necessarily mean that the church will experience explosive growth as a result. Churches are always bound by their available talent, context, and situation.[5] Not all pastors are dynamic preachers and organizers. Not all churches are located in growing areas. Not all churches have the resources to provide exceptional and groundbreaking programs. All that matters is that we do what we are called to do, how we are called to do it, and where we are called to do it.

Finally, in some situations you, the reader, will not be able to get the whole church to become more grounded in God because the senior or solo pastor and other key leaders are resistant. If you can't change the whole church, you can make sure that you and your committee, task force, team, or ministry are grounded in God's purpose. Do what you can and leave the rest up to God.

Ultimately, the foundational focus of a church in communion with the Trinity is to be grounded in God's purpose by forming a deep relationship with God as Purpose. By doing this the church community begins to encounter the Creator as they experience God's blessings in their midst. It all begins with grounding ourselves in God the Eternal Purpose.

Reflection Questions

1. To what extent do you sense that your church has a clear purpose?
2. To what extent do you sense that your church's purpose is grounded in God's purpose?
3. How would you describe, succinctly, God's purpose for your church, even if you have never formally discerned your church's purpose?
4. What concrete things can you do to ground yourself and your church in God's purpose and steep the church in a relationship with God as purpose, with God the Creator?
5. What particular steps can your church, and especially your leadership, take to become more open to and guided by the spiritual dimension of life?

Chapter 4

Alive to God's Presence

It is amazing what can happen in churches that are grounded in God's purpose. They form a strong sense of identity and are filled with a sense of direction. Their leaders and members exhibit humble conviction and resoluteness, even when trying to do something new and different. A church grounded in Purpose is connected to the source of living water. It has the potential to become a conduit that allows living springs of water to flow in and through people's lives. When a church is grounded in Purpose, it connects to the source of living water, but that does not mean living water—grace—will automatically flow through people's lives. More needs to take place. Being a church of Purpose connects the church to living water, but it is by becoming a church of Presence that the conduit between living water and the people of God is opened. To be a church of Presence means to be a church that intentionally tries to awaken people to God's presence and grace in their midst so that they can connect with Christ more powerfully in their daily lives.

Churches that become alive to God's presence may not be perfect (no church is), but even in their imperfection they are alive because Christ—God as Presence—is in their midst. In these churches, the presence of God becomes tangible and evident to those who are ready to discover it. These churches have life and give life; they deepen and revive people in amazing ways.

Becoming alive to God as Presence, to Christ, is not synonymous with creating a large, fast-growing megachurch. In fact, becoming a church of Presence can actually inhibit growth, at least at first. The focus of a church that's alive is spiritual growth—the deepening and transformation of people's lives—not necessarily physical growth (although the two are not incompatible). Some seekers will turn away from a church of Presence because they do not want depth and transformation. Many want simple rules to follow and quick, easy, and clear answers to their deepest questions. A church of Presence offers neither.

A church of Presence offers a pathway for people to experience Christ. It calls them to commitment, prayer, sacrifice, love, and transformation. It teaches people that Christ is among us and in us, but that we cannot encounter Christ with the depth that Christ desires unless we adopt practices and lifestyles that allow the life of Christ to grow in us. The example of what happens when we become alive to Christ comes through Paul's instruction to the Colossian church:

> As God's chosen ones, holy and beloved, clothe yourselves with compassion, kindness, humility, meekness, and patience. Bear with one another and, if anyone has a complaint against another, forgive each other; just as the Lord has forgiven you, so you must also forgive. Above all, clothe yourselves with love, which binds everything together in perfect harmony. And let the peace of Christ rule in your hearts, to which indeed you were called in the one body. And be thankful. Let the word of Christ dwell in you richly; teach and admonish one another in all wisdom; and with gratitude in your hearts sing psalms, hymns, and spiritual songs to God. And whatever you do, in word or deed, do everything in the name of Lord Jesus, giving thanks to God the Father through him.
>
> Colossians 3:12-17

Ultimately, Paul reminds us that as we practice faith together and share a Christlike lifestyle, we become alive to Christ in our midst. Becoming alive to Christ's presence is central to becoming a blessed church.

Too many of today's Christian leaders believe that bigger is better— an attitude that is a product of our culture—but some of the most deeply blessed churches are smaller congregations. Of course, many blessed churches are large, but in many cases the larger and faster a church grows, the less blessed it becomes because the focus is on breadth, not depth; on quantity, not quality. The appearance of blessing on the surface may obscure the fact that these churches are frenetic, showy places with lots of bells and whistles, filled with people who are not all that committed to Christ, but who have become addicted to stimulation and entertainment in their spiritual walk. They want to experience Christ's presence, but only if it comes wrapped in an exciting package.

Many Christians tend to think that contemporary is better and that offering a contemporary worship service is the answer to all our churches' ills. If only we become more contemporary, people will flock back to us. The flaw in this belief is that the youngest generation, the millennials (those born since 1982), are showing less interest in contemporary worship than they are in ancient rituals that connect them with something deeper that draws them into a more tangible experience of God. According to Neil Howe and William Strauss, generational researchers, millennials are "drawn to such complex ancient rituals as the Jewish Kabbalah, the walk of the labyrinth, the meditations of St. Ignatius, or the mantralike recitations of Taizé, in which kids sit in a candlelit room and sing the same songs, over and over."[1] For millennials, ancient rituals are new, and contemporary is old. In fact, some "seeker" churches (those that emphasize reaching out to unchurched people, or "seekers") are beginning to offer more traditional worship services to attract those millennials who want stained glass, crosses, candles, art, sacraments, rituals, and the like. This desire for the mystical and symbolic explains why more and more younger people are attracted to the liturgies of the Orthodox, Roman Catholic, and Episcopal churches. They want an experience of Christ that touches all their senses. They want more than music and a message. They want a tangible sense that Christ is in their midst.

What people really want in worship and a church is an encounter and experience of God. The extent to which people sense Christ's presence and life through worship matters more than the style of worship. Of course, given the choice between a shallow but entertaining contemporary worship and a stodgy traditional service, neither of which really enlivens them to God's presence, people (including me) will choose the contemporary because at least it is stimulating. Unfortunately, we too often offer people a contemporary or a traditional style but little substance.

Forming a church that enlivens people to Christ's presence means offering a church experience that invites and incarnates God as Presence, God as Christ. And make no mistake, many churches do not invite or incarnate Christ. They are more focused on maintaining denominational and congregational traditions than they are with letting Christ in—and Christ will not enter our churches uninvited. In Revelation he says, "Listen! I am standing at the door knocking; if you hear my voice and open the door, I will come in to you and eat with you, and you with me" (Rev. 3:20). In churches that ignore the knock or bar the door with a pattern of chronic conflict or indifference, Christ generally seems content to stand on the outside waiting. Only rarely will Christ surprisingly enter uninvited to transform the church. When Christ is left on the outside, churches become empty of Presence. Sermons are preached, hymns are sung, and rituals are followed, but Christ is rarely encountered because he has been prevented from being present. Blessed churches open their doors to Christ and let Christ become a deep and life-giving presence in their midst, bringing life to the church and all who inhabit it.

Awake, Aware, and Alive!

I have heard many people in many places complain that their churches are dead, the sermons are boring and irrelevant, the music is laborious and archaic, the pacing is slow and tedious, and the people are lifeless. I've not only heard this criticism from others. I've made such complaints myself. I left the church at age 15 because of such experiences, and returned to the church at age 24 despite them.

Churches feel dead when they are dead to Christ's presence. Sadly, spiritually dead churches can remain physically alive for many years, but eventually their spiritual death leads to physical death. Of course, members don't make the connection between a congregation's spiritual and physical deaths. They say that the church died because the congregants got old, the neighborhood changed, or the church was afflicted by a scandal years before. But these problems, while difficult to overcome, are not what caused the church to die. If the parishioners had been alive to Christ, they would have found a way to enable the church to survive and thrive, even in the face of the direst challenges. Ultimately, churches have died because leaders and members were not willing to seek Christ's presence, which would lead and guide the congregation not only to survive, but to thrive through the changes. Christ is present at the core of all our churches like a slumbering child, wanting to be awakened, wanting to play, wanting to bless us with his presence. When we realize that that Christ is in our midst and ready to be awakened, and then open ourselves to Christ and Christ's guidance, amazing things begin to happen in our midst. If we are to tap into this core, we have to take Christ's presence seriously enough to prayerfully seek and follow Christ's guidance, which is available to all who seek to follow.

Becoming a blessed church means becoming awake, aware, and alive to Christ's presence in our midst, giving us guidance, life, and love. I became aware of this truth after reading Thomas Kelly's *A Testament of Devotion* in 1989. Kelly was a college theology and philosophy professor at several Quaker colleges during the 1920s through the 1940s. His life was mostly unremarkable except that during the last three years of his life he delivered a series of talks to Quaker meeting houses in the Philadelphia, Pennsylvania, area that awed all who heard him. After he died, people realized that they had heard something authentic and true in his talks, and so the talks were collected in a book. Kelly's vision of church was so different from anything I had ever heard that it changed my whole way of seeing church.

Kelly had an understanding of Christ's presence in the church that was truly radical. He said that at the core of every true church lies a "blessed community"—a community of people at the center of the church who are so deeply grounded in Christ that the life of Christ flows through them into the rest of church. As he says, "Yet ever within that Society, and ever within the Christian church, has existed the Holy Fellowship, the Blessed Community, an *ekklesiola in ekklesia,* a little church within the church."[2] Perhaps you've met these people in your own church. They are deeply spiritual individuals whose connection with God causes them to radiate God's love and presence. They may not be leaders who sit on church boards and committees, but if they were missing, the church would crumble because they are the ones who embody the life of Christ. The more a church nurtures and cultivates this blessed community, this little church within a church, the more it becomes a blessed church that leads people to an encounter with Christ. Whenever the blessed community grows within a church, the whole community becomes transformed as more and more people encounter and experience Christ in their midst.

As the blessed community grows within a church, it becomes a transformed place, even if it looks the same. As Kelly says:

> On all the wooing love of God falls urgently, persuadingly. But he who, having will, yields to the loving urgency of that Life which knocks at his heart, is entered and possessed and transformed and transfigured. The scales fall from his eyes when he is given to eat of the tree of knowledge, the fruit of which is indeed for the healing of nations, and he knows himself and his fellows and comrades in Eden, where God walks with them in the cool of the day. . . . And these are in the Holy Fellowship, the Blessed Community, of whom God is the head.[3]

In a blessed church the focus moves from maintaining right practices or beliefs to leading people to a communion with God. What matters most is allowing the life of Christ to flow through the church. People no longer become divided by theology, but as Kelly says:

> Holy Fellowship reaches behind these intellectual frames to the immediacy of experience in God, and seeks contact in this fountainhead of real, dynamic connectedness. Theological quarrels arise out

of differences in assumptions. But Holy Fellowship, freely tolerant of these important yet more superficial clarifications, lives in the Center and rejoices in the unity of His love.[4]

What is the nature of a blessed church—a church that is awake, aware, and alive? It is *awake* to Christ in that it responds to Paul's admonition to wake up: "Besides this, you know what time it is, how it is now the moment for you to wake from sleep. For salvation is nearer to us now than when we became believers" (Rom. 13:11). A blessed church is not content to do merely what has always been done. It truly wants to do what Christ has equipped it to do. The people of the church, and especially the leaders, deeply believe that Christ is in their midst, guiding, directing, and blessing them. They expect that something wonderful and mystical will happen in worship, meetings, classes, and small groups. They don't necessarily know what will happen, but they know it will lead to an encounter with Christ.

Blessed churches aren't just awake. They are also *aware*. They have what I would call a "mystical awareness" that God is present. This mystical awareness may not be a conscious awareness, but it is present nonetheless. These congregations look around and see evidence of God. They sense Christ's presence in the music, prayers, sermons, meetings, groups, fellowship, ministry, and mission of the church. They have "Aha!" moments during the sermon and are aware that God has just spoken to them. They connect with someone in church, and they know that they have just experienced communion with God. They help another member in need, and at some level they know that they have just borne Christ to that person. This mystical awareness again emanates from the pastors and leaders of the church because they are constantly pointing out where God is present. When coincidences or small miracles occur, the leaders point them out and say, "There's Christ in our midst." In blessed churches, the people become increasingly aware that not only is Christ present in every person, but also that they have become the body of Christ (1 Cor. 12:12-31), and that Christ is working through everyone, even the least involved.

When a church becomes aware, a majority of members recognize that they are on a journey for, to, and with God, and that to sail across the waters they must keep Jesus as their North Star. No matter where they are, they keep their eyes on Christ, even if they don't know to call this Presence "Christ." To them all that matters is that God is present among them and that they must follow where Christ leads.

Finally, blessed churches are *alive* to Christ, and because they are, Christ is alive in them. John 15 offers a powerful metaphor for this kind of aliveness. Jesus says that he is the vine and we are the branches, that those who live in Christ and allow Christ to live in them will bear fruit that feeds the world. This is a superb metaphor for being alive to Christ, telling us that if we become awake and aware of God's presence in our midst, the life of Christ will flow in and through us as we become alive in Christ. Our lives take on a new character and quality. When we become alive to Christ as a church, we are infused with an energy, a dynamism, that becomes apparent. Thus, becoming a blessed church is more than an approach or style of ministry and worship. It is a way of living as a church.

When the leaders of the church, both pastoral and lay, become awake, aware, and alive to God's presence in their midst, they create the conditions for astonishing things to occur. People begin to experience blessings in every part of their lives, and especially in the church. They continue to struggle. They still may become ill. They still may find themselves unemployed or divorced, or suffer some other form of loss. But something else also happens. They become aware that God is with them, blessing them despite the pain and suffering of their lives. In the midst of suffering they experience faith, hope, and love. When a church is alive to Christ, its members notice God's grace and blessings working in their midst.

A story illustrates what it means to be an alive church: Years ago a small monastery was nestled in the mountains of France. Once it had been the center of inspiration for pilgrims and seekers yearning for God. People came from all over Europe to discover God in the monastery. But then the monastery changed. It became proud. The brothers took themselves too seriously. Instead of being truly humble, they became proud of their humility. So began their decline. Fewer and fewer pilgrims sought their wisdom, and few monks joined their ranks. The brothers became rigid. They worshiped their past. They were spiritually dead and physically dying. In another generation all the monks would be dead, and the monastery would die with them.

One day a scraggly stranger came to the door. He smiled a toothless smile and asked for a place to rest for the night. He was invited in. The monks thoroughly enjoyed his presence at dinner and sensed a spiritual depth in him, though he was outwardly rough and smelly.

The next morning, as he was leaving, the stranger thanked the abbot profusely. Taking the abbot's hand, he leaned forward, and said in a soft whisper, "I need to tell you a secret, one that God has given me permission to tell you. Christ is here in your midst. The Messiah is masquerading as one of your brothers." The abbot was shocked: "The Messiah? Here? In this place? No, it isn't possible!"

He told the other brothers what the stranger had said. They also couldn't believe it. Then they began to think: Could it be Brother Joseph? No, he's too selfish. Could it be Brother John? No, he's much too strange. Is it Brother Bernard? No, he's too clumsy. No matter which monk they thought of, they couldn't imagine that brother being the Messiah. Still, what if the stranger was right? What if Brother Joseph is really Christ, and just pretending to be selfish? What if Christ is Brother John, and he is just pretending to be strange? What if Christ is Brother Bernard, and just pretending to be clumsy? So they started to treat one another as though each was possibly Christ, lest Christ be revealed as one of them. As they did, the monastery changed. The monks began to focus more passionately on God during worship, lest Christ catch them slumbering. They read Scripture with renewed fervor, lest Christ catch them daydreaming. As they did, they grew spiritually. Their prayers took on a new life. So did their teaching and service. And people noticed. Soon pilgrims and seekers came to their door to learn from their wisdom. New monks joined their ranks to learn the spiritual secrets. They became alive once again, and once again the monastery became a center of spiritual life for all of Europe. They became alive to Christ.

In churches that are alive to Christ, people encounter Christ because they seek Christ. Obviously we can encounter Christ elsewhere because Christ is everywhere, not only in churches. If we are alive to Christ, we can encounter Christ at home, in the workplace, on a mountaintop, in a park, on a golf course, in the supermarket—and anywhere else. Nonetheless, certain places are designed for holy experiences; their architecture and atmosphere are designed for holy encounters. What gives the architecture and atmosphere the power to reveal the sacred is the intention of worshipers. When people become part of these holy places with hearts alive to Christ, they can encounter Christ there with a power that surpasses the Presence they find in most other places.

When there is no expectation of encountering Christ, the church atrophies and dies. In many churches, despite their architecture and atmosphere, the members have little expectation of encountering Christ. As Ben Campbell Johnson, a writer and teacher on spirituality and evangelism, says, "When there is no sense of the Divine, people go home empty. Soon they forget the main reason for church and worship. As the awareness of God withers, joy evaporates and persons find it increasingly difficult to speak of God to one another."[5]

To Preach, Teach, and Heal Life

How do we specifically help people in a church become alive to Christ's presence? We do it by engaging in the same ministry Christ did, but in a way that is appropriate to our own situation and context. Essentially, we do it by forming communities that preach, teach, and heal *in* Christ's presence, as opposed to what many modern Christians do, which is to preach, teach, and heal according to their own abilities and insights. To preach, teach, and heal in Christ's presence means to embody Christ in what we do. As the following section will make more clear, when we become open to Christ's presence in our lives, we allow Christ's voice and power to be incarnated in us and our ministry, and we join Christ in his preaching, teaching, and healing ministry.

1. Preaching Christ's Presence

I have a confession to make. Most of the preaching in the mainline church bores me. This potentially embarrassing confession also implicates me. I'm sure I am guilty of boring quite a few members when I preach. Still, what bores me about most mainline preaching is that we pastors have turned an event that it supposed to reveal Christ into a dry, academic, intellectual activity focusing on abstract theological topics that have little relevance to real life. That doesn't mean that these topics are unimportant, or that solid theological thinking and articulation aren't important. In fact, people in the pews need to be taught to think theologically as well as to become open to God spiritually. Good theology should lead to spiritual openness, and spiritual openness should lead to good theological thinking. The problem in so many churches is that the practitioners of much mainline Protestant preaching have forgotten to balance the theological with the spiritual, or even more important, to ground theological thinking and teaching in spiritual practice and experience.

It is not hard to see how theological thinking that is ungrounded spiritually can create uninspired preaching. For example, too many mainline Protestant pastors are guilty of "preaching their papers in public." They were taught in seminary to structure their sermons like academic papers that posit and prove a theological point, which they then read to the congregation while standing stiffly behind the pulpit and staring mainly at the manuscript. Even though many mainline Protestant preachers have utter disdain for televangelists and their preaching style, at least those preachers understand what sermons are.

Televangelists understand their role in helping people encounter Christ. I'm not suggesting that we mainline preachers have to jump, shout, and prance like many of the televangelists, nor am I saying that I support their teachings, especially the teachings of the more fundamentalist ones. I, too, find many of the messages they preach offensive and simplistic. Still, we have to pay attention to something they understand: sermons are *oral* (and in some cases, when using multimedia resources, *visual*), not written, messages that lead to an encounter with the living Christ. They are meant to offer imaginative experiences in which people sense Christ and the Holy Spirit not only through words themselves, but also through dramatic stories, gestures, inflections, and cadence.

What made Jesus' preaching so captivating and engaging is that he spoke through people's everyday experiences. Look at every film about Jesus' life. He walked among the crowds, told parables about planting, harvesting, shepherding, and the like, which reflected their experiences. He spoke in their language literally and metaphorically. Too often today we don't preach to people's lived situations. Meanwhile, magazines like *Guideposts* and books like *Chicken Soup for the Soul* reach millions of people because they use stories about people just like them who have encountered God's presence in their lives.

The problem for many of us mainline preachers is that we think it is beneath us to talk about ordinary people who experience God's presence in miraculous and dramatic ways. We think these *Guideposts* and *Chicken Soup* stories seem sappy and happy. But if we choose not to use these kinds of stories, nor speak to people's everyday experiences, then we need to recognize that people aren't flocking to hear us precisely because we are so abstract.

Despite the strength of the evangelical style, which is often more dynamic than the style of most mainline preaching, it overemphasizes the entry into the Christian life by being so "seeker focused" that it ignores the call to spiritual depth. Mainline preaching generally has the opposite problem. As an evangelical friend once said to me, "The problem with us evangelicals is that we never let people grow to spiritual maturity. As soon as they become spiritual adolescents, we tell them to turn around and bring in the spiritual babes [the new Christians]. As a result, no one ever really grows to spiritual adulthood. On the other hand, you mainliners assume that everyone is in spiritual adulthood, and so you never really help people grow from spiritual infancy into adulthood. We need to find a way to lead people from infancy into maturity."

How do we preach Christ's presence? We do so by constantly and consistently saying to people, "Look, there's Christ in your midst, and there, and there, and there!" We do it by showing people that even if they are in darkness, they can find Christ's light shining through the love of a family member, the kindness of a friend, a phrase in a book, or the inspiration from a song. We can also preach Christ's presence by reminding people that Christ is in Scripture, in the sacraments, and in all of worship. We preach Christ's presence by pointing to the incarnation of Christ in everything: our sufferings, our joys, our relationships, and our hearts.

Whenever we preach Christ's presence, we also need to introduce the church members to practices they can embrace, attitudes they can adopt, and habits they can form that will lead them to experience Christ. We can use our sermons to introduce laity to practices of prayer, fasting, confessing, centering, simplifying, and other spiritual disciplines. Teaching people how to grow spiritually, especially through the use of spiritual practices and disciplines, may require that we share our own struggles to grow spiritually (a practice that may have been taboo in seminary preaching classes). When we *humbly* share our own personal struggles to encounter Christ, we tell people that they can trust us as guides and follow our guidance—because we share their struggle to grow spiritually and to encounter Christ.

Finally, it is important that we preachers become people of spiritual depth. We need to be people of prayer who preach out of prayer. For me, this meant drastically changing the way I traditionally prepared my sermons. Years ago I used to spend much of the week poring over biblical commentaries, trying to uncover the essential biblical message by researching the history, context, situation, intent, and focus of a biblical passage. I spent hours in preparation. Over time I realized that I was focusing so much on historical and biblical scholarship that I was not attending to God's message. Today my approach is different. I focus on praying through the Scripture, allowing myself to be led by Christ and the Holy Spirit to preach God's message. Sometimes this method leads me to do research, but at other times it means spending time in solitude reflecting on my experiences and using them as a template to guide others. Prayerful reflection can be research. The practical effect is that my sermons have became much more dynamic and piercing because Christ is much more present in my preaching.

In preparing a sermon, a preacher can ask several simple questions to help compose blessed sermons that lead others to encounter Christ:

- Have I prepared this sermon in prayer, asking God to speak through me?

- Have I taught something that will tangibly help people live healthier, more balanced, and more loving lives?
- Have I taught people how to follow Christ in practical ways that make a discernable difference?
- Have I preached out of my own spirituality, leading people to encounter Christ as I have?
- Have I preached in a way that makes people aware of God's purpose for them and Christ's presence in and with them?

2. Teaching

Much of what I just said about preaching can be applied to teaching in a church. There is a similarity between the styles of preaching and teaching in most churches, especially when it comes to adult education. My focus here will be mainly on educating adults, but I think the message can also be applied to children's Christian education.

The problem inherent in most mainline church education programs is that they emphasize *information* over *formation*. Informative education is interesting, helpful, and important, but for the most part it doesn't change lives. For example, the daily newspaper is informative. I read it every day, but it rarely changes my life (except, sadly, to make me more cynical). Formative education emphasizes teaching and learning that open people to discover how God wants them to live. It teaches people how to "form" their lives in God-directed ways that embody faith, hope, and love. It opens people to God so that they can be transformed to incarnate Christ's presence and love.

Informative teaching rarely has an eye toward how information will form learners' lives. Classes on what the books of the Bible say, how to read the Bible in its historical context, Christian theology, and history often neglect what the Bible says to us about how to live life in meaningful and loving ways that serve Christ. When we teach informatively about outreach and social justice, we might help people better understand the impoverished and oppressed, but we often don't teach them how God is calling them to reach out to those in need. Such teaching also doesn't teach us how our own lives need to be transformed if we are to have compassion for the poor, the oppressed, and the outcast.

Informative teaching emphasizes concepts and constructs for their own sake. Formative teaching introduces concepts and constructs in the service of transforming lives, both ours and those of others, according to God's purposes. Formative classes have a direct impact on how people live, and specifically how they live in a way that allows Christ to live in them. They deal with topics such as the formation of healthy marital, parental, friendship, and work relationships; prayer; forgiveness; recovery from addiction; discernment; practical servanthood; personal and communal evangelism; and community outreach. Even children's education can move from informatively teaching "just the facts" to formatively teaching how the facts invite us to live in greater openness to God. Formative teaching does not preclude teaching about doctrines and mission. In fact, it strengthens them by giving them a spiritual foundation.

Stressing formation over information also applies to forming small groups. Resources need to be chosen that emphasize spiritual growth in practical ways. Material such as the Bible, devotional books, and the writings of the mystics, when approached formatively, change lives because God uses them to form and transform us. When we offer classes, groups, workshops, and retreats that emphasize formation over information, we change lives by opening people to Christ's transforming power.

3. Healing

While most mainline churches truly understand that Jesus came to preach and teach, and that they are to be places of preaching and teaching, they've forgotten that Jesus spent as much time healing as he did preaching and teaching.[6]

Our churches have abdicated their role as places of healing, which was part of the original church's calling. You can see this calling expressed in Jesus' teaching the disciples and followers to heal. The early church, as recounted in Acts, took seriously the calling to heal the sick. The apostle James even gives instructions to the church about healing prayer: "Are any among you sick? They should call for the elders of the church and have them pray over them, anointing them with oil in the name of the Lord" (James 5:14). Unfortunately, modern Christianity has given to the field of medicine the whole responsibility for healing, while failing to recognize that we Christians have a role in healing, too. We are called to complement the healing that Christ does through medicine with the healing that Christ brings through prayers and relationships.

What does it mean to be a healing church? Using Calvin Presbyterian Church as an example, I can offer several answers. First, it means that we take healing prayer seriously. Most churches are afraid actually to pray for God's healing power. Their members are skeptical about prayer's effectiveness. Their faith in healing prayer has been poisoned by false Christians who have used healing prayer to bilk gullible people out of their money. The true church, though, is called to make healing prayer part of its ministry. Increasingly, mainline churches are offering healing prayer as part of healing worship services and in their regular worship services, and they are experiencing the healing of people.

For example, one person who opened me up to the power of healing prayer, especially as part of a church's ministry, was a friend in New York who had a healing experience as a result of a mainline church's healing service. My friend had years ago gone to a doctor who diagnosed her as having an illness that would probably be chronic. She was devastated. A few days later she was out walking in Manhattan, and while thinking about her illness and the ramifications for her life, she passed Fifth Avenue Presbyterian Church just as it was having its "Healing of Iona" prayer service. She entered the church and sat in the back, watching the people go to the front for prayer. Eventually she decided also to go forward, though she was skeptical. She received healing prayers from a minister and sat back down, thinking that nothing would happen. Suddenly, she felt something like electricity go through her, filling her with a kind of peace and joy. The feeling remained for a few days. When she went to the doctor the next week for a follow-up exam, he found no trace of the illness. She had been healed, and it happened because a church had the courage to offer the healing ministry of Christ as part of its ministry.

At Calvin Church we have two kinds of healing ministries. First, we offer a healing prayer ministry. We have called forth particular members of the congregation who we have discerned are called to this ministry to offer prayers for those suffering with illness or other difficulties. We then train them in the tradition and practice of healing prayer. Requests for healing prayers come from sick and suffering members and nonmembers alike. Our healing prayer ministers visit those requesting prayer once a week for a 15-minute visit. As part of the visit, the healing prayer minister prays for the person, anointing him or her with oil, and also trains the person to pray for his or her own healing. (For a sample of a resource for teaching people how to pray for healing, please see appendix I, "A Guide to Healing Prayer.")

Second, we offer healing services on the first Sunday of each month as part of our celebration of the sacrament of communion. As people come forward for communion down our two aisles, a healing prayer minister and I stand in the center ready to offer healing prayer. Anyone who would like healing prayer before receiving the elements of the Lord's Supper steps into the center and can receive prayer from either of us. We ask what the concern is and try to make the prayer succinct but powerful. Afterward, we anoint the person's forehead with oil, making the sign of the cross in the name of God the Father, Son, and Holy Spirit. Then, the one prayed for re-enters the line and receives communion, allowing the sacrament to complete the healing prayer. The initial decision to offer healing prayer as part of the sacrament of communion was not easy because we were like most other churches. Healing prayer was not part of our ministry. Still, we decided to offer it because we realized that healing is an essential part of our calling.

I also am involved in offering healing prayers as part of my own ministry. The amazing and wonderful thing is that we have had many healings in our church as a result of our various prayer ministries. I'm not talking about the "throw-your-crutches-away-and-dance-on-the-floor" kind of healing seen on television. Sometimes the healing is physical, but just as often it is mental, relational, or spiritual. The point is that as we've emphasized healing, people have been healed in many ways, and so has our church. For more information on healing prayer, two good resources are Agnes Sanford's classic, *The Healing Light,* and John Wilkinson's study of the biblical basis of healing, *The Bible and Healing.*[7] (Wilkinson is a medical missionary and consultant on public health in Scotland.) Also, most mainline denominations offer resources for integrating healing rituals into worship services. For more practical help on this topic, you might explore the Order of St. Luke, an ecumenical organization devoted to fostering healing ministries (*www.orderofstluke.org*).

Becoming a healing church also means emphasizing health and holiness in all that we are doing. For instance, staff and leaders in congregations need to emphasize healthy relationships, along with an intolerance of dysfunction. We need to be clear that we expect staff and leaders to treat each other with Christ's love and care—the foundation of a healthy, holy church. Rabbi Edwin Friedman, a family systems therapist and congregational health expert, has published some wonderful resources on how to overcome congregational dysfunction, including his book *Generation to Generation: Family Process in Church and Synagogue,* and the video "Family Process and Process Theology: Basic New Concepts."[8] Ultimately, we need to remember that since churches are always about relationships—relationships with God, all of God's people and creation, and one another—the leadership and staff must exemplify good relationships. Sometimes modeling healthy relationships can mean letting go of leaders and staff who cannot relate with others in healthy ways— often a painful process. Still, when we hire people, we want to assess potential staff members' ability to relate healthily to others.

A final way that churches are called to be places of healing has to do with our understanding of the ministry of the laity. We need to reclaim their call to healing ministry. The past 100 years have seen a growing emphasis on the pastor as the agent of healing and health in a congregation. The pastor does all the visiting. The pastor is the one who cares for those in need. Unfortunately, this emphasis on the pastor as the main agent of healing and health keeps many churches from growing. All that time the pastor spends caring for individuals not only prevents her from attending to other aspects of ministry, such as preaching, teaching, and leading the church to be a place of healing, but it also keeps the church as a whole from taking responsibility for healing. The ministry of care and compassion in a church, what we today call pastoral care, is a ministry all the members need to be engaged in.

What I am proudest of is that Calvin Church is a community that loves, and therefore heals. The people here understand that they are called to love, and so they do. I'm not going to say it is perfect, because I know that some people haven't felt loved by the church, but they are generally the exception. Many times I visit someone in need, only to discover that a member of the church has already been there. I have been told on quite a few occasions, "Graham, you can't do everything. We can care for people, too. If you can't visit someone, we understand. We're all responsible." Those are the words of a healing community. Ultimately, an alive, blessed church is a place where Christ can heal, teach, and preach, a place where everything we do somehow connects people to Christ's presence.

Calling Alive Leaders

If we are to become a church that is alive to God as Presence, where do we begin? Everything begins with leadership. If the leaders, lay or pastoral, are not alive to Christ, the church won't be either. As I said previously, too many churches cut off the spiritual dimension, and nowhere is this lack clearer than in the process of nominating and calling forth leaders. Typically, the questions nominating committees ask about candidates run along the lines of "How organized is he? Does she have management skills? Is he good with his hands? Will she be able to coordinate the church dinner?" In some cases we don't even ask those questions. We just ask, "Will she or he say yes?" We don't ask, "Is she a person of deep faith and commitment to Christ? Will he prayerfully seek God's voice and lead us to follow God's will?"

We changed the way we call leaders at Calvin Church several years ago, and it has led to a dynamic change in our leadership. Since I came to Calvin, we have always had good people on the church board, but for many of them it was a whole new idea that we should prayerfully seek God's voice to lead us to follow God's will. They hadn't thought of church leadership in that way before. One of the foundational changes we made when I came to Calvin was to ask leaders to put aside their own egos, as well as what they thought their pastor wanted, and instead to emphasize prayerfully seeking and doing God's will. I stressed that they were called to listen for and to do God's will. They were not to be political representatives of the congregation or groups within the congregation, seeking mainly to do their will, but to be spiritual leaders. It was when we began seeking leaders who already had a willingness to seek God's will first that this church really became transformed. Our leadership was not bad before we changed our nominating focus. In fact, our leaders were exceptional. But now our leadership has a depth that is tangible, especially in times of crisis.

A guide to forming a more spiritually grounded nominating committee is included in appendix J, "Nominating Committee Members." We begin by inviting the nominating committee members to spend time in prayer, asking God to reveal whom God is calling to become an elder. (In the Presbyterian Church [U.S.A.], elders are laity ordained to lead the church by serving on the session, the church's governing board; only elders can sit on the session.) At Calvin Church we use the same process for calling forth any committee member whose position, because of requirements by our denominational constitution or the church's bylaws, requires a nomination and vote by the congregation. In our congregation this includes nominating committee and long-range planning committee members.

Returning to the work of the nominating committee, we ask it to assess the faith of the candidates first, their functional abilities second. The priority is on calling people of faith who will focus on doing God's will, not necessarily on getting people with organizational skills. We are looking for people who are Christ bearers. After inviting the members of the nominating committee into a time of discernment, we ask them to come together and share their discernments and to form a list of potential candidates. The members of the nominating committee prayerfully come to a consensus about whom they sense God may be calling to be candidates. The committee then sits down with the candidate, explains the leadership position, and encourages the potential leader to spend time in prayer to discern whether she or he similarly feels called by God to become an elder. (Appendix K, "Becoming an Elder at Calvin Presbyterian Church," is a sample of the guide we give potential nominees to help them in their discernment.)

The impact of the change in our process has been amazing. It is obvious that our leaders are people deeply committed to prayerfully discerning God's will. We have different perspectives and disagreements, but in the end the elders are committed to working in prayerful unity. We have gone through some difficult times and a few crises. It is important to remember that blessed churches aren't immune to crises. But because of the leadership's faith, commitment, and trust in God's leading, we have always found God's answers—answers that are deeper and more creative than anything we could come up with on our own.

Not only is it important to ask prayerfully whom God is calling to serve as leaders; we need to be just as discerning about who serves on a committee, team, or task force. Although the process of calling these people is less formal, the candidates still can be sought in prayer. The leaders need prayerfully to consider whom God is calling to serve with them and then recruit members based on their own prayerful discernment.

Meetings That Come Alive

Leaders in a blessed church need to be people of faith, but they must also guide others in a way that helps them form a prayerful faith. How meetings are run is crucial in teaching people how to be open to and trust God. Most churches are overfunctional in the way they run their meetings, from the church board on down. In the blessed church, the focus is not solely on following guidelines like *Robert's Rules of Order*, but on heeding God's guidance. (For guidance on how to create a more spiritually open and alive meeting where people seek God's guidance and voice, see appendix L, "A Guide to Holding Spiritually Grounded Meetings," as well as appendix D, "Discerning Direction for a Particular Issue.")

In short, the way we try to hold meetings at Calvin Church (although we are not strict about it) is to invite people to discuss the issues, but in the end to focus on seeking what God wants. Sometimes this process involves prayer, although often the answer becomes apparent without prayer. We try to avoid what happens in many churches: figuratively and literally committees in most churches begin a meeting by inviting God into the room in prayer. Then, by what they do and how they discuss proposals and make decisions, they basically tell God to wait outside in the hall until they have made a decision. Finally, through their closing prayers they invite God back in to bless their decisions. In contrast, spiritual leaders ask God to be a part of the whole meeting. They ask God to become thoroughly part of the process, so that they may seek and do what God is blessing, not ask God to bless what they are doing. This process rightfully restores Christ to being head of the church.

Alive to Presence in Worship

While it is crucial for the leaders to become alive to Presence, the foundation of the blessed church's life is worship that is alive to Presence and that embodies Christ. Unfortunately, too many churches try to take a shortcut by focusing mainly on the *style* rather than the *soul* of worship. The question at the heart of a blessed church is not "What style of worship should we offer?" It is "What kind of worship are we called to offer that will lead people to encounter God as Purpose, Presence, and Power?" The latter question is the one that addresses the soul of worship by emphasizing that the focus of worship is God, not us.

At Calvin Church, our order of worship is grounded in our Presbyterian, Reformed tradition, but it also integrates elements from other traditions. We begin worship with a Taizé chant and lead people into silent prayer. Our worship service and space integrate the ancient and the contemporary. When we renovated our sanctuary, we asked, What is God calling us to do? Prayerfully looking at our demographics and community, we felt called to design a sanctuary that combined traditional symbols, ambience, and architecture with contemporary lighting, sound, and music systems. This blend fits our community, although it might fail in more traditional or transient communities.

We have also continually asked this question in regard to our selection of hymns, anthems, and other music, choosing music that we sense will best help the community as a *whole* to experience Christ. The focus in many churches is on choosing music that appeals to one segment of the congregation over the others. We try to avoid idolizing one style or era of music—classical, contemporary, or something in between—but to use whatever we sense will best help people encounter Christ. What matters to us is God's call, not the desire to idolize past traditions or to imitate current trends.

Another area in which Christ's presence is truly sensed and encountered is in the sacraments. It's unfortunate that in the zeal to move toward contemporary worship, sacraments such as communion have been de-emphasized in some congregations, especially in nondenominational ones. The irony is that even as many congregations have moved toward an emphasis on "seeker-friendly" worship, elsewhere in the church we see an emerging movement back toward ancient practices. More and more evangelical, nondenominational authors, such as Robert Webber and Dan Kimball, are calling churches to recover ancient practices to reach younger generations that seem to have an appreciation for experiential practices such as communion.

The spirit in which we offer communion and other sacraments is important. Sacraments can be offered in a ritualistic and dry manner that fails to create the conditions in which people can experience Christ's presence. There are ways of offering sacraments that make Christ's mystical presence in and through the sacraments more apparent, especially to newer or newly recommitted Christians. For example, at Calvin sometimes we serve communion in the traditional Presbyterian way, distributing the elements through the pews, but sometimes we call people forward, especially during our monthly healing services. The question for us is how to go about leading people to encounter Christ through these sacraments and to offer an experience of worship that helps people encounter Christ.

Alive to Presence in Ministry and Mission

The final element in becoming a church that is alive to God's presence is maintaining a focus on what Christ is calling the church to do in ministry and mission. Ministry is generally considered to be how we serve God in the church—our pastoral care and programs targeted at the members—while mission is how we serve God outside the church by reaching out to those who are unchurched, hungry, poor, or otherwise in need. I have heard both laity and pastors complain that their church isn't sufficiently committed to ministry and mission. They grumble that their people are too self focused. The problem may be not with the people, but with the particular ministry and mission. The leaders may be pushing other members to engage in ministries and missions that are not God's call for them. Part of becoming a blessed church means actively listening to Christ's call to mission, whatever it is. As noted in the previous chapter, God has a purpose for everything, and the key to effective ministry and mission is discerning and responding to God's call for this congregation in this place.

Mission and ministry first need to be grounded in prayer. A large problem in the mainline church is that in sermon after sermon people have been told to feed the poor, change the political system, and reach out to the unchurched; offer generationally sensitive programs for the divorced, single, grieving, and addicted; build this, transform that, solve this crisis, and eradicate that problem. People get overwhelmed by all the needs of the world. We should realize that we are only *part* of the body of Christ, not the whole body. God gives us specific ministries and mission to do, while giving others different ministry and mission opportunities.

As I mentioned in the discussion on formative education, we need to reclaim the ability to discern how God is calling us to reach out to the world around us. The ministry and mission of Calvin Church are certainly not the same as that of a rural or an urban church. We are in another context and situation. We are called to different ministries and missions. If we are truly Christ's church, we need to focus on what we can do and are called to do, rather than on the work we do not have the calling or talent to do. We ought to be aware that a lack of talent often reveals a lack of calling. We should ground what we do in prayer, seeking Christ's active guidance. The key is discernment that leads to activity for Christ's sake, not for activity's sake. When we direct our efforts to the ministries and missions to which Christ calls us, the work becomes God's work, not ours.

It is important to define our service to God first in spiritual, rather than purely functional, ways. The functional is an important component, but it must emerge from a spiritual yearning and aspiration to do God's will. Too often we functionally characterize ministry and mission as planned programs. When a church becomes truly blessed, ministry and mission just happen, whether planned or not. Our service to God is not restricted to activities that have been cleared by a committee or board (although what boards and committees do certainly is service to God). In a blessed church, ministry and mission have the opportunity to emerge more organically, meaning that the members are given permission and encouragement to respond to needs as they feel called, and the role of the church is to support them. For example, while the church may feel called to start small groups by creating a comprehensive small-group program, in the blessed church you will also find some people taking it upon themselves to gather once a week for prayer or Bible study. These spontaneous groups can serve as the seeds for a more extensive small-group program, or they can simply be the church's small-group program. Ministry becomes more flexible and spontaneous as people seek to encounter Christ in their own ways.

In mission, people look for opportunities in all areas of their lives to reach out to those in need. For example, one woman I know, who teaches children in a depressed area, took it upon herself to raise funds to buy shoes for poor children. Another family, seeing the struggles of a family with an unemployed father, gave a sizable and anonymous financial gift to help them through their tough times. Mission becomes organic, growing, and flowing in unexpected places and ways. It's not that Christ isn't present in churches where meticulous planning takes place through a centralized board; but by opening up the process and encouraging people to discern and respond on their own, we create the context in which Christ's presence grows stronger and moves in its own direction.

A problem facing many churches today, my own included, is that we tend to look at mission through "Christendom" eyes that recognize only overseas mission to the economically impoverished and hungry as valid outreach. We fail to recognize that we are in a post-Christendom era in which the people of our own culture have become increasingly impoverished and hungry spiritually. Because we do not always pay attention to God's call, we fail to respond when God calls on us to reach out to the spiritually starving on our doorsteps. We get caught in 1950s philosophies of mission and outreach, rather than responding to God's present call.

The best example of someone who discerned God's call and responded in a unique way is Mother Teresa. Most people don't know much about her life. They think that she must have been born to be a nun and to reach out to the poor in Calcutta. The fact is that before she began her mission to the poor, she was the headmistress of an elite girls' school in Calcutta. Each day she looked out her window and saw the poor, and her heart broke. God used her breaking heart to transform her gradually and to call her to minister to the poor. Eventually she responded to God's call. She didn't do it by creating an elaborate organization. She did it the only way she knew how. She left the school armed with a bag of rice. She stopped at a corner and, using a stick, began writing in the dust to teach the children to read. At the end of her lesson she gave the children rice. Over time, her mission grew. She was able to carry out this mission because she had a formative outlook on life that allowed her to be transformed by God.

Ultimately, being guided by the presence of Christ in ministry and mission requires members to be willing to discern how God is calling them to respond to the world's needs, whether as part of a committee or in their personal lives. (For help in understanding how to discern, see appendix M, "Four Principles of Discernment.") In a blessed church the members increasingly and creatively look at the world around them to see how God may be calling them to respond in their own ways. They respond to opportunities that seem in tune with God's calling.

Of course, when we look for opportunities, it is easy to become overwhelmed by the problems around us. We cannot take care of the whole world, but we can take care of that part of the world for which God has given us a passion, a calling, and an ability. When we are alive to Christ, God makes our mission and ministry clear. It is important, then, for pastors and leaders to nurture spiritual readiness on the part of the other leaders and members, stressing that God is constantly calling us to serve, whether as part of the church or in our own unique ways through our acts of love. True ministry and mission are a response to Christ, who is embodied in us and who seeks to reach out to others through us.

Are We Alive?

The hardest part of forming a trinitarian church, a church of Purpose, Presence, and Power, is forming one that is alive to God as Presence. It is hard because so many in the mainline church do not believe that God can be tangibly sensed in their midst. They focus on God in heaven, or on Christ in history. Becoming a blessed church means being a church that reveals God's presence in everything, so that people can encounter and experience Christ in every facet of their lives.

When a church becomes truly alive to Christ, it becomes a dynamic, creative place. It may not necessarily become a place of explosive growth, because the factors that foster that kind of growth are not present everywhere. What does happen is that in worship people sense Christ's presence in their work for the church. They form deep relationships with others in the church, and they sense God's love in the relationships. They struggle and suffer the pains of life, and discover God touching and caring for them through the people of the church. And as they do, they discover that they are not only in a place of God's presence, but that they are living more and more according to God's purpose and are experiencing God's power flowing in and through them.

Reflection Questions

1. To what extent do you sense Christ's presence in your church?
2. To what extent do you sense that your church is purposeful about being alive to Christ's presence in preaching, teaching, and healing?
3. In what ways does your church close the door to Christ as Presence?
4. What concrete things can you do to help your church become more alive to Christ in its leadership, worship, ministry, and mission?

Chapter 5

Open to God as Power

In 1990, I first read about an amazing man who gave me a whole new vision for what is possible in a church. His name was George Müller, and he served God throughout the 19th century in Plymouth, England.[1] I mention him here because of how his life demonstrated what is possible when we become open to God as Power, to God the Holy Spirit.

Müller was born in Prussia in 1805. When he was a young adult, his experience of God's presence through a group of Christians he had met revolutionized his life. He became a Christian, eventually moved to England, and became a pastor in Bristol. It was there that God's purpose, presence, and especially power transformed him. From that moment on, he decided to center his life in Scripture and to pattern his life on Matthew 7:7, where Jesus says, "Ask, and it will be given you; search and you will find; knock, and the door will be opened for you." Müller realized that if this passage was true, then God's power must be available to all, even if most Christians ignored it. If Scripture was true, then God must want to provide miracles. God must want to bless our work.

Müller decided to test his theory by relying on God's purpose, presence, and power for his life and ministry. His first experiment was to refuse a salary for his ministry. He decided instead to rely on God for his welfare as he continued to serve God. Over time, he discovered the extent to which God can bless what we do. He discovered the power of the Holy Spirit, God as Power. Although Müller received no salary, the Spirit took care of him. Whenever he needed something, whether money, food, clothes, medical care, or anything else, the Spirit responded. For example, a man he barely knew might come up to him on the street and say, "I'm not sure why, but I feel that something is telling me to give you this," and then give him several shillings or a pound—exactly what he was praying for. Müller didn't engage in this experiment because he was lazy. In fact, he was anything but. He never prayed for anything beyond his most essential needs. Through prayer he discovered God's Spirit blessing him in everything.

A few years later, strengthened by his experience of God's power, Müller embarked on a new venture in faith—one that eventually made him known worldwide. He felt called by God to start an orphanage that would be rooted in prayer and providence, and that would be a model of faith and love. According to his plan, discerned in prayer, the children would receive three meals a day, have their own beds and cubicles, own several pairs of shoes and changes of clothes, learn to read and write, and receive loving and respectful treatment. This radical idea was one for which he would be severely criticized, because, according to the conventional wisdom of the time, orphans were little more than street urchins to be ignored at best, abused at worst. Caring about them and educating them was considered a waste of time. Even more radical was his vision of grounding the orphanage in prayer. The orphanage solicited no donations, practiced financial accountability, focused always on the welfare of the children, and centered all decisions and actions in prayer. So instead of aggressively raising funds, the orphanage board and staff would instead go to God in prayer whenever they were in need.

Over the course of Müller's life, the orphanage grew substantially from the initial four orphans to more than 2,050 residents living on a campus of 25 acres. The leaders never asked for money, no matter how dire the need, but would always respond to their need by praying and trusting God in faith. Relying solely on prayer and faith, they raised the equivalent in today's dollars of from $50 million to $80 million. Müller was a man of amazing faith who relied on God's power to flow through all he did.

Müller provided me with an alternative vision of what could happen in a church when we are truly open to God's power, the power of the Holy Spirit. For many mainline Christians who have been led to believe that God is distant and uninvolved in life, Müller's story is unbelievable because it says that God is involved. It says that God works miracles in our midst that we don't expect. For people stuck in a functional view of God, this message is hard to swallow. What Müller taught me is that if I became a person of prayer who tried faithfully to expect God to bless my ministry and life, God *would*, even if the blessing wasn't always what I expected or envisioned. I began to see a possibility for the mainline churches: they could become houses of prayer through which

God's Spirit blew, blessing their members, ministry, and mission. They would face struggles and tests, but if congregations did their best to believe and have faith that God could make the impossible possible, even if that faith was imperfect, wonderful things could happen. As I look back at 14 years of ministry since I first read about George Müller, I can confidently say that I have never been disappointed. When I've asked, I've received, although not always in ways I anticipated. When I've sought, I've found, although not always in ways I expected. When I've knocked, surprising doors of opportunity and possibility have always been opened, even if what was behind these doors was not what I had envisioned.

My faith in God as Power was confirmed in 1997 when I read Rick Warren's book *The Purpose-Driven Church*. Warren has helped thousands by offering a vision of how to create a church of purpose, but what I found most helpful and enlightening was the story of how he started the Saddleback Valley Community Church in Orange County, California.[2]

In 1979, as Rick Warren was finishing up his last year of seminary, he felt called to start a dynamic new church for the unchurched. He spent time in prayer, sincerely seeking God's will. Afterward, he put a map of the world up in his living room and began praying with his wife for God to show them where they were to start this church. For six months they prayed, and slowly God's purpose became clearer. Using a process that included prayer, faith, and demographic studies that showed the locations of the largest populations of unchurched people, they eventually discerned that they were called to plant a church in southern California, and specifically in a town called Saddleback Valley. In 1981 Orange County was the fastest-growing area of the country. Warren knew that God was calling them to go there.

Being a Southern Baptist, he decided first to contact the Southern Baptist director of missions in Orange County, a man named Herman Wooten. The young minister called and said, "My name is Rick Warren. I am a seminary student in Texas. I am planning to move to south Orange County and start a church. I'm not asking for money or support from you; I just want to know what you think about that area. Does it need new churches?"

Wooten's reply clearly revealed how God as Power responds when we prayerfully act according to God's purpose and presence. Warren's call had interrupted Wooten as he was writing a letter that said, "Dear Mr. Warren, I have heard that you may be interested in starting a new church in California after seminary. Have you ever considered coming to

Saddleback Valley in south Orange County?" God's purpose, presence, and power were clearly evident.

Finally, after more research and several visits to Saddleback Valley, Warren and his wife, by now parents of a four-month-old baby, packed up their belongings and drove to California, praying along the way. They pulled off the freeway and stopped at the first real estate office they found. They walked in and met a real estate broker, Don Dale. Warren said to him, "My name is Rick Warren. I'm here to start a church. I need a place to live, but I don't have any money." Dale laughed out loud and said he would see what he could do. Two hours later, Dale had found them a condominium to rent, with the first month's rent free, and Dale had agreed to become the first member of Saddleback Church.

From there the church grew in response to prayer. Another church in the area agreed to sponsor them. A man they had never met agreed to pay their rent for two months, and people they didn't even know sent money to help them, often in the exact amount they had prayed for. From these humble beginnings, Saddleback Valley Community Church grew from a few members to a congregation of 5,000 that has a worship attendance of 10,000 every Sunday.

The important lesson I learned from Warren is not how to build a 5,000-member church. That is his calling, not mine. What I learned is that when we respond to God's purpose and rely on God's presence, divine power flows through everything we do. I learned that God wants to bless our churches, but too often we reject the power of the Holy Spirit. So nothing happens. I've also discovered in my own church that when we pray, amazing things happen in our midst—events that could come only from God.

Recapturing Pentecost

Forming a church filled with the Holy Spirit was Jesus' promise. It is the power of the Holy Spirit that truly distinguishes the Christian faith from most others. While Jesus was alive, he taught his followers to follow the will of God, love others, and be Christ's servants in the world, but that was only the foundation of what was to come. His real focus was on opening them to the power of the Holy Spirit. Especially in the Gospel of John, we hear Jesus teach his disciples about the power of the Holy Spirit, a power that would allow them to preach, teach, heal, and perform miracles in the name of Christ. The disciples experienced the truth of Jesus' teaching on the day of Pentecost. We are told in Acts that after Jesus ascended to heaven, his followers gathered and waited in faith for the coming of the Holy Spirit. Before ascending, Jesus said, "But you will receive power when the Holy Spirit has come upon you" (John 1:8). So they waited. And then it happened. The power of the Holy Spirit came upon all of them on the day of Pentecost. This power filled their souls and gave them the passion and power to give their lives completely to God. From that moment on, they manifested God's power in their lives.

They preached with a power and a voice that was more than their own. They were able to live in the unity of the Spirit. They healed the sick. They had visions. Amazing things happened as the church grew and spread. It is clear from the events recorded by Luke in the Acts of the Apostles that the power of the Holy Spirit was available to all who had faith, and sometimes, as in Paul's case, even grabbed hold of people unawares. The breath of the Spirit transformed the church from its dogmatic, legalistic roots into a vital faith that connected people with God, allowing God's power to flow through their lives.

Unfortunately, over the past 2,000 years our denominations, with some exceptions (Quakers, Pentecostals, and charismatics), have slowly pushed the Holy Spirit to the margins, limiting the Spirit's power by emphasizing functionality, hierarchy, organization, and adherence to tradition. We are guilty of this omission in our modern mainline churches. To what extent do we expect or invite the Holy Spirit to act? To what extent are we open to God's power, to God as Power? To what extent are we willing to have God's power flow through what we do, bringing blessings, miracles, and transformations?

Our churches are meant to be churches of power. God's original intent was that the divine Purpose and Presence be manifested in works of power in which God blesses us, and the world through us. But this cannot happen unless we, as spiritual leaders, make a crucial decision to let God's Spirit work in our midst. If pastors are not open to the power of the Holy Spirit, the power of the Spirit will be limited in their churches, for the Spirit of God generally enters only in a limited way those churches that remain closed to the Spirit. If lay leaders will not open up to the Spirit, their churches will become stale and dry as God stands outside looking in. The Spirit generally will not blow through closed doors and windows.

Understanding the Holy Spirit

To become a blessed church, a congregation must become a place that is open to the Holy Spirit; but to do so means understanding the nature of

the Holy Spirit, for the Holy Spirit is the least understood and appreciated of the three persons of the Trinity (especially by mainline Protestants).
It helps to look at what Scripture has to say about the Holy Spirit. What
we get in Scripture is not a complete picture, but a glimpse of Spirit-
experiences. We discover that the Holy Spirit is the person of God, the
power of God, that affects the world, transforms life, and showers grace
and providence on those who are sincerely trying to open their lives to
God. This is no aloof and distant God, but God who is immersed in the
world and actively present in every moment and detail of life. This is
God who blesses, saves, and becomes apparent in miraculous events.

When we open our hearts, minds, and souls to the Holy Spirit, it
fills us with the life of Christ. We become temples for the Holy Spirit to
become incarnated in flesh. We live at the same time both in God's kingdom and on the earth. We may live the same physical life that all other
creatures live, but we simultaneously live in God's realm. This life in
two realms gives us the potential, however imperfect, to follow God
and live according to God's plan, even if we don't understand completely what it is or where it will lead.

For example, the Holy Spirit filled Jesus and led him into the desert
at the beginning of his ministry, even though Jesus didn't fully understand why (Matt. 4:1-11). That time in the desert was a crucial time of
preparing Jesus for his ministry. The Holy Spirit opens people up to
whole new ways of living that make us one with God and open us to a
renewed life and a deeper truth (John 3:1-9; 14:17-31). The Holy Spirit
sets us free from the power of sin that corrupts and tempts us to seek
our own will over God's (Rom. 8:1-17). When we pray, it is not only we
who pray to God, but also the Holy Spirit praying within us (Rom. 8:15-
16). The Holy Spirit also cultivates in each of us unique gifts that allow
us to incarnate Christ in our own ways and spread God's blessings
throughout the world as we bear God's fruit (1 Cor. 12:4-11; Gal. 5:16-
26). Finally, it is through the power of the Holy Spirit that we become
united and share in the unity of the Spirit (Phil. 2:1-5).

Ultimately, the Holy Spirit leads us all to a mystical truth: God is
before us, in us, with us, and through us, blessing us and life around us
whenever we are open to the power of the Holy Spirit. The potential
impact of the Holy Spirit on the life of our churches is amazing. The
practical message of the mystical truth cited above is that our churches
can be places of blessing and power where God works miraculously to
heal, save, and transform lives as we come to union and communion
with God and one another. This is not an idealistic pipe dream, but a
reality when we become open to the Holy Spirit in our midst.

Here I want to explore how we can become more open to the Holy Spirit so that our churches can become places of unity and community where people glimpse God's mind and manifest spiritual gifts for the blessing of all.

Unity and Community

Many churches today are fractured and fragmented as conflict reigns. A friend of mine once said that the most wonderfully loving and the most hate-filled people he had ever met were all within the church. I know many pastors who have been unfairly and cruelly skewered by members of their congregation over matters that amount to nothing, and more than enough laity who have been terribly abused by their pastors. I see the power of this division taking place in my own denomination, the Presbyterian Church (U.S.A.). It is filled with passionate people on the left and the right who are so consumed with their own vision for the church that they sow seeds of division everywhere. Chronic conflict is not the vision God had for the church. Christ did not create the church so that it could be a community divided against itself. The church was created to be a place of united community in which Christ's love and God's Spirit reign. What happened? The church became closed to the Holy Spirit.

In most of our denominations, unity in the Spirit has been replaced by a striving for purity of practice and doctrine. In some places fights erupt over practice: who preaches the right way, who offers the sacraments the right way, who plays the right kind of music, who uses the proper order of worship, and who engages in the right kind of ministry and mission. In other places fights erupt over theological belief: who has the right view of Christ, who is more righteous, and who has the right view of Scripture. These kinds of arguments kill the Spirit. Unity cannot be found through right practice and belief. Unity can be formed in a church only when the Holy Spirit is present. Eberhard Arnold, the founder of the Bruderhof movement—a community of Christians in Germany who opposed the evils of the Nazi movement and later emigrated to North America to escape Nazi oppression—has said:

> Full community, full agreement, is possible! It is possible through faith in God, in Christ, and in the Holy Spirit. . . . This unanimity is only possible because of our faith that God uses His Spirit to say the same to each individual. Mutual persuasion does not do it. God does it, speaking to us through the Holy Spirit.[3]

The Holy Spirit wants us to be united, but we cannot create this unity solely through our own powers. It comes only as we collectively open our hearts to the Holy Spirit. Plenty of books are available that teach group process, conflict resolution, and systems approaches, offering a vision of unity grounded in the insights of psychology, family systems, and organizational research. I have been influenced by many of these theories through my training and work as a counselor and social worker. I recommend that any leader become versed in these theories. They can offer new insights and information on how to deal with conflict. Still, true unity and community in the church can come only through the power of the Holy Spirit, which binds hearts and minds together. Psychology, family systems theory, and organizational theory can take us only so far. Ultimately, unity comes through the work of the Spirit.

Unity in the Spirit emerges when we, as leaders and a church, are willing to put aside our own egos to accept the power of the Spirit working in our midst. When moderators and other leaders of congregations, boards, committees, task forces, and teams encourage their members to become open to the Holy Spirit by putting aside their own egos and desires to seek only God's will, the Holy Spirit begins to sow unity and community. As Eberhard Arnold says:

> Only if we have willing, sincere, and open hearts will we find unanimity in our convictions. We have never found it disturbing when people have come to us representing convictions that differ from ours. On the contrary, that is more fruitful than if we had no chance to hear opposing ideas. We believe that a free exchange of ideas can help people to recognize the truth, thanks to a Spirit that does not originate with us human beings. Then, no matter how diverse our opinions may have been, through the ultimate truth we will all be united. . . . A united conviction can never be produced by forcing anyone to comply. Only the Holy Spirit with His power of inner persuasion leads people from freedom of opinions to true unity.[4]

I have seen this kind of unity work in our own church. The members of our church session hold a variety of opinions and generally feel free to express their own views and insights. Discussions can range widely as we explore various options and ideas. Still, it is when they are asked prayerfully to let go of their own expectations and desires and to do what God wants that an amazing unity emerges. It is not just a unity in which we all choose one option to avoid conflict. Instead, through prayer we often discover new options and possibilities that we did not consider at first. When pride and a need to have decisions go "my way" are put aside to allow the Spirit's power to work in our midst, we discover an amazing creativity and openness to possibility. Putting pride aside requires something important from me, though. I must be willing to let go of my own desires and wants. I have to be willing to let go of my own plans whenever I sense through my own prayerful discernment that the Spirit may be talking through others.

For example, several years ago we were faced with a growth problem. We were becoming so full during our second Sunday worship service (about 80 percent of capacity) that we were running out of seats and parking spaces. As most church-growth experts report, when a congregation exceeds 80 percent of capacity, growth stalls because of a perceived lack of space. We had to find a way to get more people to come to our early service, which averaged 20 percent of capacity. We invited members to come together for a meeting to discern possibilities. We looked at a lot of options, but in the end it was the suggestion of one member that held sway. He suggested that we do what was done in his previous church, which was to have the children's education program begin halfway through our first service so that children would be in worship for the first part of the service, and then go to Sunday school after the children's sermon. Besides offering us a new alternative, this proposal addressed the complaints of many parents who wanted a way to worship without always having to spend sermon and communion time telling their kids to be quiet.

When our worship committee met, I was very much against the change of schedule. I was involved in adult education on Sunday mornings, and the change would kill our Sunday adult-education hour and my engagement in it. As I argued against the change, the chair of the committee stopped me and said, "Graham, maybe you need to consider that this is something God is calling us to do. Maybe you are being called to lay aside your teaching for the sake of the church." I was stunned, not because he had crossed me but because he was right. I could sense the Holy Spirit speaking through him. And so we changed, and it was wonderful for the church. Our two services now seat 50 and 65 percent of capacity respectively, and both are growing—an outcome that has given us room for growth without the need to build a new sanctuary. When we are open to the Holy Spirit, a new kind of unity forms that is grounded in God's call and possibility.

Whereas this kind of unity comes through the work and power of the Holy Spirit, there is another power that does not want unity in the church: the power of the demonic. Growing up, I was never much of a believer in the demonic, but the more I have become involved in a ministry of prayer and spiritual formation, the more I have seen this darker force at work in the church. Whether you call it the demonic, the power of division, or the dark side of the force, something out there does not want the church to be unified in the Spirit as a community of Christ.

I was given a great awareness of the power of the demonic through a series of lectures given by Adrian van Kaam that I heard while was studying at Duquesne University for my doctorate. The demonic had never been mentioned in any class I had taken in seminary. Still, when I heard van Kaam talk about it, I knew he spoke of something real that threatened the unity of the church, but only if we let it. Basically, the demonic is a force whose only real power is to sow division through our fears.

The demonic is a force, energy, or entity that seeks to pull humans away from God and to prevent people from loving God and experiencing God's grace in their lives. According to van Kaam, the demonic works through two means: demonic possession and mini-obsession. Demonic possession is extremely rare and was exemplified in the 1972 film *The Exorcist*. When a person is possessed, her mind is either partially or totally overwhelmed and invaded. I have never witnessed a possession myself, and I hope I never will, although I have met people who have experience with possessions. They occur only in rare circumstances, usually when families or individuals become open to the demonic through their own extreme dysfunction or by dabbling in satanic practices. According to van Kaam, the purpose of possession is to blind people to the possibility of demonic mini-obsession. Possession attracts such attention that people become blind to how the demonic is working through mini-obsessions to sow division in the body of Christ.

It is through mini-obsessions that the demonic works to set Christians against one another. A mini-obsession occurs when a seemingly *minor* psychological obsession over something relatively small becomes so strong that it gets blown out of proportion in a way that creates fear, anger, and anxiety.

It is important not to confuse a mini-obsession with obsessive-compulsive disorder. That disorder is an almost incapacitating psychological illness that can be treated through psychotherapy and medication. A mini-obsession does not incapacitate or otherwise interfere with one's ability to function in everyday life. Rather, it causes one to become so obsessed with an issue, event, ideal, or ideology that all who do not agree are regarded as the enemy. For example, a mini-obsession may be at work in the church when a person or group has a legitimate concern to address, but in the process the member or group becomes so obsessed with it that the matter begins to bring division into the body of Christ. People may obsess over the church budget, a mission of the church, the use of contemporary or traditional hymns, a perceived slight by the pastor, abortion, homosexuality, or orthodoxy. Whatever the focus of the obsession, they become so consumed with it that they make it a church-dividing issue, forcing people to take sides. In their minds, all who take the side opposite their own are wrong, evil, or, ironically, in league with the devil.

Probably the most obvious mini-obsession dividing the church today has to do with the whole issue of homosexuality and ordination. This serious and important topic should be discussed, prayed over, and resolved. Yet in many denominations and churches it has become a dividing issue as people acrimoniously attack each other's character and faith in their efforts to win the battle. People who agree in 95 percent of the areas of their faith can become sharply divided against each other in this one area; as a result they become be suspicious of others' motives, as well as the genuineness of others' faith. As one person, reflecting on the acrimonious fights in my own denomination over the issue, said to me, "The demonic is having a field day over all of this. Look at how we attack each other in the name of Christ."

The demonic gains entry into our lives through our pride and ego. It uses human pride by leading humans to see themselves as more and more self-sufficient apart from God. For example, with the issue of homosexuality, the entry for the demonic is the pride of those on the right and the left who believe that they are so right that they quit praying and seeking God's will in the matter. They believe that their reading of Scripture, their theological acumen, and their moral stance are so unassailable that anyone who disagrees must be immoral or evil.

The demonic also can gain entry by hooking into existing conditions, such as negativity, cynicism, envy, hunger for power, problems with authority, and the reactivation of earlier traumatic experiences such as child neglect and abuse that lead to distrust of others and "acting out" in divisive ways. I've seen these manifested on a congregational level many times, even in my own church. One pastor who came to me for spiritual direction struggled with a woman who was plagued with most of the conditions cited above. She was an extremely negative and cynical person who had problems with authority, served on most of the committees in the church, and constantly hungered for more power. Over the course of a few years she falsely accused the pastor of embezzling funds (including surreptitiously building a $70,000 home library), verbally attacking her in public (even though witnesses to the event all said that the pastor had treated her respectfully), and purposely acting against the constitution of the denomination (despite the fact that she couldn't say how).

In spiritual direction we discussed how the demonic had been using her and how to overcome it. This pastor wanted to defend himself
by verbally attacking and accusing the troublesome woman in front of
the church board. I shared with him van Kaam's theories on overcoming demonic mini-obsessions, which this woman clearly had. Van Kaam
says that we overcome mini-obsessions and the demonic by becoming
aware of their power and increasing our openness to God in faith. In
other words, we overcome it through prayer and faith. We cannot overcome the demonic purely by human powers, because the demonic rev-
els in human power and works. If you try to fight the demonic with
outward power, human power, the demonic twists your efforts and
causes you to become just as obsessed as your enemy, thus consuming
you in a mini-obsession. Eventually the desire to attack the demonic
tears you away from God, and leads you into sin. If the pastor had at-
tacked the woman, using his position of authority as a pastor to crush
her, he would have relied on human powers, not on God as Power. He
could have become just as much a pawn of the demonic, creating an
even greater division in the church.

We overcome the demonic by becoming humble, acting in faith, hope,
and love, and immersing our lives in prayer. In other words, we follow
Jesus' guidance: "So make up your minds not to prepare your defense
in advance; for I will give you words and a wisdom that none of your
opponents will be able to withstand or contradict" (Luke 21:14-15). The
pastor and I developed a strategy that he would respond to this woman
with faith, hope, love, and prayer—a counterintuitive response. The
pastor would not respond defensively and attack her, but would respond
in love and patience, while also asking the board of his church and the
denomination to get involved. The pastor would trust in God and let
God take care of him.

What he experienced was clearly the work of the Holy Spirit. The
more he responded in faith and love, the more she accused him, but the
accusations were becoming more preposterous. The congregational
council got involved. Seeing how she was trying to hurt the pastor and
divide the congregation, council members surrounded the pastor and
insulated him from the attacks. Eventually, they brought a case
against her to the synod (the regional authority), and the synod had
to step in and reprimand the woman while telling her that she could
not be involved in any committees of the church for six months. She
was also prohibited from accusing the pastor in public. Violating this
edict would lead to her excommunication—an extreme punishment in
most denominations. Throughout, the pastor simply trusted and prayed,

letting the council care for him and the church. Ultimately, the pastor discovered that the Spirit does work and take care of us, even in the face of the demonic. As of this writing, the woman has left the church to go elsewhere.

In the end, we can overcome division and live in unity only through the power of the Holy Spirit. The Spirit wants unity in the church, and only the Spirit has the power to overcome the power of darkness that sows seeds of division and disunity.

Glimpses of God's Mind

As we become more open to the power of the Holy Spirit, we receive an amazing gift. We increasingly gain glimpses of God's mind. What it means to glimpse God's mind is hard to explain, and people can easily manipulate others by falsely claiming that they've glimpsed God's mind. You've witnessed this behavior in people who falsely report hearing God's voice as a means to gain power, money, or influence. Others become so pridefully convinced of their own righteousness that they assume whatever they want must be what God wants, and that their thoughts must be God's thoughts. Despite the reality of manipulative and self-righteous people, people of deep faith do get glimpses of God's mind through the power of the Holy Spirit.

Rufus Jones, a Quaker spiritual writer, has said, "God is always revealing himself, and that truth is not something finished, but something unfolding as life goes forward."[5] We are never able to capture in our conscious minds God's whole plan for creation, the world, or us. Even if God revealed this plan, it would not make much sense to us because God's plan is like an eternal tapestry woven beyond our ability to comprehend all at once, and much of this tapestry has yet to be completed. Our concerns in life constitute a tiny thread of that tapestry, and much of life is spent trying to find that thread and to discern its meaning.

The questions for us: How do we first discover the thread that pertains to our life, and second, how do we understand it in the context of the tapestry of all of life? In other words, how do we gain a glimpse of how we are to live according to God's plan and purpose for life? Many people expend much mental energy in trying to figure out their lives and how they are supposed to live. They work hard at this task, but discerning God's plan is not so much a process of hard work as it is a process that begins with relaxing and trusting in God. It continues through faith, humility, and prayer (as almost everything spiritual does). Churches, and especially their boards, can glimpse God's plan when they collectively put aside their egos, demands, and expectations simply to seek what God wants. God then gives these glimpses as gifts.

You have had these glimpses, as have most people in most churches. Unfortunately, it is easy to ignore them. The ones who discover God's power at work in their lives are the ones who have had a sense, however small, that God was calling them to act, and then responded in faith. For example, in 1998 Calvin Presbyterian Church embarked on a capital campaign to raise $250,000. We glimpsed *the possibility* that God was calling us to create the conditions for growth by renovating our sanctuary and much of the church. Many in our congregation were hesitant and reluctant because this church hadn't participated in any capital campaign in more than 50 years. Still, we stepped forward in faith. In fact, acting prayerfully in faith was so important to us that in choosing a fund-raiser, we rejected our denomination's program and used a nondenominational one that emphasized Scripture, prayer, and faith. The denomination's program focused on teaching us how to approach members in a functional way to help them figure out what they could afford to give. We went with a group that would teach us prayerfully to lead people to ask what God was calling them to give. This group would teach us how to put faith and response to God's grace at the center of the campaign. In the end, we raised more than $330,000, which was pure providence: that was exactly how much we finally needed, since our costs for renovation were higher than anticipated, and our plans changed during the campaign as we sensed God offering us other opportunities. For example, a house next door to the church that came on the market could house much of our youth and education program. God had given us a glimpse, and when we acted in faith, God provided exactly what we needed, no more and no less. When we glimpse God's mind and act in faith, God as Power can work in wonderful ways in our lives, both as individuals and as communities of faith.

Spiritual Gifts

A hot topic among many growing (and trying-to-grow) churches is spiritual gifts. The term "spiritual gifts" comes from 1 Corinthians 12:4, where Paul says, "Now there are varieties of gifts, but the same Spirit; and there are varieties of services, but the same Lord; and there are varieties of activities, but it is the same God who activates all of them in everyone." Over the past decade or so, more and more churches have used "spiritual-gift inventories"—forms that members of a church fill out, and that identify what spiritual gifts they have that can be used in service to the church. The reasoning behind the inventories is that some-how we can categorize and organize spiritual gifts so that people can be matched with particular ministries of the church. The identified gifts range from teaching, leading, organizing, building, fixing, and singing, to accounting, praying, visiting, and mission. The idea is a good one, and one that could benefit most churches. Some of these inventories are relatively helpful, but they raise a problem. They focus more on the func-tional aspects of ministry, such as one's physical and psychological skills and abilities, but they don't identify anything spiritual such as depth of faith, openness to God, ability to discern God's voice, and other spiri-tual attributes. The lack of focus on the spiritual is ironic since they are "spiritual" gift inventories. The inventories take something (a spiritual gift) that is given by the Holy Spirit and is unique to each person, and then try to categorize the gift in a standardized way by identifying it according to function. Having taken the inventory, a person may be iden-tified as having a "spiritual" gift for finance, teaching, cleaning, or some-thing else, but the inventory doesn't reveal the true calling of the Spirit. Such instruments assume that a person's functional skills are the same as her calling. What happens if a person has functional skills in teach-ing, but God is calling her to reach out to the poor, a ministry for which she may have no apparent skill? That's what happened with Mother Teresa in the story recounted in chapter 4. If she had taken a spiritual-gifts inventory, it probably would have identified her as having a spiri-tual gift for teaching and organizing, but it would not have disclosed her calling to help the poor. Spiritual-gift inventories can be helpful, but we must take care not to assume that functional gifts are the same as spiritual gifts.

By their very nature, spiritual gifts arise out of God's special call to each of us, a call that is also bound to God's call for all churches and the universe. Typically, people become increasingly aware of their gifts as their relationship grows with the God of purpose who calls forth these gifts, with the God of presence who creates the need for them, and with the God of power who cultivates and nurtures them.

The more a church becomes open to God as Power, the more spiri-tual gifts are empowered to emerge organically in each person and in response to God's purpose for him. I am not suggesting that spiritual-gift surveys and programs should never be used. They can be helpful to those who understand their limitations. What I suggest is that as your church becomes more open to God's purpose and presence, you should recognize that people will emerge to serve in the church according to their real spiritual gifts, gifts that often aren't included in surveys and that are a response to God's call. People will answer God's call to serve in the church in ways that are right for them, not necessarily in the ways we think are right for them. A person identified by a spiritual gifts survey as a teacher may find her ministry in building a Web site. A lawyer with personnel and financial experience may hear a call to develop spiritual retreats. A mathematics teacher, who would be identified as strong with finances, may become involved in church drama projects. Use these surveys, but more important, let the Spirit work in your midst to raise the right people with the right gifts for the right tasks.

The more we trust in the power of the Holy Spirit, the more it allows us as a church to break free of the functional categorizing that afflicts so many mainline churches and traps them in a cycle of functionalization (described in chapter 2)—a state that can lead eventually to dysfunction and to what I have called *disfunction*. We become much more open to all sorts of potentials and possibilities. We become more creative as we willingly take faith-based risks, allowing the power of the Holy Spirit to work in our midst.

Providence

One of the greatest experiences I have had as pastor of Calvin Presbyterian Church is the privilege of witnessing and experiencing God's providence at work in the church. This is perhaps the hardest facet of becoming a blessed church for Christians to accept because of our functional approach and our unspoken expectation that God will remain distant and uninvolved in our congregations. Plainly put, when we have faith and trust in God's power, amazing providences (what some people might call coincidences, but which people of faith know are not coincidental because they come from God—what might be called "God-incidences") take place in our midst. William Temple, archbishop of Canterbury early in the 20th century, once remarked about these kinds of providences, "I notice that when I pray coincidences happen. When I stop praying, coincidences stop happening." This is exactly the experience I have had at my church and in my life. God works to bring about coincidences, providences, and miracles. The more prayerful we are, the more events both unexpected and unexplained just seem to happen to bring about blessings.

Here's an example of how God as Power can work in our midst when we humbly pray and expect God to work. Walt Kallestad, senior pastor of Community Church of Joy in Glendale, Arizona, experienced this providence in his church. Community Church of Joy was, at one point in the early 1980s, a 200-member church in a suburban, blue-collar area of Phoenix. Today it is one of the largest churches in the Evangelical Lutheran Church in America, with more than 10,000 members. As the congregation slowly grew, its members seriously sought God's will in prayer. What they discovered was a call to move the church further out into a developing area of Glendale where they could build a church complex on over 150 acres. They prayed for God to show them where to go. Eventually they found a tract of land that seemed to be exactly what God wanted. They had little or no money. But they had their prayers.

They prayed for God to reveal the property God had chosen for them, and soon they found a perfect spot. But would the people sell? They initially focused on one farm of five acres that was key to the project. Kallestad drove up the narrow dirt road belonging to the owners, and found a run-down trailer. He knocked on the door, and slowly the door was opened. According to Kallestad:

> An elderly man dressed in farmers' bib overalls stood in the doorway. I introduced myself and explained that I was the pastor of Community Church of Joy. I explained that many at the church were praying about his orchard, wondering if God would provide a way for us to buy it and build a new center for mission with a worship center, a Christian school, a seniors' center, a place for youth, and much more.
>
> The old gentleman grabbed my arm and pulled me in. He told me his name was Scotty and asked me to follow him to the kitchen table where his wife, Ruthie, was sitting. As I entered the kitchen Scotty said, "Reverend, please tell my wife what you just told me."
>
> So I told Ruthie about our dream of purchasing the land in order to build a new center for ministry. Ruthie started to cry. I noticed Scotty was crying too, large tears running down his grizzled face.
>
> Trying to regain composure, Scotty eagerly said, "Reverend, my wife Ruthie and I moved to this land forty years ago. Five acres of these orchards belong to us. Nearly every day for the last forty years we walked around our orchard holding hands and praying that one day there would be a great church built here.
>
> I lost my composure and joined my tears to theirs. It was one of those holy moments when you sense the mysterious moving of God's spirit.[6]

Afterward, God's providence continued to work. Even though they had an agreement to buy over 150 acres, they still had to finance the purchase. They secured a bank loan for $9 million but were told that they still had to raise about $3 million on their own. As the time drew closer for them to produce their part of the deal, they were $2 million short. Kallestad describes what happened next:

> One day as Community Church of Joy's leaders were in my office talking and praying about that seemingly insurmountable goal of $2 million, the telephone rang. It was a trust officer from a local bank, calling to inform me that a 102-year-old client of the bank's had recently died and left a bequest for Joy in her will. He paused for effect and then told me that this woman was a devout Catholic and had never been to Community Church of Joy. Another pause, and he went on to explain that although she had never worshiped at Joy, she had heard stories about what we were doing for the children. The needs of the children, it seems, were a special passion of hers. Believing that God was working through our church to meet our needs, Gladys Felve left over $2 million for the mission purposes of Joy![7]

This is the kind of thing that happens when we are open to the power of the Holy Spirit working in our churches. I have experienced many similar occurrences in my own church, although not to the extent that the Community Church of Joy did. What I do know is that at Calvin Presbyterian Church we try to be open to the Holy Spirit in our meetings, worship, and all other aspects of our congregation's life. God responds through all sorts of miracles and providences. Over time, the blessed church becomes a place where these kinds of providential occurrences are accepted, expected, and anticipated. In other words, these kinds of divine coincidences don't surprise people anymore because they happen so often.

God wants our churches to thrive, and to be places of deep love, grace, and the power of the Holy Spirit. God wants our churches to succeed, but for that to happen we have to believe it, be open to it, and depend upon it in faith. A man once said to me: "God never sets you up to fail." I've discovered the truth of this promise. When we trust in God and rely on God in faith, believing and acting on that faith no matter what obstacles appear before us, God comes through. Our part is to trust and act in on that trust. When we do, God doesn't let us fail.

Becoming a Church of Power

So how does a church set out to become a church of Power? It does so by taking three steps that are like turning on a fan: "plug in," "click on," and "bask in the breeze." First, we need to *plug in*. This means that we have to be mindful of connecting with the power of the Holy Spirit through prayer. As pastors, our primary responsibility is to pray. It's amazing, though, how strongly both pastors and laity can resist making prayer a priority. In fact, one pastor told me about a time he was in the sanctuary praying. The church secretary came in and interrupted him, announcing the arrival of a member who was waiting for him. The pastor told her he was praying and couldn't meet with the man for at least 20 minutes. After the pastor had finished praying, the member confronted him in his office, saying, "How dare you keep me waiting while you pray! Your job is to be available to me when I need you, not to be off at leisure praying." It's amazing that people can think prayer is leisure. For me, prayer is hard, but it is also the foundation of everything I do.

Prayer opens us to these kinds of divine coincidences. Obviously, in the life of every church, even in those that are struggling and dying, all sorts of providences are given—family, home, food, health, meaningful work, friends, and more. Still, prayer opens us to more miraculous gifts that go beyond the blessings God bestows on us every day, providences that reveal how wonderful God really is.

Prayer opens the door for Christ, who stands knocking. I know that I can sense a difference in my church between the times when I am more prayerful and the times when I am not. I have a Ph.D. in spiritual formation, I have been trained in all ways of praying, and I am adept at many, but I still struggle with prayer. I struggle to make the time for it. I struggle with distractions when I pray, and with the feeling that I don't know what I am doing. No matter how much training I get or how much expertise I gain, I'm still a novice in prayer. Yet when I pray despite my inadequacies, providences happen, and when I don't, they don't. As a pastor I have to make sure that I set a discipline of prayer in which I try my best to be centered in God, and then pray for the church, its members, my family, and myself.

One of the greatest boons to the ministry of Calvin Church was the prayer group we started within the church. Each Wednesday morning a group of from nine to 11 members gathers to pray for the church, the staff, the members, and the world. Recently we formed a second group that meets at noon on Wednesday. I believe that in many ways they are the hidden heart of the church. These two groups keep the church connected with God, and through them the power of the Holy Spirit remains strong in the church. I believe that these groups are as responsible as anything else for opening us to the power of the Spirit. I also believe that any church that forms a similar group can similarly become more open to the power of the Spirit. (If you would like to begin a similar group in your own church, you can find a process in appendix N, "A Guide to Creating a Prayer Group.")

While prayer is the way we plug in, we *click on* through faith. Our faith, our surrendering trust in God, turns on God's power much as turning on a lamp in a house fills the room with light. When we turn on a lamp, we trust that the lamp will work. If it doesn't work, we are momentarily befuddled. That's how strong our faith in lamps is. When we have a similar kind of faith in God, then God as Power can flood us with grace and blessing.

It's not enough just to pray. Many churches and Christians pray, but they pray without faith. In other words, they pray but they are not really trusting that God can work. They pray much as we might wish on a star or read a horoscope. They don't believe something will happen. When we click on, we not only believe that something will happen, we act in faith, *knowing* that something will happen.

The first thing we need to do to "click on" as a church is to act in faith. When we act in faith, we trust that God will do something. We haven't yet seen the results, we've had nothing but a glimpse of a possibility, but still we trust. To trust, we have to let go of our fears about "what if": What if God doesn't come through? What if this idea is just our own? What if we trust and nothing happens? Instead, we trust and allow the power of God to begin to work. The distinction that separates people like George Müller, Rick Warren, and Walt Kallestad from most of us is that they had a solid, if not audacious, faith that God would act despite the obstacles. God does amazing things for those with faith. As Jesus said, "Truly I tell you, if you have faith and do not doubt, not only will you do what has been done to the fig tree, but even if you say to this mountain, 'Be lifted up and thrown into the sea,' it will be done. Whatever you ask for in prayer with faith, you will receive" (Matt. 21:21-22).

When I refer to amazing things, I'm not necessarily referring to numerical growth. Some churches won't grow numerically, no matter how blessed they are, because that isn't their calling. But what does happen is that they experience God's blessings in other ways, such as creative mission, a loving environment, or a transforming impact on the surrounding community. We also need to be aware that having a strong faith and trust in God's power does not necessarily bring an end to all difficulties in a church or a ministry. If we are engaged in a difficult situation, it is not automatic evidence of a lack of faith, prayer, and discernment. God sometimes calls people of faith to ministries that are full of suffering and difficulty. Most of the people of the Bible were called precisely to such ministries. Not everyone with a strong faith will experience exuberant blessings and growth. Still, the people of faith, prayer, and discernment who are called to these ministries often have the ability to experience God's blessings amid the turmoil by noticing the more subtle blessings God gives them to keep them going and to make small inroads.

To many people, the providential response to faith exemplified by Walt Kallestad and Community Church of Joy sounds impossible, but God makes the impossible possible. With God all things are possible: growth in the midst of decline, healing amid disease, stability amid turmoil, and more. To experience these occurrences in our churches, we have to have the courage of faith to trust and "click on" God's power. We have to have the courage to dream God's dreams, and to act on them in faith. If we don't, all we will have is the power of God's potential, not God's power making that potential a reality.

Finally, when we have plugged in and clicked on, we can *bask in the breeze.* Whenever we plug in and click on the power of the Holy Spirit, our churches begin to experience God's Spirit blowing through everything we do, much as we sit in front of a fan on a hot day and let it cool us. When we bask in the Spirit's breeze, we become a church that learns to expect God's power to work through everything we do. We cease being anxious. The church becomes a place of joy and laughter as we do our work in faith and power. Decisions lose their ability to stress us because we know that God will make everything OK if we pray and have faith. Because we witness God's power working everywhere in great and small ways, our congregations become places of Power, places of the Holy Spirit.

Power as a Path to Purpose and Presence

The more we become blessed churches of God's Power, the more we also become blessed churches of Purpose and Presence. There is a wonderful trinitarian concept called *perichoresis.* It means in part that even though we can experience and form a relationship with each person of the Trinity, we still experience and relate to the other two persons through that one person of the Trinity. The Creator and the Holy Spirit are in the presence of Christ. Christ and the Creator are in the power of the Holy Spirit. And the Holy Spirit and Christ are both in the purpose of the Creator. While we can relate with and experience each one separately, we cannot separate them.

What does this truth mean for us on a practical level? It means that the more we try to become a church of Power, the more we also become a church of Purpose and Presence because the Purpose and Presence that are in the Holy Spirit lead us to do so. It also means that when we are intent on becoming a church of Purpose, we also experience God as Presence and Power in our midst; and as we become a church of Presence, we will discover Purpose and Power. Ultimately, in becoming a church of one person of God, we become a church of all three.

In a church of Power, the leaders sincerely try to discern God's will for the church, and that church simultaneously becomes a place where people experience Christ and the power of the Holy Spirit, even if only in small ways. The church's pastors and leaders try to reveal to others Christ in their midst. They also end up helping people to discern their own life's purpose and to discover more explicitly God's power working in their lives. As the church's pastors and leaders seek ways to become more open to God's power, they simultaneously create the conditions in which the church and its members become more aware of their purpose and know that Christ is in their midst making possible the realization of that purpose.

Reflection Questions

1. To what extent do you sense that your church is truly open to God's power?
2. To what extent do you sense that your church is willing to experience the power of the Holy Spirit?
3. What events in your church have demonstrated the power of the Holy Spirit to you and other members of the church?
4. What concrete things can you do to open yourself and your church to God's power and to steep the church in a relationship with God as Power, with God the Holy Spirit?
5. What steps can your church, and especially your leadership, take to become more open to the Holy Spirit?

PART III

LEADING A CHURCH TO BLESSEDNESS

Over the years, I've had both the privilege and the burden of helping pastors and their congregations become blessed churches. It's been a blessing to share with them this vision for what is possible when we become churches that let God's purpose, presence, and power transform our churches. Still, it is a burden figuring out how to help these churches take the most practical steps toward becoming blessed churches. Most churches and church leaders are so caught up in a functional style of ministry and life that even if they envision what becoming a blessed church might mean for them, they can't quite see how to do the practical things that lead others to share this vision. Most church leaders don't even know where to begin at a practical level.

Becoming a blessed church begins with leadership. It requires leaders who genuinely want their congregations to bear the love, grace, and life of Christ in their midst. They yearn for it, because they are tired of the kind of life present in far too many churches.

Still, yearning is not enough. Leaders need to take certain practical actions that will lead the church to blessedness. They need to offer healthy leadership, grounded in practices that lead people to spiritual health. To this end, two things are crucial. First, healthy leaders must have particular personal dispositions—deeply formed qualities that allow them to be people God can use to lead others to blessedness. Second, they must possess certain leadership skills that enable them to motivate and move people to blessedness. *Leadership dispositions* are formed through a relationship with God as we move more deeply into the spiritual life. *Leadership skills* are developed as we strive to be the best we can be in guiding others to God. Dispositions are rooted in the spiritual dimension, while skills emanate from the mental and relational dimensions.

117

Ultimately, leading a church to blessedness means living and leading in such a way that God's purpose, presence, and power flow through everything. An example of leadership dispositions connecting with leadership skills to guide a church to blessedness comes from Claude King, who, with Henry Blackaby, wrote the book *Experiencing God*. King has been a leader among Southern Baptists in Georgia in planting new churches, while Henry Blackaby is a writer who has focused much attention on spiritual leadership and on guiding people to become more open to the power of the Holy Spirit. King tells how he discovered an alternative way of leadership—a way that relied less on his own efforts and more on God's grace.[1] After graduating from seminary in 1984, King felt the call to become a tent-making pastor who would plant new churches while supporting himself financially through a secular career.

To prepare himself, King studied all the books he could on planting and growing churches. He spent time envisioning what these churches' worship and life would be like. He spent 18 months developing his step-by-step "business" plan. He worked hard, did all the right things, and nothing happened. He was unable to start a new church. No one seemed interested in his plans. He still felt called to plant churches, but his field remained barren, so he took a job as an editor for the Baptist Sunday School Board. The job frustrated him for six years because it confined him to a desk and didn't allow him to do what he felt called to do. Meeting Henry Blackaby turned things around for King. Blackaby taught him that God's mission begins in prayer and faith, not in our own plans and deeds.

Eventually King had the opportunity to serve as a volunteer in a local organization devoted to starting new churches. This time he and his colleagues grounded their work in prayer. Instead of spending an inordinate amount of time developing plans, they offered themselves to God in prayer and asked God to guide them. They visited local churches and encouraged the members to join them in praying for God to lead them in a mission of starting new churches to reach the unchurched. In contrast to their earlier efforts, they offered no plans or timetables, just an invitation to pray. To their amazement, after three months they had a list of 14 towns or groups that were interested in starting new churches. Where did these people come from? People just started coming up to King, saying that they were interested in a new church, not knowing that he was interested, too.

Afterward, King reflected on the difference between leadership grounded in human plans and actions, and those grounded in God:

God allowed me to follow my *own* plan in Georgia, and I failed miserably. He had an important lesson to teach me, and I chose to learn the hard way. I found that I could not plan or even dream how God might want to do His work. I found that my relationship to God was of supreme importance. I learned to love Him more dearly, to pray more faithfully, to trust Him fully, and to wait on Him with anticipation. When he was ready to use me, He would let me know. Then I would have to make the necessary adjustments and obey Him. Until then, I would watch and pray. His timing and His ways always would be best and right.[2]

Ultimately, leading a church to blessedness begins and ends with leadership that recognizes that it all begins and ends with God. The next three chapters are devoted to helping you discover ways to nurture leadership within your own church. In chapter 6 we will look at dispositions of personal leadership that are crucial to unleashing God's blessedness. Chapter 7 examines the attributes that are crucial if we are to lead others to discover God and God's blessings. Chapter 8 offers a strategy for nurturing blessedness in your own church.

Chapter 6

Becoming a Blessed Leader

Annie Dillard, in her book *Teaching a Stone to Talk*, tells a wonderful story about an expedition of two ships led by Sir John Franklin that set sail from England in 1845 with a crew of 138 men.[1] The expedition embarked amid great fanfare with the hope that it would ultimately find the mythical Northwest Passage across northern Canada. Many believed that if such a passage existed, it would allow ships from Europe to avoid having to sail around the southern tip of either South America or Africa, thus cutting thousands of miles off the trip to the Far East.

The expedition's two ships were a marvel. Each was a three-masted barque carrying auxiliary steam engines. Each contained a 1,200-volume library, a hand organ playing 50 tunes, enough china place settings for the whole crew, cut-glass wine goblets, and ornate silver settings for the officers bearing their initials and family crests. The explorers carried a 12-day supply of coal. What the ships didn't contain: winter clothing, larger coal reserves for hardships that were sure to extend their journey for more than 12 days, and other crucial provisions for a passage through the Arctic.

As observers watched from England's shore, the expedition soon passed out of sight. Over the ensuing years, word of the party's fate filtered back to England by way of explorers who had heard vague rumors from the Inuit tribes near the Arctic. For example, some crew members had been seen pushing a wooden boat across the ice. Similar boats were seen at Starvation Cove, in the Northwest Territories of Canada, along with the remains of 35 men. Thirty bodies were found at Terro Bay. Apparently the Inuit had also seen one of the three-masted barques protruding from the ice at Simpson Strait.

Over the next 20 years, search parties recovered skeletons from all over the Arctic. Slowly, the story was stitched together. With his ships frozen solid in the ice and unable to move, Franklin died aboard ship. Their supplies exhausted, the remaining officers and enlisted men out-fitted themselves from the ships' stores and set out to walk to safety. Eventually, their frozen bodies were found along with their supplies. What they took with them was often bizarre. For instance, many were found with remains of chocolate, tea, guns, and oddly, the place set-tings of the opulent silver flatware. In the end, no member of the expe-dition survived.

What was the one crucial element missing from the Franklin expe-dition right from the start? *Leadership*. It's amazing that such an accom-plished and respected ship's captain as Sir John Franklin could have been so inept in leading this expedition, yet he was. He wasn't pre-pared for what he and his crew were about to face because of his arro-gance, ambition, and selfishness. He was arrogant about his ability to overcome anything he faced. He was a slave to his ambitions, thinking only of the glory he would receive if he found the Northwest Passage, and not the wisdom of seeking it. He was selfish in that he thought only about his and his officers' welfare, comfort, and glory (as evidenced by the organ, library, and eating accoutrements), rather than his crew's safety. Similar personal qualities sink many of our own attempts to form blessed churches.

The key ingredient in becoming a blessed church is leadership. With-out good leaders, our churches become akin to sailing ships captained by men like Sir John Franklin. They become lost and end up drifting aimlessly. They fall prey to the destructive effects of the inevitable storms. At worst, they become stalled in an ice-locked sea of this-is-how-we've-always-done-it, unable to move forward or backward. The leaders, victims of their own arrogance, ambition, selfishness, or fear, either provide no direction or strive endlessly and manipulatively for power, creating a divided and fragmented church. Following Christ isn't factored into the equation.

Many mainline churches suffer from poor leadership. The leaders of these churches, especially the pastors, either resist accepting the leader's role, or they lead in egocentric and dysfunctional ways. Much of this poor leadership is a result of the psychological and spiritual im-maturity of those responding to the call to become leaders—and of the fact that few mainline church pastors receive any practical leadership training in seminary or beyond.

I've been amazed at how many pastors who have taken my courses on spiritual leadership resist the idea of being a leader. As I've talked with them, I've discovered that for many, "leader" is a dirty word. They think that to aspire to leadership is akin to being overbearing and manipulative. They believe that pastors should merely be facilitators, not strong leaders (despite the fact that good facilitators in any field *are* good leaders). This resistance to leadership is, I believe, a hangover from the 1960s and 1970s. Many boomers who grew up in these decades became severely disillusioned by the plague of scandals, manipulations, conspiracies, and lies that afflicted the political, religious, corporate, and cultural leadership of those decades. To them, becoming a leader meant becoming part of the growing corruption they saw everywhere. They therefore responded to the call to ministry while resisting the call to leadership. Consequently, many mainline pastors are divided against themselves. They try to lead by taking a backseat to others. They want to guide their churches to health and growth, but at the same time they fear being seen as manipulative and coercive. Thus, they end up becoming ineffective and eventually cynical when people don't follow them. They are afraid to lead.

I've seen many examples of self-divided leadership. I've worked with individuals who tried to transform their churches into blessed churches and then complained that people resisted what they were offering. They moan, "Why don't these people follow the program? Don't they see how important this is? Why do they complain that the church is too much like a business, but when given a more spiritually grounded alternative, they won't grasp it?"

What is so hard to get across to these pastors is that often the problem doesn't lie so much with the members as it does with the pastor. They want their members to be spiritually deep, but they themselves fear spiritual growth. As one pastor said when invited to walk a labyrinth, "I'm a bit leery of it, you know. I'm kind of afraid I might have some sort of spiritual experience and lose control." Because of their own fear of growing spiritually, they don't have a clue how to lead their members, especially their leaders, to grow spiritually. Still, they get frustrated when their members, and especially their leaders, seem to lack faith. How can they expect lay leaders to lead the members to spiritual depth when the pastors are afraid of leading the lay leaders to spiritual depth? True leadership finds a way to say lovingly and resolutely to people, "This is where we have to go if we are to become healthy."

Look at the model given to us in Scripture. Almost all great leaders in the Bible were reluctant and resistant, but in the end they were adamant that to receive God's blessings, people had to follow them. When Moses led the Israelites into the desert, he insisted that the only way to the Promised Land was for them to follow his lead. At times he inspired the people with God's vision. At times he pointed to God's miracles in their midst. At other times he rebuked them in love for their fear and lack of faith. Moses praised, disciplined, encouraged, guided, rescued, and embraced them. He led. Like many pastors, he was afraid of leading at first. He shared his fears with God: "But suppose they do not believe me or listen to me, but say, 'The Lord did not appear to you'?" (Exod. 4:1). In the end, though, Moses led. Good leaders aren't afraid of leading, or at least they don't let their fears prevent them from leading. Good leaders also lead by being grounded in God's purpose, alive to God's presence, and open to God's power. So how do we become blessed leaders? It all begins with taking seriously the idea of spiritual leadership.

Spiritual Leadership

What is spiritual leadership at its core? Henry and Richard Blackaby, in their book *Spiritual Leadership*, give what I think is the best definition I've found: "Spiritual leadership is moving people on to God's agenda."[2] Spiritual leaders ground their leadership in God's will, lead people to move from where they are to where God wants them to be, teach them to depend upon the Holy Spirit, hold them accountable to God, and so influence all people, not just church members.[3] Ultimately, the focus of spiritual leadership is in leading others, especially other leaders, to spiritual maturity. As the Blackabys say, "The ultimate goal of spiritual leadership is not to achieve numerical results alone, or to do things with perfection, or even to grow for the sake of growth. It is to take their people from where they are to where God wants them to be. God's primary concern for all people is not results, but relationships."[4]

Still, it is difficult to lead people to a place where we ourselves haven't been, especially when we are leading people to grow spiritually. If we are spiritually immature, how do we lead others to maturity? As a leading writer and speaker on Christian leadership, John Maxwell, says, "Who you are is who you attract."[5] In other words, if we want to lead people to spiritual maturity, we have to work on becoming spiritually mature ourselves. If we want to lead others to a deeper relationship with God, then we have to work on our own depth. We have to be willing to engage in spiritual practices and to cultivate an active and alive prayer life. Otherwise, all our good intentions will fall flat. Too many pastors want the members of their churches to become spiritually deep, but they aren't willing to start with themselves. Too many pastors become frustrated with church members for being spiritually immature—for seeming to be lazy, petty, and lacking in commitment—but they don't recognize that the answer may lie in the pastor's spending more time prayerfully seeking God's purpose, presence, and power. To be a spiritual leader means to be a person of spiritual maturity first, a leader second. And the only path to spiritual maturity is time spent in prayer, study, reflection, solitude, and service.

Above all, good spiritual leaders lead others to become spiritual leaders. As the Blackabys say, "Leaders lead followers. Great leaders lead leaders."[6] The more effective we become at spiritual leadership, the more we focus on leading leaders to spiritual maturity, so that they can lead the others to spiritual maturity. Where spiritual leadership has the greatest impact is on church boards and committees. Pastoral leaders must always lead other leaders to seek what God wants. Left on their own, most church lay leaders will use leadership skills and strategies from the realm they know best. They will lead according to the functional ways the world generally calls people to lead. Typically, laity (and too often clergy) don't ask what God wants, but make pragmatic decisions based on what makes sense, seems fiscally possible, or will do the least damage. Good spiritual leaders allow people to consider the functional merits of a course of action but still encourage and push their leaders prayerfully to ground their decisions and leadership in God's will and ways. As church leaders experience God responding to their faith- and prayer-based actions, they will lead others to the same kind of faith and experience.

Ultimately, spiritual leadership is grounded in the model of Jesus' leadership. As the Blackabys say, "Jesus did not develop a plan nor did he cast a vision. He sought his Father's will. Jesus had a vision for himself and his disciples, but the vision came from his Father."[7] Jesus had a quality and a character about him that grounded his leadership in the spiritual rather than in the functional, physical, or even relational realm. He led by allowing himself to be led by the voice of the Creator. He led by allowing himself to be led by God as Purpose.

Jesus' leadership was supported by seven key spiritual dispositions that served as the pillars of his ministry. A spiritual disposition is a natural, God-endowed inclination toward God or the divine. Nurturing a disposition through disciplines and spiritual practices enables us to grow in God's ways. For example, love is a disposition, and when we nurture it, it leads us to love God and others more fully in every area of life. The foundation of Jesus' ministry was his relationship with the Creator and the Holy Spirit, but the pillars of his leadership were his dispositions of faith, hope, love, discernment, prayerfulness, humility, and servanthood.

I believe that to become spiritual leaders we need deliberately to nurture these seven dispositions. While they may be God endowed and natural, they are also mostly potential. The more we nurture them, the more fruit they bear in our ministries.

1. Becoming a Faith-Filled Leader

Faith is the primary pillar of the journey toward spiritual leadership. If we are lacking in faith, we cannot lead others to God, because faith is primary to Christian life. Faith isn't mere belief that God exists. Faith is active. It is fluid. It is our live-wire connection with God. When we have faith, we ground our lives in God so that our work, friendships, partnerships, marriages, parenthood, and service are all grounded in God. When we have faith, we form an abandoning trust in which we rely on God for everything. Many members and leaders of the church don't realize how crucial faith is. Erwin McManus, the pastor of Mosaic (a thriving multicultural and multi-ethnic church in Los Angeles), says:

> We have primarily related to "faith" as a noun rather than a verb. The church tends to live by "the faith" more than it lives by faith. The goal has become to make sure beliefs are doctrinally sound and people have a growing knowledge of the Bible, rather than to live in a dynamic, fluid relationship with God through which we learn to hear the voice of God and move in response to him.[8]

In other words, we have made faith functional. Too often we consider it an assent to a set of creeds and doctrines, not a living connection with God that involves our minds, bodies, and souls.

For Jesus, faith was a surrendering connection with God the Creator. He constantly taught people to form a vibrant faith and rebuked people for their tepid faith. For instance, after most of his healings he told people that *their faith had made them well.* He didn't say, "Go, I made you well. Go, God made you well. Go, you made yourself well." He told them that it was their surrender and connection with God in faith that made them well, that created the conditions for healing to involve the person and God *together.* When a storm battered their boat on the Sea of Galilee, and the disciples panicked, Jesus stilled the storm and rebuked them: "Why are you afraid? Have you still no faith?"

When the disciples failed to heal a young epileptic and asked Jesus why they had failed, he replied, "Because of your little faith. For truly I tell you, if you have faith the size of a mustard seed, you will say to this mountain, 'Move from here to there,' and it will move; and nothing will be impossible for you" (Matt. 17:20-21). With faith anything is possible, but without it nothing is possible. Spiritual leadership is faith-filled leadership. It realizes that to accomplish what God is calling us to do in a church means surrendering to and relying on God's purpose, presence, and power. Spiritual leaders ground their leadership in a rock-solid faith.

As faith-filled leaders, we don't have faith only when things are going well. We especially have faith when things are going badly. It is in times of turmoil and difficulty that faith truly makes a difference, for those are the occasions when faith is tested and strengthened. That is when God acts the most powerfully and lovingly. I've discovered this connection between turmoil and faith in my own ministry. Many times my ministry, leadership, and even life have been threatened, and all I wanted to do was to panic and take matters into my own hands. It's during these times that I've had to make the gut-wrenching decision to surrender to God and trust in faith, despite doubts that scream out to me: "But what if God doesn't really exist and I'm wasting my time? What if I trust God and God doesn't help me?" What I've learned through experience is that every single time I've overcome my fears and anxieties and simply trusted, God has always come through.

Too often we get faith backwards. We say to God, "Show us what you are going to do, and I'll have faith." God says in response, "Have faith and I'll show you what I can do." In the end, the only way we come to know what God can do is through faith. As we are told in Hebrews, "Faith is the assurance of things hoped for, the conviction of things not seen" (11:1). Faith is the doorway through which we eventually see what God can do.

A faith-filled leader-pastor grounds his ministry in faith and leads others to ground theirs in faith. When leaders are faith filled, they remain calm in the face of crisis. Churches are forever facing crises. Some are small, but some of the large crises can threaten to divide the church. As mentioned in chapter 5, the demonic loves crises, especially crises that lead to conflicts between and among leaders—crises that weaken and kill the body of Christ. Faith-filled leaders respond to crises with calmness. That doesn't mean that they repress their fears and other emotions. They are still afraid and anxious, but in the end they remain calm and act calmly because they trust God to guide them to the right course of action.

For example, during the summer of 1999 our church faced a financial crisis. The budget was balanced, but we had serious cash-flow problems. Summers are usually the time when people fall behind on their pledges, and because we had dramatically increased our expenditures by increasing our staff, we didn't have enough money to pay our bills. Our session met one evening in June to decide what to do. Should we have an emergency meeting to apprise the members of the situation, asking them to give more so that we could make it through the summer? Should we make announcements each Sunday through the summer, telling the members of our financial situation? As it happened, for that session meeting, we had done a study of the life of George Müller. I had not intentionally offered this study as a way to guide us through our crisis. It was simply one of those divine coincidences. We spent 40 minutes discussing George Müller and how his example might touch our church. Then we put the book aside to focus on the other matters on hand.

When it came time to discuss our financial situation, we talked for 40 minutes about what to do. Finally, one of the session members said, "I think we are facing a 'George Müller moment.' Do we panic and try to take control ourselves, or do we have faith?" In the end, we decided to have faith. We decided to pray over the matter, trusting that God would get us through. We also decided to put nothing more than a simple sentence in our July newsletter: "Please remember to keep up your pledges during the summer months." We didn't tell the congregation of our situation. We didn't make announcements. We decided to trust God to get us through, since we believed that God had led us to increase the staff in the first place. We barely made it through the summer, yet we ended the fiscal year with a significant surplus. We believed that this surplus was God's grace responding to our faith. We faced the crisis calmly as faith-filled leaders, and God responded.

As faith-filled leaders, we also face confusion with conviction—a conviction born in faith. In other words, during times of confusion we seek God's way in faith, and even if all we gain is a glimpse of how to respond, we respond with a sense of flexible assurance in following what we sense to be God's plan. We respond in assurance that if God is with us, nothing can be against us. We are flexible enough to refine our discernment continually so as not to be convinced only of our own righteousness. Church leaders often face the future with no clear idea of what to do. There's usually no blueprint for the decisions we face. Should we increase or cut staff? Should we buy or sell property? Should we create or discontinue a ministry? When we are faith filled, we ground our decisions in prayer and then act with a conviction based on what we sense as God's answer. That does not mean that we justify irresponsible acts by saying that we are acting in faith. True acts of faith are grounded in serious prayer, discernment, and wisdom. They are acted upon only when we sincerely believe that a particular course of action is God's plan.

Finally, when we are faith-filled leaders, we face commotion with communion. At times we have disruptive and destructive members in our midst. They try to sow division, intentionally or unintentionally. They can create commotion by challenging leaders' authority, criticizing pastors and other leaders, and complaining about everything that takes place. Faith-filled leaders respond through communion. In other words, they try to unite their hearts and minds with God's so that their actions can be God's actions. For instance, a pastor I know had a parishioner who constantly created a stir in the church. The man was involved in quite a number of activities and chaired a committee. He took every opportunity to publicly criticize and complain about the pastor and the church board. When he really got going, he could cause quite a commotion. The pastor spent time in prayer, seeking God's guidance. What she sensed in prayer was God advising that despite the commotion this man caused, he had no real power in the church. People didn't respect him, they didn't follow him, and they allowed him to chair a committee only because they didn't want to organize it themselves. In the end, the pastor decided that the best course of action was simply to try to care about this man. She would be pleasant to him, compliment him, and thank him for his work. Then something happened in worship one Sunday. The pastor was looking at the man, feeling defensive and angry about him, and suddenly she felt the urge to pray for him. So she did. She prayed for God to bless the man. She prayed for God to care for him. Afterward something happened to the man. He sought out the pastor and asked her to pray for him. He became more pleasant. And the pastor continued to pray for him.

This incident suggests what faith-filled leadership does. It responds to crises, confusion, and commotion with faith, knowing that God is present. Spiritual leadership is faith filled because it attempts to rely on God for everything. Spiritual leaders try to seek God's guidance in all situations and to follow that guidance with calmness, conviction, and communion.

2. Becoming a Hopeful Leader

A pastor came to me for spiritual direction for a while, and during each session it seemed that all we talked about was how bad his church was. He complained that the members resisted everything he suggested. He would tell the board to do something, and either the board wouldn't do it, or they would find ways to resist his suggestions. Then the members began to complain that he was always complaining about them. In his mind, they were an ungrateful people who were accustomed to the laziness of the previous pastor. No matter how much I tried to redirect the discussion toward what responsibility the pastor might have for the attitudes of the members, he deflected any blame onto the members. They were the problem. They were bad people who didn't care about God and didn't care about faith. All they wanted was a social club. It didn't surprise me that within a few years he left ministry entirely. He tried to be a leader, but in the end he was a cynical, negative, disparaging leader, and it's no wonder that no one followed.

Sad to say, all too many pastors are like him. They complain about the laziness, lack of faith, lack of vision, and lack of passion in their members. Such a pastor stays in ministry for 20, 30, or 40 years, hating every moment of it because of the people's failure to do what the pastor considers to be good for them. These pastors rarely stop to consider that the problem may not be with the members but with their own negative leadership.

To be true spiritual leaders, we need to be hopeful—not negative, cynical, angry, bitter, depreciative, and hopeless. Too many churches are led by angry cynics. It's no wonder that these churches are declining. Who wants to be around negative people who sap life and kill faith?

If anything, the model of Jesus is a model of hope. No matter how silly or ridiculous his disciples were, he treated them with tender hope, even when reproaching them. He constantly encouraged them. He constantly pointed them in God's direction, telling them that if they had faith, anything was possible. Even when he was ready to die, he gave them hope, assuring them that the Holy Spirit would come to guide them to truth and instill them with Christ's power. This hope is what keeps us following Christ 2,000 years later. Even when we are part of negative, dying congregations, we keep coming back, because we believe that in Christ there is hope.

To become hopeful leaders we have to be willing to let go of anger and disappointment, so that we can be instilled with what Adrian van Kaam calls *appreciation*.[9] When we are appreciative, we look at our lives and at the world with grateful, thankful eyes, seeing the possibility and potential of every situation. We recognize how we've been blessed. To be appreciative literally means to recognize the inherent value in everything. When we are *depreciative*, we look around at life and see only the bad and the impossible, as well as the failures, flaws, and faults of others and ourselves. Depreciative leadership is deadly, but appreciative leadership is alive.

To become an appreciative, hopeful leader means to see everything that happens in the church as a potential blessing, even if it seems detrimental at first. For example, at times I've had ideas to rejuvenate the church, only to find the members resistant. My initial reaction was, "How can they be like this? Don't they see how this would benefit their lives?" After thought and reflection, I realized that they didn't see. How could they? While I had been practicing spiritual disciplines for 15 years and had made spiritual growth and maturity a priority, it was all new to them. I had to learn that they could take only small steps, not the giant leaps I expected. I had to learn to appreciate the steps they had taken and to build upon what they could do, rather than complain about what they couldn't. Most pastors, including me, want our churches to have 10,000 members with 100 percent attendance every Sunday. We want everyone in our churches to have our passion and yearning. We want our churches to be like gardens of Eden on earth. But they never will be. We have to learn to be appreciative of what we do have: the relationships, love, faith, and life that do exist in our churches and our lives. We can't spend our ministries complaining about what our churches aren't. We have to appreciate what they are.

Ultimately, being hopeful as a leader means facing every situation with a belief that no matter how bad things are, no matter how bad things get, no matter how difficult the path ahead of us, good things will happen. We appreciate God's involvement in our lives and in the world. As leaders, we see and believe in the good, instead of dwelling on the bad.

It is amazing how much a hopeful attitude can affect our ministries. Hopeful leaders instill hope in others and give them life. Despairing and depreciative leaders repel people and cause them to escape as quickly as possible. In my own leadership I have found that if I can frame or reframe the situation in a more positive light, people begin to hope. In preaching, my focus is always to give people hope, every Sunday, even if I am preaching on the reality of pain and suffering. I point out to people that God is with them and that God will bring laughter and joy back to them. In the face of crisis, I remind people that in the end God will come through and that good things will happen. Even when surrounded by negative people, I try to counteract their negative energy by supplying my own positive energy. The focus of leadership always has to be on people's essential goodness, the good that they do, their possibilities, and God's presence is with us in everything.

In the end, I think the most helpful passage from Scripture is 1 Thessalonians 5:16-18. This passage lies at the core of my ministry: "Rejoice always, pray without ceasing, give thanks in all circumstances;

for this is the will of God in Christ Jesus for you." The more we are able to rejoice, pray, and give thanks in our lives and throughout our leadership, the more we give people hope. And the more we give people hope, the more our churches thrive.

3. Becoming a Loving Leader

Walt Kallestad is a wonderful example of the power of love in church leadership. When Kallestad first came to Community Church of Joy, he found a church that was not quite ready to go where he was leading.[10] He had just graduated from seminary and was armed with creative ideas. Unfortunately, the church members didn't like many of his ideas. He tried to push them to follow, but they resisted. Eventually many left, causing the church to dwindle from 200 members to 100. He was so discouraged that one day he called the bishop, asking for help in finding a new pastoral call. "If I stay here another six months," he said, "I'm sure I'll be able to close the place down." Fortunately, the bishop encouraged Kallestad to stay. When the church kitchen caught fire one day, Kallestad found himself almost elated. Here's how the events were recounted by a member of Community Church of Joy:

> If the church burned to the ground, he could move on. He could leave the people who had hurt him and slandered him and fought him in the dust and ashes.
>
> On the other hand, if the church was saved from the flames, he could ask the bishop for a transfer. Hopefully to a perfect church somewhere. A church whose members would appreciate him for the wonderful person he was. "Thankfully," he thought, "there are the faithful in this church. I do have some solid support."
>
> Without warning, his thoughts were interrupted. He was so overwhelmed by the presence of God that he burst into tears. "What do you want of me?" he asked God. And God answered, "I want you to be faithful to your calling. I want you to really love the people in your church."
>
> The pastor said to God, "That's not exactly going to be easy."
>
> And God seemed to tell him, "If it were easy, I wouldn't have called you."[11]

So Kallestad changed the way he did ministry. His sermons became sermons of love. Instead of just shaking parishioners' hands every Sunday, he hugged them. He made a concerted effort to be loving in everything he did, and it made a difference. Slowly the church began to grow again. People wanted to be in this place of love. As Kallestad began to love people, God loved them through him. He incarnated God's love, and it made all the difference in the world.

Spiritual leadership is loving leadership. If we do not ground our leadership in love, then our churches cannot become places of love, and ultimately that is what they are called to be. So many writers on church growth emphasize the Great Commission: "Go therefore and make disciples of all nations, baptizing them in the name of the Father and of the Son and of the Holy Spirit" (Matt. 28:19-20). What they fail to mention is that before we can go out and make disciples of all nations, before we can bring people into our churches to encounter Christ, we have to be sure our churches follow the Great Commandment to "Love the Lord your God with all your heart, and with all your soul, and with all your strength, and with all your mind; and your neighbor as your-self" (Luke 10:27). We cannot make disciples out of our neighbors un-less we first love our neighbors with a love rooted in a love for God. Walt Kallestad couldn't lead anyone to Christ until he decided to love them as Christ loved them.

Loving leaders ground their lives in the spiritual desire to fall in love with God. The main focus of the Great Commandment is not sim-ply for us to love our neighbor, but to love God with everything we have. When we fall in love with God, God's love flows through us. It is this love flowing through us that attracts others to Christ, for Christ's love becomes a presence within us. Love cannot originate in us but has to originate in God: "Beloved, let us love one another because love is from God; everyone who loves is born of God and knows God. Who-ever does not love does not know God, for God is love. . . . God is love, and those who abide in love abide in God, and God abides in them" (1 John 4:7-8, 16). I've learned this lesson well in my own church. Years ago I heard a pastor of one of the largest churches in our denomination say that if we simply fall in love with the members of our church, the church will take care of itself. I've always taken that lesson to heart. I truly believe that I am the pastor of the greatest church anywhere and that the members are the most wonderful anywhere. I truly love them and love being with them. What I've noticed is that this love spreads. I think that what makes our church special is that the people love each other, too. I've found that as I love them and they love one another, many of the problems that afflict churches simply melt away. Love's power is amazing.

Love goes beyond merely liking the people we serve. It means find-ing a way to love those we like and especially those who irritate, resist, and work against us. The more we fall in love with God, the more we discover God loving through us those whom we cannot love. When we abide in God and God's love, God loves through us.

There's a wonderful story that Corrie ten Boom tells in her book *The Hiding Place*.[12] Ten Boom lived in Harlaam, in the Netherlands, while it was occupied by Nazis during World War II. As the war progressed, she and her family sensed God's call to hide Jews from the Nazis. Eventually, she and her family were caught and placed in concentration camps. There they suffered and witnessed things no one should ever have to suffer or witness. Yet Corrie ten Boom did so with faith, hope, and love. She never lost faith that God was with her. She never lost hope that God would free and heal her. She had a solid conviction that God was calling her to be a conduit for God's love in the concentration camp. After the war, ten Boom traveled throughout Germany, preaching God's forgiveness for even the worst sins that had been committed during the war.

On one occasion, she gave a speech about forgiveness in a Munich church. She told the congregation that God was calling on them to give their sins to God, so that God could forgive them. Afterward, a man worked his way through the crowd to talk with her. Immediately she recognized him as one of the most brutal guards of the Ravensbruck concentration camp, where she had been an inmate. He told her that he appreciated what she had said, that he knew he had committed terrible sins, and that he felt forgiven by God but needed to be forgiven by her.

Ten Boom was stunned and paralyzed by a combination of fear and revulsion. As he extended his hand to her, she tried to raise her hand to grasp his but couldn't. She couldn't love or forgive him. After standing for what seemed like an eternity, she finally prayed to God, saying she couldn't forgive the man and that God had to forgive him through her. Suddenly, a light like an electric current seemed to flow into her. Her arm rose as if controlled by some other power, and she clasped the man's hand. Then a current of love from God flowed through her into the man. With God's power she forgave him and was herself overwhelmed by God's love.

The love of spiritual leadership is like this. It is not just we who love, but God who loves through us. When we lead with this kind of love, anything is possible. On a practical level, it means that we have to let go of defensiveness, as well as the tendency to be offended, irritated, and hurt by the actions of others. Being in leadership positions means that others will say offensive things to us. They will irritate, hurt, and attack us, sometimes intentionally and sometimes unintentionally. The more we are able to love them with God's love, the more we can recognize that they are just like us—broken people in need of God's love. When we do this, we become God's delivery system, delivering God's love to the world and leading others to this love. It all happens when we fall in love with God and let God's love lead us in our lives.

4. Becoming a Discerning Leader

So often we hear the term "visionary" applied to leaders, but the truth is that true spiritual leaders are not visionaries so much as they are "vocationaries." In other words, their vision emerges out of their vocation, their calling (vocation literally means "calling"). In chapter 3 we observed that God has a purpose for us as well as for our churches. True vision emerges out of our connection with God, which enables us to discern God's purpose. As we become vocationaries who discern God's plan for the church, we are then called to lead people to live into that plan.

Too often leaders lead from a power source other than God. For instance, far too many leaders are rooted in their own ego needs for power and popularity, or in their fearful need to appease people around them. Spiritual leaders root themselves in a continual discernment of God's call. This fundamental issue is one that too few pastors and leaders recognize. To be a spiritual leader means to realize, "I can only do what God calls me to do, so my leadership must emerge out of discerning the purpose God has for the church and me, which are intricately intertwined." For example, a pastor who is called to pastoral care—to love those around her—may not be able to build a church with dynamic programs and mission projects. She may not have the organizational ability to do so because that is not her calling. She needs to lead out of a continual discernment of her calling to create a church of love that makes love and pastoral care its program and mission.

I have seen far too many pastors burn out by not being true to their calling. No pastor or leader can do everything. No pastor can be a perfect preacher, prophet, teacher, pastoral caregiver, missionary, administrator, mentor, counselor, model, and spiritual guide all at the same time. God simply doesn't give everyone every gift. God calls us as leaders to a specific ministry focus. We have to lead out of the gifts we have been given and trust God to take care of the rest. I've learned this principle well in my own ministry. There are only so many things at which I am adept, but I've discovered that when I trust in God, God seems to respond by raising up people to take care of the other ministries that I cannot.

True calling emerges from God. The more we spend time discerning and acting on God's purpose for us and our churches, the more we and our churches thrive. Spiritual leadership is discerning leadership that follows the guidance of Proverbs 3:5-6: "Trust in the Lord with all your heart, and do not rely on your own insights. In all your ways acknowledge him, and he will make straight your paths." The more our leadership is rooted in a discernment of God's purpose and plans rather than our own, the more God finds ways to make things happen—to make our crooked paths straight.

5. Becoming a Prayerful Leader

As I have said, true spiritual leadership must be rooted in a deep prayer life. The more the pastors and lay leaders of a church take their prayer lives seriously, the more they let their leadership be Christ's leadership. As the Anglican mystic Evelyn Underhill writes, "A real man or woman of prayer, then, should be a live wire, a link between God's grace and the world that needs it. . . . One human spirit can, by its prayer and love, touch and change another human spirit; it can take a soul and lift it into the atmosphere of God."[13] In other words, it's not so much by our own efforts that transformation and growth occur in our churches, but through our prayer. When we pray for the church, its ministries and mission, and ourselves, God enters and immerses the church in God's kingdom.

Walt Kallestad echoes this idea: "For a Christian, all things begin and end in prayer because all things begin and end in God. It is here that you must begin if you are serious about claiming your community of faith for God and the purposes of God."[14] Prayer unleashes God's power in our midst. I have noticed the power of prayer in my own church and especially in my leadership. The more I give my ministry to God in prayer, the more God seems to take care of my ministry. For example, some of the best sermons I've preached have been those in which I was so overwhelmed with activities that I had no choice but to go desperately to God in prayer: "God, I have no time to think or work. I have to visit this person in the hospital, pick up my kids from kindergarten, go to my in-laws' for a party, and do the laundry. I only have these 20 minutes to work on my sermon. Help me." When I've been stumped for direction on how to surmount some problem, I've always found help from God through prayer. When I've been overwhelmed with appointments and tasks, and have prayed for God to help me, I've been amazed at how often someone will call and cancel an appointment, or the need to accomplish a task will suddenly evaporate in the light of an unforeseen situation, as if in answer to prayer—which it was.

Prayerfully leading others to prayer has an amazing impact on the church. Coincidences, providences, and miracles happen when we pray. To become prayerful leaders we need to do three things.

First, we need to set a time and a place for prayer. This determination can be extremely hard for many of us. I've found that even a church can be a difficult place to pray. Our church is active with many people in and out of our sanctuary for a variety of reasons (rehearsals and plays, for instance). Leaders need to assess continually the active and passive barriers to prayer within a church. Many of our modern churches have put such an emphasis on building functional space as such classrooms, nurseries, offices, and storage rooms that we forget the need for sacred, spiritual spaces. It is important to create spaces for prayer. In 1998 we built outside the church a prayer labyrinth, which has become a sacred space of prayer for many. Recently we turned a small and little-used entry vestibule into a prayer room. Still, as leaders we can't just *take* time for prayer; we have to *make* time for prayer. And when we do, this time spent in prayer can transform our leadership and our churches. Martin Luther used to say, "I am so busy today that I must spend more time in prayer." Apparently, he spent up to three hours a day in prayer. He understood that spiritual leadership is prayerful leadership.

To be prayerful leaders we also have to let prayer flow through our ministries. In other words, don't just rely on formal times of prayer, but keep up a prayer dialogue with God all through the day. I've discovered the power of this practice. For five years now I have made a concerted effort simply to talk with God throughout the day. If I'm counseling or spiritually directing someone, I pray silently. If I'm working on a sermon or project, I pray throughout, asking God to guide me. If I'm in a meeting, I silently ask God to guide us. And on every occasion, God does.

Finally, to be prayerful leaders we need to bless our churches with prayer. We need to pray regularly for our churches, staffs, members, ministries, and missions. For example, choose one day a week and simply walk around the church praying for everything that takes place in the places you are passing. Spend time in worship praying for the church. Keep a list of church prayer concerns. However you do it, pray for God to bless the church or, better yet, for the church to do what God is blessing.

6. Becoming a Humble Leader

To become a spiritual leader means to become a humble leader. In fact, a lack of humility can squelch the Spirit in the leaders. A leader can have faith, hope, love, a calling, and a prayerful heart, but if she is prideful God cannot break through. The simple reason is that prideful leadership makes the leader, not God, the focus of the church. Humility is crucial. The modern church has ignored the value of humility so long that we are now plagued by far too many prideful leaders.

To many people "humble leader" sounds like an oxymoron. How can we be humble and be leaders? Doesn't humility turn us into mild-mannered, spineless, weak-willed people? Doesn't being humble mean walking around with a placid smile on my face, while keeping my hands folded in front of me like a cloistered monk? The belief that being humble means being placid is a common misconception. A major reason that humility has gotten a bad rap in our modern culture is that it seems antithetical to the way modern Westerners think of leadership. Much of the modern model of leadership comes from the business and political cultures, where being strong, in charge, tough minded, thick skinned, and stiff backed is often valued. Even in the political and business culture, however, this model of leadership is being questioned. There is a growing recognition, especially in the corporate world, that the best leadership is collegial, cooperative, encouraging, empowering, and humble.

Richard Florida, a Carnegie-Mellon University economist, also underlines the point that good leadership is humble leadership. In his ground-breaking book *The Rise of the Creative Class*, he writes about the challenges of managing employees in the postmodern age.[15] He stresses that the old style of managing in which employers ruled the roost and everyone else jumped is gone, because the modern economy is moving toward what Florida calls a "creative economy"—one in which creativity is prized and central to growth. Increasingly, workers are demanding that their employers treat them as colleagues and manage in a style that is flexible, compassionate, encouraging, and empowering—allowing them to learn from failure and to take risks. They expect an employer to solicit their opinion and insights and to integrate them into the product of the company. Ultimately, they want their leaders to be people who seek what is best for the company *and* the workers, not only what is best for the leader.

When Florida describes creative leadership, he is describing humble leadership. Humility is not being spineless and weak. Humility means having a spine and being strong *to bring about what God values*—faith, hope, love, discernment, prayer, humility, and servanthood. To be humble means to put aside willingly our own desires, expectations, and demands to seek what God wants. We willingly put aside our own egos, and by so doing become encouraging, cooperative, collegial, and compassionate. The root of the word "humility" lies in the creation story of Genesis. God scoops up some dirt, or *humus,* and forms it into the shape of a *human* being. Then God breathes God's Spirit into that human being, giving the human life and an awareness of God. *Humans* come from *humus,* and *humility* means recognizing our earthiness. When we are humble, we recognize that it is only the gift of the Spirit dwelling in us that gives us our unique perceptions, abilities, and characteristics. In our created state we are nothing more than dirt, a collection of carbon molecules like everything else. To be humble means to be aware of our grounding. We humbly recognize at the deepest levels that only God matters, for everything comes from God, including us.

Humble leadership is grounded in this awareness that only God matters, in aspiration rather than ambition. When we lead from our *aspirations,* we lead from a yearning for what God wants. The word "aspiration" comes from the same Latin root, *spiritus,* as spirit and breath. Aspirations are rooted in the spiritual dimension. When we aspire to something, we seek God's will. When we lead from *ambition,* we lead from the functional, mental dimension. The origin of the word "ambitious" is related to "seeking honor or power." In other words, our ambitions are rooted in wielding power and accomplishing deeds to gain notoriety and acclaim in the eyes of others. Ambitions aren't bad, but when they are disconnected from the spiritual, they can become driving forces that consume our lives, erode our relationships, and devalue life as we greedily seek only our will rather than God's.

Still, ambitions can serve our aspirations. When we have ambitious aspirations to achieve good things for God, they can motivate us to accomplish wonderful things for God. I certainly have ambitions to create a healthy church that is attractive to others, but my ambitions are tempered by my aspirations to do so only in a way that God wants, in a way that is open to God's inspiration.

Humble leadership roots our work in a recognition that what we are and achieve comes as a gift from God. As humble leaders, we try to exercise our one true freedom, the freedom to choose between God-guided and inspired ways and our own, world-driven ways. Thomas Kelly, a Quaker writer and mystic of the mid-20th century, says:

Humility does not rest, in final count, upon bafflement and discouragement and self-disgust at our shabby lives, a browbeaten, dog-slinking attitude. It rests upon the disclosure of the consummate wonder of God, upon finding that only God counts, that all our self-originated intentions are works of straw. And so in lowly humility we must stick close to the Root and count our own power as nothing except as they are enslaved in His Power.[16]

7. Becoming a Servant Leader

Finally, spiritual leadership is servant leadership. Jesus models this as he washes the feet of his disciples, saying, "Do you know what I have done to you? You call me Teacher and Lord—and you are right, for that is what I am. So if I, your Lord and Teacher, have washed your feet, you also ought to wash one another's feet. For I have set you an example, that you also should do as I have done to you" (John 13:13-15).

In the end, spiritual leadership is focused on the welfare of others, not ourselves. We are in ministry for others, not ourselves, which makes sense, since the word "minister" literally means servant. We are called to become servant leaders willing to sacrifice our own welfare at times for the good of the body of Christ. Becoming a servant leader can mean having a vision and a desire for the church, but tempering or putting them aside if accomplishing them threatens to divide the church. Becoming a servant leader can mean sacrificing time with our families or time alone to care for others (although we have to be careful here not to sacrifice our families and ourselves—that's not servanthood but slavery to the demands of others). It can also mean sacrificing our ambitions in order to do what God really wants.

Sacrificing our ambitions for God can be difficult for many pastors, because success in ministry is often measured by the size of the church the pastor serves. Many pastors end up playing a game of ambition as they continually seek to serve in bigger and bigger churches to be seen as a success. I've seen the effects of this game time and time again in pastors of small churches who feel like failures because their church is small, especially if they are serving yoked parishes of two or more churches. True servants focus on service to God, not size. God measures success not by how large our church is (that's a human measurement), but by how well we have served. Have we prayerfully served with faith, hope, love, and humility, and according to how God has called us? This is all that matters. In the end, God measures our success by our service and servanthood, not on the size of the organization we managed.

The apostle Paul constantly talked about the centrality of servanthood in the leadership of the church. In explaining how we live together as the body of Christ, he says that "the members of the body that seem to be weaker are indispensable, and those members of the body that we think less honorable we clothe with greater honor, and our less respectable members are treated with greater respect; whereas our more respectable members do not need this. But God has so arranged the body, giving the greater honor to the inferior member, that there may be no dissension within the body, but the members may have the same care for one another" (1 Cor. 12:22-24).

In the end, servant leadership emerges out of spiritual leadership that is grounded in faith, hope, love, calling, prayer, and humility. The more our leadership is grounded in these, the more they lead us to become servant leaders.

Reflection Questions

1. To what extent do you sense that you and your church leaders are faith filled? Hopeful? Loving? Discerning? Prayerful? Humble? Servant led?
2. What concrete things can you do to form leadership as an individuals and a church that is more faith filled? Hopeful? Loving? Discerning? Prayerful? Humble? Servant led?
3. What particular steps can your church, and especially your leadership, take to encourage faith, hope, love, discernment, prayer, humility, and servanthood among its leaders?

Chapter 7

Leading the Blessed Church

To lead a church to blessedness a leader must become grounded spiritually in God's purpose, presence, and power by forming deep dispositions of faith, hope, love, discernment, prayerfulness, humility, and servanthood. Spiritually shallow leaders cannot lead others to spiritual depth, though many try. Still, while it is essential that spiritual leaders form deep dispositions, that is not enough. Many deeply spiritual people, people of prayer and faith, are not very good leaders. They genuinely want to serve God, but they have weak leadership qualities.

Being adept at the deepest forms of prayer and reflection does not necessarily qualify a person to lead others onto God's agenda. Even the most deeply spiritual people can be overcontrolling or too permissive. Becoming a blessed leader requires developing key leadership qualities.

Leadership *dispositions* root us in God's purpose, presence, and power—in a deeply loving relationship with God. Leadership *qualities* enable us to motivate and move others. Most good leaders have a variety of qualities that make them effective, but the best—especially the best spiritual leaders—appear to share seven specific qualities. Such a leader has become trusting, encouraging, compassionate, visionary, able to articulate that vision, sacrificially selfless, and committed to outreach.

Leaders who nurture and develop these qualities usually accomplish a great deal. They enable people to feel safe amid turmoil, crisis, transformation, and change. They give people the confidence to believe they can have an impact. They let people know that they are valued and supported, despite mistakes and failure. They help people to glimpse possibilities beyond what they had been able to grasp on their own. They give people a sense of purpose and meaning. They lead people to become selfless and sacrificing. Finally, they lead people to make reaching out to others the main goal of their lives.

1. Becoming a Trusting Leader

The most fundamental leadership skill is the ability to trust and to build trust. Many people in leadership positions simply do not trust others, and when people do not feel trusted, they do not respond. Think of the times you were most responsive to those in authority. Was it when your parents trusted you with a responsibility? Was it when you were entrusted with a project at school or work? Was it when you were given a position of authority and allowed to succeed or fail on your own merits? The importance of trust cannot be overestimated. Leaders who trust others create the conditions for positive things to happen. Fostering trust is even more important than having a sense of vision, which runs contrary to the often asserted belief that good leaders are visionaries first.

Too often people think that good leaders always have a compelling vision, but the truth is that while *great* leaders often have such a vision, many *good* leaders don't. What they do have is the ability to trust others, to build trust among others, and to engender trust in themselves. John Maxwell, in his book *The 21 Irrefutable Laws of Leadership*, underscores the importance of laying a foundation of trust in what he calls the *leadership law of buy-in*.[1] In essence, this principle ("buy-in" is his term for "trust") shows that those who build trust are successful, while those who don't are not. Here are Maxwell's four axioms of the leadership law of buy-in:

1. *Leaders with no trust and no vision will be replaced by leaders deemed more trustworthy and visionary.* In other words, no trust and no vision equals no job.
2. *Leaders who* are *trusted but have no vision will be retained and a new vision will be sought.* A group may wander for years with no vision, but that shortcoming doesn't matter if the leader is trusted. The church can be healthy and happy, even if it really doesn't know its purpose.
3. *Leaders who are* not *trusted but have a compelling vision will be replaced while the vision is retained and a new leader is sought.* Unfortunately, in such a situation, the church may go through a period of turmoil and dysfunction while it searches for a trustworthy leader who can help the church follow its vision.

4. *Leaders who are trusted and whose vision is accepted end up leading churches through deep and broad growth.*

As seen in Maxwell's axioms, the key element is trust, not vision. A church can be healthy without a vision, but it cannot be healthy without trust. The ability of a leader to trust is the key to being trusted by followers. The more a leader trusts, the more he will be trusted.

Spiritual leaders must be like good parents, who intuitively understand that the foundation of their children's future lies in building trust. According to Erik Erikson, the great psychologist, the development of trust is the most crucial element of raising a psychologically healthy child. According to his theory of psychosocial development, children move through eight stages of development, and as they do they must resolve certain conflicts that arise in each stage, or the conflicts will remain unresolved for the rest of their lives. The conflict to be resolved in the first stage is *trust versus mistrust.* For the first 12 to 18 months a child's main developmental task is to learn whether she can trust her parents, others, and the world. If she learns to trust, she will form a solid foundation for a healthy life. If she doesn't (because of mistreatment or abuse), she will have a chronic inability to trust anyone—family, friends, spouses, or strangers—and will struggle to form healthy relationships.

Churches seem to exhibit a similar developmental challenge each time they get a new pastoral leader. When a leader first comes to a church, the first few months to a year are vital in determining whether the leader can be trusted. A leader who comes in, changes everything, criticizes members and leaders, and generally seems suspicious of the church and its members will sow seeds of distrust that strain the life of the church. Similarly, a leader who comes to the church, honors what is already in place, praises the members and leaders, and generally seems to embrace the church and its members will sow seeds of trust that help the church to grow.

The declining level of trust between clergy and laity is one of the most critical issues facing mainline denominations, both at denominational and congregational levels. Many mainline denominations have experienced breaches of trust in their hierarchy and in their congregations. They have been rocked by scandals in which priests, pastors, or church leaders have become embroiled in affairs, sexually molested children and youth, embezzled and absconded with funds, denigrated members, or otherwise proved themselves to be untrustworthy. It's no wonder that people distrust the church, its pastors, and its leaders. The lack of trust in traditional mainline congregations has contributed to the flood of people moving their membership to nondenominational churches. Many in our population simply do not trust the traditional, institutional mainline church, believing that it is corrupt. So they opt for nondenominational churches that seem free of the corrupting influence of the institution. Of course, some nondenominational churches are afflicted with scandals, but these are considered exceptions, while denominational scandals seem to be part of the system. The whole point is that the many breaches of trust at denominational levels have led, in part, to the decline of affiliated local churches. Exacerbating the situation has been the past failure of denominations to respond adequately to congregational scandals, allowing problems to continue unaddressed for years, or to be repeated even after a problem has been addressed.

I have seen how an inadequately addressed problem that leads to a breach of trust can damage a congregation. A student of mine, as part of his doctor of ministry project, did an excellent analysis of the struggles of leading a small church in Appalachia. He discovered that Appalachian churches don't as a rule trust pastors and church leaders, or institutions and leaders in general, because of ongoing patterns of dysfunction in their culture, and especially in their churches.

Using his own congregation as an example, he chronicled the four years before his arrival, during which three sexual affairs had occurred in the church, involving respectively a previous pastor's wife, members of the church board, and a music director. Throughout these scandals the denomination's annual (regional) conference didn't appear to respond or even to care much about the congregation's plight. Eventually the members began to accept and expect that their leaders would lack integrity in their personal lives, and that the conference would do little to intervene. To add to their skepticism, over the previous 20 years pastors had come and gone so quickly (several in a matter of six weeks to three months), with conference officials seemingly oblivious to the congregation's instability, that members learned to expect pastors to stay only a short time and for the conference to ignore their plight. This church had learned well the lesson of mistrust: you can't trust pastors, leaders, or conference officials. Many left the church, and those who stayed said, in essence, "I'm just going to go to church, try to live the best I can, and never again trust those church folks."

The implication for the larger church is that when members experience chronic dysfunction in their local churches that the regional decision-making authorities seem powerless to overcome, they conclude that leaders can't be trusted, pastors can't be trusted, and the denomination can't be trusted. Over time this chronic dysfunction can lead members to conclude that even God can't be trusted. They have been let down by so many of God's servants that they wonder when God will let them down.

To build trust in a church requires two essential elements. The first is the leader's integrity. Integrity is everything in spiritual leadership. Leaders who lack it immediately become captains of foundering ships, while leaders who live lives of integrity instill a sense of trustworthiness in the church. A leader with integrity is as honest as possible in all matters, refuses to accept or expect "perks," and never becomes manipulative or crassly political, no matter how important the cause. In severely damaged churches, learning to trust may take a very long time because the pastor and staff must prove their integrity and trustworthiness to deeply skeptical people. The pastor mentioned above had served the church for over seven years, the longest tenure in the church's 110-year history, and he was just beginning to feel trusted. He had shown integrity over seven years and had done what many flashier and more charismatic pastors could not have done: he instilled a sense of integrity in the church.

Many pastors never take seriously this issue of integrity and the time it takes to demonstrate it. They believe that their holding a holy position should be enough. What they don't realize is that bearing the title of priest, pastor, deacon, elder, warden, or vestry or board member is not enough anymore. People don't trust titles. They trust people who have proved over time that they are trustworthy. As a writer on team-based ministry, George Cladis, says:

> Postmodern people recognize the right of others to lead them more on the basis of trust and relational credit than of titles and credentials. The clerical vestment, a symbol of the ordained office and the authority granted by the church to a pastor to preach and administer the sacraments, is not nearly so meaningful today as it was years ago. The postmodern world wants to know the heart of its leadership. Words like *authentic* and *genuine* are being used to describe effective and able leaders. The most important question for those who would follow a leader is no longer, "Does she have the educational and professional requirements to fill this position?" but rather, "Is she trustworthy and will she listen to my concerns?"[2]

Personal integrity is central to leading a congregation. In churches damaged by scandals or affairs, building trust can take years. In churches that have had a relatively healthy history, building trust may take little time. As spiritual leaders, we have to be sensitive to church members' level of trust, and we must be agonizingly patient in rebuilding that trust if it has been damaged.

The second element in building trust is empowering others. Trusting leaders give people the authority to "own" their own ministries, no matter how large or small. Trusting leaders gently guide other leaders, while allowing them to lead their ministries their own ways, thus empowering them to serve with God's power. Such leaders respond to success by praising others more than themselves. They respond to failure by taking responsibility on themselves, even if they aren't culpable. They accept culpability because they are more focused on empowerment than on personal recognition. The trusting leader remembers that churches are families in which all people serve and help each other to God's glory, rather than organizations that reflect the leader's glory. Churches exist to nurture people to seek and find God, to live deeper and better lives, and to love others. Ultimately, the best leaders strive to empower others, but paradoxically empower themselves by building trust, because trusted leaders are empowered leaders.

What does it take to empower others? It takes a willingness to relinquish control and the need to have authority over others. It takes a willingness to let others be responsible and to receive credit for the results of their own efforts. It takes the willingness not to interfere or look over a shoulder when things are going well, and sometimes to let a failing ministry fail, even if that ministry seems crucial to the church. For instance, if the members simply will not take responsibility for the youth group, especially in a small church, then the trusting pastor may have to say, "Then we don't have a youth group," rather than burn himself out trying to support it. The trusting leader does not try to do everything himself, but shares ministry with others. He or she also lets others make decisions while trying gently to guide them to seek God's will and to pay attention to their own inner wisdom. Sometimes empowering others means going with the decision of others, even when we disagree. On countless occasions the session of our church has gone against my guidance, and I've always seen my role as letting go of my desires to support theirs. In the end, I have never encountered a situation in which their decision wasn't better than my own. My trust in them has led to better decision making.

Ultimately, building trust is the foundation of good spiritual leadership. For that reason, I have spent much more time discussing trust than I will any of the ensuing qualities of spiritual leadership. When a foundation of trust is built between a church's members and its leaders, blessings can eventually flow. When trust crumbles, so does the ministry of the church.

2. Becoming an Encouraging Leader

After they have built a foundation of trust, good spiritual leaders then build the pillars that support the work of the church. Perhaps the most critical pillar is the willingness and ability to encourage others. Good leaders know how to get the best out of people by continually encouraging them to take steps of faith in their service to God in the church and elsewhere. Again, in many ways good spiritual leaders are like good parents teaching their children to walk, talk, and experience success in their own efforts. Such parents encourage their children: "Go ahead, you can do it, you can do it." And when the children do it, they celebrate: "Yaaaaay! You did it!" They also encourage their children by pushing them to accomplish things on their own that they didn't think they could.

I was reminded of this parental tendency one day when I took my children to a "soft play place"—a multilevel indoor structure with elaborate, padded, child-friendly obstacle courses. Children climb padded tiers, crawl around padded blocks and cones, crawl through tubes, and slide down twisting slides. My four-year-old twins love these contraptions. Once, one of my daughters was scared to climb a set of padded tiers. The first few times I hoisted her up, but then I began to push and encourage her to climb on her own. I showed her how to pull herself up and spent 15 minutes softly urging and encouraging her: "You can do it, Shea. You are so big. Look at you. Yes, now swing your leg up. Go ahead, you can do it! And . . . *you're up!* Look at that! You are *so* cool!" By the time we were ready to leave, she was climbing with gusto. When I asked her later what her favorite part of the day was, she said, "When you showed me how to climb by myself."

I have witnessed the power of encouragement in many arenas of life, but in none more frequently than the world of sports. Growing up, I had many coaches, and I had always heard that the best coaches were the ones who knew how to "kick a little fanny." My experience, however, was that the coaches who yelled, screamed, and criticized rarely got the best out of their players, especially over the long haul. My best sport was lacrosse. I was good enough to play on a national championship college team—with and against the best players in the country. The coach most responsible for my becoming a good player was the varsity coach during my sophomore and junior years of high school. He was

the kind of person who continually barked out words of encouragement no matter what happened. He was strict in teaching us how to do
things right, and he pointed out our mistakes, but when we made even
simple good plays, he was the first to smile and say, "That was fantastic,
Standish! That's it exactly!" As a result, I developed into a good high
school player. With his encouragement I became fearless, creative, motivated, and dynamic.

But when I made the college lacrosse team, I encountered a coach
who was much more the "kick the fanny" kind. He yelled at the players
and benched us for simple mistakes and rarely handed out compliments.
I was praised by him only once in four years. Often, when I made a
good play in practice, he mocked me. I guess it was his way of trying to
motivate me, but it robbed me of my self-assurance. As a result, even
though I eventually became a starter, I never felt confident. I was always
more afraid of blundering than eager to make a great play. The coach's
constant criticisms made me hesitant and fearful. I was so scared of
making mistakes that I made many. I don't mean to say that this coach
was a bad man. I think he was a good man, and I certainly learned a lot
about lacrosse from him, but he didn't know how to encourage any but
the few top players. As a result, I believe that I never reached my potential as a college player. But I did learn a crucial lesson: great leaders
encourage. I have never forgotten that.

What does it mean to be truly encouraging? The answer may seem
obvious, but many leaders don't get it. They have great expectations for
their followers, but they offer little positive support. An encouraging
leader helps people to believe in themselves, and instills in them a sense
of confidence—for confidence literally means to have faith (*fidelis*) with
(*con*) another person. When we encourage people, we not only have faith
in them, but at deeper levels we instill in them a faith that God is with
them. And when God is with us, who can be against us? Our faith in
people engenders the confidence that can lead them to achievements of
which they didn't think themselves capable.

For instance, several years ago I sensed that it was time to start a
prayer group in our church for people who would be willing to pray
weekly for the church. My inspiration came from an older member who
had told me that the small church in Indiana where she grew up had
thrived throughout the Great Depression. She was convinced that it
thrived because every Monday morning a group of four women showed
up for an hour to pray for the church, its members, and the world. Inspired by this example, I sought someone to lead a prayer group for our
church to help it thrive. I called a member who I sensed would be good

at it. She was surprised: "Me, lead a prayer group? I don't know how to pray. Why would you ask me?" I could only respond that I sensed something about her that would make her the perfect leader. She was reluctant, intimidated by the idea of leading others to pray. I began to encourage her by saying that there is no such thing as an expert in prayer. None of us knows what we are doing, including me, though I had been trained in prayer for many years. The only way we learn to pray is by praying, and it is God who leads us.

The woman thought and prayed for a week about whether she was called to start a prayer group. She finally came back and said she would do it. I developed guidelines for her (see appendix N, "A Guide to Creating a Prayer Group"), and talked to her about how to invite others to join. Then I let her go. I continually tried to encourage her through the first few months. When she needed help figuring out how to recruit members, I offered guidance and a list of names, but let her do the recruitment. When she wanted to change the weekly agenda, I supported her ideas, even though they deviated from my initial suggestions. If a member of the group became too focused on her own concerns, I suggested ways that she could lead the group away from that person's agenda and back to other prayer concerns. Eventually the prayer group took off; it has been a strong presence for the past four years. I believe it is a vital part of our own blessedness, because we now have two prayer groups, each of six to 12 people, who pray each week for the church, its ministry, the world, and me.

Encouraging leadership builds on trusting leadership by positively supporting the members we have also empowered. Encouragement arises from trust, even if the person fails. While we let the members take responsibility for what they do, we also take the burden of failure off their shoulders when they fail. For example, if a leader failed to accomplish something she was entrusted with, I might take the burden off her by explaining that a large part of the problem had been that I wasn't very clear myself about how to do it. Or I might tell her that it's my fault because I should have prepared her better. I don't offer such assurance falsely but with a realization that often the failures of lay leaders are related to the pastor's lack of clarity or failure to prepare them. The willingness to lift burdens off other leaders arises from our remembering that churches are places of relationships, not production. Many leaders fail to encourage other leaders because they seem to believe the church is responsible for a product—salvation, worship, ministry, or mission—rather than for nurturing a relationship between members and Christ. Encouraged and empowered people create an atmosphere of faith, possibility, excitement, and joy. Criticized and berated people create an atmosphere of fear, discouragement, disgust, and even hostility.

When things are not going well, it is essential that we as leaders find ways to encourage, even if only in small ways. That means sending thank-you notes, complimenting a person's minor achievement, praising people in public, and celebrating small accomplishments. Obviously we don't want to overdo it, lest people think our praise is a con; and we need to tailor the praise to the personality. The more leaders are willing to encourage others, the more they form a church that becomes encouraging itself—where members find ways to encourage each other.

3. Becoming a Compassionate Leader

An indispensable element of spiritual leadership is emphasizing relationships over rightness, empathy over effectiveness. I am amazed at how often pastors make the mistake of treating ministry and mission as more important than the people serving. Still, I shouldn't be surprised, since making our work more important than the people we work with is a natural outgrowth of our culture. We live in a functional society, rooted in the mental dimension of life. Our society is consumed with effectiveness, efficiency, and production. Western culture, especially American culture, is consumed with the bottom line. As a result of our functional attitudes, we continually determine people's worth by what they do and what they produce.

Do you want proof of that assertion? Think of how we typically greet someone new. We ask, "What do you do?" Immediately we try to measure what newcomers do for a living, how much money they make, and how much power they have. By and large, those who are most effective and efficient in their careers are the ones who get ahead. In most sectors of the corporate world, the focus is on the development, production, and sale of the product, not on the *people* who develop, produce, and sell. In a functional society like ours, what matters is the bottom line. Still, even this tendency is changing as more and more corporations and businesses realize that a crucial element in productivity is the fostering of good relationships. Workplaces in which people feel a sense of bonding and commitment to each other often become more creative and productive than before. The key is that fostering and nurturing collegial relationships must be balanced with a clear sense of boundaries and aims.[3] In other words, while relationships matter, we can't lose sight of our goal.

Whether we are considering a business, a family, or a church, we can't become so focused on making everyone feel good that we forget our purpose. We still need to set relational boundaries, being clear about our role as leaders. For instance, as the pastor and head of staff of Calvin Church, I want to make sure that the staff members get along well with one another and with me. At the same time, though I have a counseling background and 24 years of experience as a counselor, I can't be a therapist for my staff. There are times when I have to set limits and boundaries that are in line with our purpose and say something very uncounselorlike, such as, "I'm sorry, but that's just the way it is. You're going to have to deal with it," or "If you don't want to do things this way, you may have to consider whether you want to continue working here."

It also means that I have to give some disgruntled members the freedom and sometimes the encouragement to leave. Good leaders don't go around trying to make disgruntled people happy, especially those who are chronically unhappy. Often it is better for the health of the church that these people go elsewhere, especially if their continued membership has the potential to lead the church into dysfunction. That doesn't mean that I push them out the door heartlessly or that I don't care when they leave. As my wife would tell you, I go into serious angst when someone is critical of the church or me, especially if that person's discontent leads them to leave the church. Still, as pastoral leader of the church I have to remain focused on what God is calling me to do and on my role as leader. Otherwise, the discontent these people bring will slowly cause the church to slip into dysfunction. Ultimately, there must be a balance in which fostering healthy relationships becomes part of serving the purpose of the church, and in which compassion for the people serving in the church is always kept in the forefront. Otherwise, the church can easily become too focused on functionality as it mimics the corporate culture, making what the church does more important than the people of the church.

In many churches, especially larger ones, the functionality of the corporate culture has crept in, and pastors and leaders increasingly emphasize functionality and production over people. For example, increasingly the pastors become like CEOs and executives, and the church board acts as a corporate board, while a sense of functionality absent of spirituality permeates the church's culture. The church has increasingly lost its spiritual core. The more a church takes the corporate culture as its model, the more it will emphasize programs and results, rather than people and relationships. Eventually, this approach will cause the church to make the slow descent into dysfunction because the spiritual is cut off in the church.

Churches that focus on compassion and love, that are rooted in the spiritual dimension, over time enhance their ability to offer creative and life-giving ministries and mission, but churches that focus solely on ministry and mission can lose their souls if they forget to love the people involved in them. A major component, then, of spiritual leadership is being a compassionate leader. What does this mean in action? It means remembering that loving and caring for people, especially other leaders, is always more important than anything else the church does. Compassionate leaders always lead with love. Therefore, even when they face resistance from the members, they recognize that these are scared, broken, hurting people, and they act with compassion.

There's a comment made in many churches that I've always hated: "So-and-so dropped the ball on that one." What this means is that a person agreed to do something, but then failed, for whatever reason, to accomplish it. What bothers me about the phrase is that it shows a lack of compassion. The phrase has its origins in football: a player fumbles and "drops the ball," which messes up the offense. The reality is that in football, people fumble. They don't fumble intentionally. It's always a mistake. Sometimes they fumble because they are trying too hard to do too much. Sometimes they fumble because they lose sight of the ball. Sometimes they fumble because they are anxious or afraid. Nobody fumbles on purpose. But on good teams, when players fumble, it is up to the rest of the team either to get the ball back or to prevent the other team from capitalizing on the fumble. Good team leaders tell the rest, "Don't worry about the fumble. Just focus on what we need to do, and eventually we'll get another opportunity. And if we fumble again, we *all* have to get the ball back."

Compassionate leaders recognize that people don't fail on purpose. They fail for a variety of reasons, including not knowing how to do something, trying to do too much, losing sight of the goal, or lacking confidence. Good leaders have compassion and let people know that it is OK to make mistakes or fail, that a new opportunity will eventually present itself, and that the person is still valued and important.

The compassionate leader always remembers that those engaged in ministry are human, too, and can struggle with lack of confidence, understanding, and skill when serving God in ministry and mission. A compassionate leader doesn't become so consumed with a project that she forgets to ask how things are going. She doesn't forget that those involved may be going through a divorce, suffering an illness, facing unemployment, or struggling through some other crisis. Compassionate leaders even build in time during meetings for people to share brief comments about their lives. They don't just focus on the project at hand. For example, we allot 10 to 15 minutes at the beginning of each session meeting for people to share their concerns and celebrations, and if people need more time, we take longer. It is vital that leaders be compassionate and pray for each other, and the only way that can happen is for leaders to encourage other leaders to share the concerns and celebrations for which they need compassion and prayer.

As stated above, spiritual leaders are compassionate leaders. They never forget how important love is. They try their best to remember that people are more important than ministry and mission, that relationships are more important than outcomes, and that empathy and care are more important than efficiency and accomplishment.

4. Becoming a Visionary Leader

Many people think that having a strong, clear, compelling vision is the most important facet of good leadership. It is not as important as building trust, encouraging others, and being compassionate, but that does not mean it is not important. For churches to grow and become blessed, leaders need to have a strong sense of vision. They must know their own purpose and have a sense of the church's purpose.

Unfortunately, many leaders don't really understand what vision is. They think that vision must lead to something concrete and compelling. That is not always the case. Sometimes a vision isn't clear. An old joke illustrates the idea:

> Do you now why the Israelites wandered in the desert for 40 years?
>
> Because Moses was a man, and like all men he refused to pull over and ask for directions.

Why did it take so long for Moses to lead Israel to the Promised Land? If you take a cynical view, you might be tempted to call Moses a failure. He had a call and a vision to lead the Israelites to the Promised Land, but his failure to do so in a short time suggests that his vision was incomplete. How can a person promise to lead people somewhere and then lose his way for 40 years? What most people don't realize is that leading the Israelites to the physical Promised Land was not Moses' or God's primary vision. It was Israel's destination. The vision was the transformation of the Israelites from slaves of the Egyptians with a weak and atrophied faith to servants of God with a strong and vibrant faith. To accomplish this vision, they had to wander, struggle, and suffer in the desert so that they could learn to trust God faithfully and without reservation. They had to be transformed in mind, body, and spirit before they were prepared to enter the Promised Land. A whole generation of people wedded more to Egyptian slavery than to God had to die so that a new generation could be born that would be obedient to God. This latter generation of Israelites would enter the Promised Land. The journey itself became the vision, but the details of this vision weren't clearly articulated. What was clear was the outcome: reaching the Promised Land *as people of faith.* We can see how important the transformation of their faith was in the symbolic number of years they spent wandering in the desert. Whether they actually spent 40 years in the desert is a question for biblical scholars to ponder; what is clear is that in the Bible the number 40 represents a transformation. Whenever the number 40 is used in Scripture, it indicates a time of transformation to a deeper awareness and faith in God. For example, Noah spent 40 days and nights on the water after the 40 days and nights of rain. Moses spent 40 years in the desert, and then returned to Egypt to lead the people to 40 years of wandering through the desert. Elijah spent 40 days in a cave in the desert as he waited for God to speak. Jesus spent 40 days and night in the desert at the beginning of his ministry.

It was only after the Israelites were fully prepared by their 40-year transformation that they were delivered into the land.

Sometimes a vision isn't clear. The person with the vision gains only a glimpse and has difficulty articulating it to others. Sometimes it isn't compelling to everyone—a frequent occurrence in churches. The pastor may have a vision, but certain members, especially those whose only vision is maintaining what has been, aren't interested in the vision. What matters most is not whether the person with the vision has convinced everyone, but the strength of the vision, even if its details remain somewhat hazy. Even if he can't articulate the vision clearly, others generally will follow if the leader believes strongly enough in it.

Some of the best leaders throughout history have had trouble articulating their visions, but people followed because they knew the leader had a vision. I'm not sure that George Washington could articulate clearly his vision for the military during the Revolutionary War. He led his army to very few successful battles. In most cases he fought to a draw or retreated when it seemed he was about to be defeated. But for over 10 years people followed because they trusted him and knew he had a vision. In actuality, his vision was one of practical reality rather than of decisive victory: prolong the conflict against the superior British army long enough to wear down the resolve of the British people and government. He couldn't articulate this vision primarily because it wasn't crystal clear at the time, and because telling troops to fight not to lose isn't an inspiring message. The troops might not have been told what Washington's vision was, but they did share a respect for him that motivated them to follow no matter what.

How do we form a vision? As always, the first answer is through prayerful discernment. The spiritual leader spends time in prayer, asking God to reveal what God wants for the church. But this practice is supplemented by continual reading, study, and reflection; by going to conferences, taking classes, seeking out mentors, and looking for possibilities. Vision emerges. It is not developed. In other words, for people who are visionaries, visions usually emerge spontaneously as a result of discernment, study, and reflection. Sometimes a vision emerges while one is watching a movie. Sometimes it emerges while one is reading a book. Sometimes it emerges during a walk. Real vision usually emerges over time as the leader gains an insight, and then over the years as she gains more insight about the insight. A visionary is available at any time to inspirations and revelations from God as they emerge in every facet of life.

Once a leader gains a glimpse, then she must take time to engage the vision, reflect upon it, clarify it, and polish it. This process takes time, more reflection, and prayer. Ultimately, real vision originates from someone other than us—from God—even as it emerges out of us. The leader with vision is the one who leads people to move beyond themselves so that they can take their first tentative steps toward the Promised Land.

5. Articulating the Vision

For a church to grow into blessedness, it is important for the leaders, and especially the pastor, to have a vision for where the church can and should go. Still, having a vision is not necessarily the same as communicating it to others. Some very good leaders have had strong visions but were not able to articulate and communicate them clearly. Part of the problem may have been that they simply did not have good communication skills, but a more likely problem is that often people with strong visions ascertain them more intuitively than cognitively. They have a somewhat unconscious and even spiritual understanding of where they need to go and how to get there, but the path is not clearly outlined. They move forward like a creature using antennae rather than eyes. They sense where they are and what the markers are on the way but don't see fully where they are going.

Sometimes visionaries simply cannot articulate a vision because they can't find words or concepts to describe what they see. For example, it is easier to articulate a vision during times of crisis than in comfortable times. During times of crisis people desperately seek a solution to their problems and a visionary who can supply it. Sometimes they are so desperate for a visionary they will cling to someone destructive. During more prosperous times solutions to problems are much more ambiguous and unclear because the problems are much more nebulous. Sifting through the more mundane details of life becomes more important to followers than finding answers. During these times, people often sift through visionaries because the lack of a compelling process gives people the luxury of shopping around for answers.

Still, the greatest leaders are those who not only have a vision but also can articulate that vision simply and clearly. Not everyone may share that vision, but unless a simple, clear alternative vision is offered by a more trusted leader, people will follow whatever vision seems the simplest and clearest. In other words, people would rather follow a simple, clear, but flawed vision than no vision at all. Leaders who articulate positive and socially beneficial visions can change the world in wondrous ways when they articulate these visions clearly. Unfortunately, articulators of evil visions can rise to power in the absence of a positive alternative, and the sad truth is that evil is often easier to articulate than good. For example, Adolf Hitler rose to power in post–World War I Germany precisely because he offered a clear and simple—even simplistic—vision for the German people that promised to lift them out of their crisis and into world prominence. No one else offered a compelling vision in those difficult times, and so people followed Hitler, though he led them down a destructive and evil path. In contrast, Winston Churchill, offering a lucid and unambiguous vision of British defiance, was able to rally a broken and discouraged British nation to stand firm and fight back against the Nazi juggernaut. Churchill offered an alternative vision to Hitler's.

In the field of religion, Mother Teresa was a great leader because she articulated her vision of caring for the poor of Calcutta and the world in a simple way: "I see the face of Jesus in the poor, and I have to reach out and love them." Great spiritual leaders such as Martin Luther King, Jr., Mahatma (Mohandas K.) Gandhi, George Fox, John Wesley, Martin Luther, and Francis of Assisi also had this ability to articulate a vision in a compelling and simple way.

What does it take to articulate a vision? First, leaders must be willing to spend time reflecting on and refining their vision. Second, they must spend equal time trying to figure out how to outline the vision in clear, short phrases. For example, I have a very clear vision for my life and my congregation, and I constantly communicate it in a short, simple question that peppers my sermons, newsletter articles, classes, training sessions, conversations, meetings, and so forth: "What is God calling us to do?" I ask our session to anchor our decisions in that question. I ask members to root their own decisions about parenting, work, and the minutiae of daily life in that question. I say it a lot, but repetition is important. I have to say it to myself often because despite how much I preach about seeking God's call, I can forget to do it myself amid life's confusion and demands. And some of my most satisfying experiences have been those times when I've struggled to make a decision and others have said to me, "Well, Graham, we'll just pray about it and God will show us what to do."

I came up with the phrase "Doing what God is calling us to do" after much time in prayer and reflection to refine my basic vision. The short phrase in fact came to me several years ago when I was teaching a seminary course on "Becoming the Blessed Church." A member of the class asked me, "If we are supposed to come up with a vision and purpose for our churches, what's your vision for your church?" I immediately said, "To do only what God is calling us to do." Hearing those words come out of my mouth awed me as I immediately thought to myself, "That's it! That's what my life and ministry are about."

So the most important thing in articulating a vision is reflecting on and refining our vision into short, simple, compelling statements. Whether we like it or not, we are "sound-bite" people. I think humans are engineered to be attracted to sound bites. We have a hard time holding too many thoughts in our heads at one time. That's why great speakers know that even if they have 17 wonderful points that could improve people's lives, it is better to share only three. People will forget all 17 because that is too many to remember. On the other hand, they will remember three. That's why most great speakers reduce their talks to three points, and why compelling phrases often come in threes. Many churches I know articulate their purpose or mission statements in threes: "Know, show, grow." "Reaching up, reaching in, reaching out."

In the end, no matter how a vision is articulated, it must be communicated extensively. Pastors must continually slip the vision into their sermons, newsletter articles, congregational letters, classes, retreats, training sessions, and other communications, so that people are inspired and instructed to embody the vision not only in the service of the church, but in the more mundane moments of their lives. Pastors must teach people how to employ the vision concretely and pragmatically in their lives. Lay leaders must be similarly trained to embody the vision in their service to the church, so that all the leaders articulate the same vision.

The more often leaders articulate a vision, especially one grounded in God as Purpose, the more the church will become a living reflection of that vision and of God's purpose. The clear articulation of a vision enables the church truly to become a place of purpose, presence, and power.

6. Becoming a Sacrificially Selfless Leader

One of the downsides of leadership is the sacrifice often required of leaders. Being a leader means sacrificing time, money, and possessions that are dear to our hearts. John Maxwell states that one of the realities of leadership is that leaders must "give up to go up."[4] All of the great religious leaders have realized this truth. For example, Gandhi sacrificed his whole life to the cause of Indian independence—to his vision of a spiritually united, independent Indian nation grounded in love. He gave up a lucrative career as a lawyer to do so. He gave up wearing fine clothes to wear a saronglike garment of homespun cotton. When standing up against British injustice, he was willing to be imprisoned, sometimes for years. In the face of violence among the Indian people, he was willing to give up his life through dangerous fasts that almost killed him. In the end, he sacrificed his life for this vision when he was assassinated.

Martin Luther King, Jr., sacrificed his time, freedom, and eventually his life for the cause of civil rights. Nelson Mandela sacrificed 25 years of his life in prison for the antiapartheid cause in South Africa. The founding fathers of the United States were willing to sacrifice their lives by signing the Declaration of Independence. Martin Luther was willing to sacrifice his life for the Protestant movement, as was John Calvin. George Fox, founder of the Society of Friends (the Quakers), was continually beaten and imprisoned because of his vision of the Holy Spirit working in everyone's life.

There is no greater model of this sacrifice than Jesus, who gave himself to save the world. In fact, the importance of Jesus' sacrifice was clearly shown in the film *The Last Temptation of Christ*, based on the book of that name by Nikos Kazantzakis. When it was released in 1985, conservative Christians gathered outside movie theaters to protest the movie's portrayal of Jesus, but they missed the whole point of the movie. What they mostly objected to was the last hour of the film. In it, a beautiful, child-like angel appears before Jesus as he hangs in torment upon the cross. She tells him that Jesus' suffering and death is not what the Father had intended. The angel then gives him the choice to leave the cross and live a normal life, which Jesus chooses, and she leads him off the cross. He marries Mary Magdalene, has children, and lives a good life. The years pass. As he lies dying of old age on his bed, he is visited by his former disciples. Suddenly, he realizes that the normal life of a family man is not the life he had been called to live. His purpose was to be sacrificed. Because he failed to be sacrificed, the world remains unsaved. In that moment he realizes with horror that the angel was not an angel of God, but of Satan. Jesus rebukes Satan, calling on the Father to place him back on the cross. Immediately he again finds himself on the cross, once again mocked as he suffers and dies. The choice to leave the cross and live a normal life was his last temptation, and in the end he transcended the temptation by choosing the Father's purpose rather than his own.

Whether we like it or not, leaders who follow Christ must make sacrifices just as Jesus did. I don't want to portray too bleak a picture, though. Few of us are called to make the kinds of sacrifices Gandhi, King, Mandela, Calvin, Luther, Fox, and Jesus made. Our sacrifices as leaders are usually more mundane. At times we must sacrifice time spent alone recharging our batteries. We sacrifice meals at home with our families, evenings watching a favorite TV show or sporting event, time with our children and spouses, and the freedom to pick up and do what we will. We sacrifice sleep, food, exercise, and sometimes a healthy diet (especially when we eat too many church dinners offering all sorts of main courses, side dishes, and desserts). So much can be demanded of us as leaders.

Still, we have to be careful not to turn our sacrifices into false idols. Too many church leaders, especially pastors, end up destroying their health, marriages, and churches because they sacrifice for the wrong reasons. People can confuse feeding an obsession with true sacrifice. They end up serving a work addiction rather than serving God. They sacrifice time spent alone or with family because of the stimulation they get from their work. That is not sacrifice. True sacrifice makes things *sacred*. When we make sacrifices in the service of Christ, they become sacred acts (to sacrifice literally means to make something sacred). True sacrifice is made on behalf of God. It isn't confined to the religious world. We make sacred sacrifices throughout our lives. For instance, sleep sacrificed to feed a baby at two o'clock in the morning is a sacred sacrifice to care for a precious human life. Sacrificing significant time at home for work *can* be a sacred act to support our families and to provide a product or service to the world, although all that time spent at work can also be a work addiction when the stimulation of work and success becomes intoxicating for us. We have to be careful to distinguish between the sacrifices to God and to false idols.

How do we determine whether a sacrifice is a sacred or an obsessive act? By determining what the focus of our act is. Is our focus, whether at conscious or deeper levels, to serve God and others? If so, then it is a selfless sacrifice. If we sacrifice simply to boost our careers, achieve our ambitions, or gain acclaim, prove our worth, win others' approval, or escape pain or difficulties, our sacrifice becomes a selfish sacrifice. We must make sure we are living balanced lives that engage in sacrifice only when God calls for it.

When our sacrifices as spiritual leaders are rooted as much as possible in unselfishness (of course most still have mixed motivations), they lead others to sacrifice. But more important, they lead others to selflessness—and that is the ultimate goal of true sacrifice. True sacrifice, even in small ways, leads people to become less selfish and self focused, and more selfless in their love for others. The sacrifice of leaders becomes the ground that allows other leaders and the church to become increasingly focused on outreach to others through ministry and mission. Sacrifice for God in our leadership leads others to experience God's purpose, presence, and power in their lives. It leads them to serve God the Creator, Christ, and Holy Spirit.

7. Leading Others to Outreach

The final goal of all spiritual leadership, even if it takes years to accomplish, is to lead others to reach out to others in love, compassion, and God's grace. True spiritual leaders lead people to reach out to others, but not in prepackaged, programmed ways. They lead people to acts of love in response to God's call and presence in their lives.

The ultimate focus of the church can never remain solely on the formation and development of the members. It must be on reaching out to others—the mark of spiritual maturity. As James says in the New Testament, "What good is it, my brothers and sisters, if you say you have faith but do not have works? Can faith save you? If a brother or sister is naked and lacks daily food, and one of you says to them, 'Go in peace; keep warm and eat your fill,' and yet you do not supply their bodily needs, what is the good of that? So faith by itself, if it has no works, is dead" (James 2:14-17). A mature faith is not self focused. The connection we have with God's purpose, presence, and power—a connection established through our faith—always leads us to love others. True spiritual leaders lead people to reach out.

While outreach to others becomes the ultimate focus of leadership, we must take care not to coerce spiritually immature people to devote their lives to outreach before they are ready. I realize that this statement can be easily misunderstood, so bear with me while I explain. One of the biggest complaints I have heard from liberal, moderate, and conservative Christians about the spiritual formation movement is that it emphasizes self-focused navel gazing. These critics complain that the study of spirituality and spiritual practices teaches people to become self-consumed rather than mission oriented. That's not true. Spiritual formation's detractors create a false dichotomy. Rarely do I find someone truly devoted to spiritual practices who isn't also devoted to outreach of some kind. A relationship with God always compels us to acts of loving sacrifice. True prayer always leads to action. The real problem arises when people act without prayer, because then the focus is on themselves, not on serving God.

When we expect spiritually immature people suddenly to become committed to outreach, we end up asking people to serve a compulsion, not God. Look at the example of Jesus and his disciples. He did not call them and immediately ask them to care for the poor, clothe the naked, visit the imprisoned, heal the sick, and make disciples of all nations. Instead, he spent the early part of his ministry preparing them. He focused on forming their faith. Eventually he gave them small missions of teaching and healing. When they failed and became discouraged, he encouraged them and taught them how to succeed. It was only toward the end of his life that he gave them the authority to fully serve him in mission, and it was only after his death and resurrection that he commanded them to go out and share the gospel. Mission and ministry were the result of spiritual preparation and maturation. In far too many mainline churches there has not been enough focus on preparing people spiritually for mission. We prepare people for mission by creating an environment of trust, encouragement, compassion, vision, selflessness, and sacrifice. Spiritual leaders recognize the importance of first forming people spiritually for their mission.

Over the years I have heard many pastors talk about their frustrations with their churches' failures to reach out in ministry and mission. They complain that their churches are too selfish and self focused. My only response is to remind these pastors that it is mature people who respond to God in mission and to suggest that perhaps they need to focus more on nurturing their people in a faith that will lead to mission. Preparing people for mission and outreach is nowhere more important than in transforming a church of elderly people to one that attracts younger folk. Often these churches are filled with old, spiritually immature people. They have spent their lives in a functional, social church that didn't necessarily expect spiritual growth. The process of getting them to transform the church into one that is more open to younger people is not an exercise in beating them over the head with the need to do whatever it takes to attract younger people. The process is one of helping the members of the church grow spiritually, so that as they mature they see their mission as reaching out to younger people in love and acceptance.

Good leaders lead people slowly, gently, patiently, and lovingly toward outreach. They recognize that it can take time—perhaps years—to get there. At the same time, good spiritual leaders subtly and consistently push the idea of outreach. Good spiritual leaders understand that true ministry and mission are grounded in mature faith—a faith that genuinely seeks out God's purpose, embodies God's presence, and acts passionately with God's power. When we lead people to faith, mission emerges on its own. People begin to live lives of compassion. They not only become involved in the mission of the church, but they also realize that the other parts of their lives—their homes, workplaces, friendships, and more—are fertile areas in which they can sow seeds of Christ's love. They begin to take seriously that God is calling them to mission and ministry beyond the church. They look for ways, big and small, to reach out in love. They look for ways to become servants.

Leading a Church to Maturity

Spiritual leaders recognize the need to nurture the church and its members to maturity. Emphasizing spiritual growth can be an especially difficult prospect in a growing church, because as members become more mature they attract new members who aren't as mature. The spiritual leader is always leading the spiritually mature and immature at the same time. Leading both is the tricky part of good spiritual leadership. The questions spiritual leaders must always ask are, To what extent are we nurturing the growth of spiritual seekers (those new to faith), and to what extent are we offering opportunities for spiritual disciples and servants (those mature in the faith)? The process of leadership is like being a parent to infants, children, teens, young adults, and older adults all at once. Such nurturing requires a sensitivity to each one's stage on the path to spiritual maturity. A large part of this process entails the leaders' attending to their own spiritual health, much as a parent must attend to his or her health.

Good spiritual leaders always keep in mind that they are called to nurture the church as a parent nurtures a child. With children we begin by creating a climate of trust so that they can learn to trust that the world is a good place filled with God's wonders. We encourage our children to take initiative in their lives so that they can become confident in themselves and their abilities, and gain a genuine sense of self-esteem. We nurture them to become compassionate and kind to others, caring for the problems of others instead of ignoring them. We teach them to develop, set, and follow their goals so that their lives will have purpose, and we teach them to become leaders who lead others to their goals. We teach them to be disciplined and willing to sacrifice for their goals, so that they don't live a random, self-consumed existence, but lives filled with meaning—for sacrifice brings meaning. Finally, we teach our children to share and to contribute to the welfare of others and society.

Spiritual leaders nurture spiritual children to become spiritual adults. As Paul said to the Corinthians, "I could not speak to you as spiritual people, but rather as people of the flesh. I fed you with milk, not solid food, for you were not ready for solid food" (1 Cor. 3:1-2). Implicit in this statement is the idea that when people begin the journey to spiritual maturity by joining a church, often they are not ready for the full impact of the gospel and what it means for their lives. We must take care not to push people to do what they are unready to do, for then we don't lead them to God but to burnout. Ultimately, when we become spiritual leaders leading a church to blessedness, we are responsible for helping all members grow into the presence of Christ in the world, and they are responsible for growing at their own pace.

Throughout this chapter I have offered a positive perspective on leadership qualities. It is important to realize that while we must be gentle and caring in our leadership, we also be must have a certain degree of holy wisdom, recognizing that each of these leadership qualities has a dark side. For instance, we cannot be so trusting that we are easily manipulated. We cannot be so encouraging that we refuse to give direction and discipline when necessary. We cannot be so compassionate that we do not hold people accountable. We cannot be so visionary that we forget the details. We cannot be so sacrificing and selfless that we lose our health, families, and minds. We must keep a balance in our lives. Finally, we cannot become so focused on outreach that we forget about those around us. As important as these leadership qualities are, there are times when we must set limits, give direction, hold people accountable, take care of our lives, and maintain balance. Holy wisdom is the ability to discern those times when God is calling us to stand our ground, give firm direction, hold people accountable, and take care of ourselves. This wisdom comes from grounding our leadership qualities simultaneously in leadership dispositions, but that is a subject for the next chapter.

Reflection Questions

1. To what extent do you sense that your church's leaders have been trusting leaders? Encouraging? Compassionate? Visionary? Have articulated their vision? Been sacrificing and selfless? Emphasized outreach?
2. What concrete things can your congregation's leaders do to be more trusting? Encouraging? Compassionate? Visionary? Communicating? Sacrificially selfless? Outreach oriented?

Chapter 8

Leading the Church to Blessedness

Leading a church to blessedness is a challenge in today's culture. So many facets of modern life distract and diffuse our attention, making it hard to make the commitments necessary to grow spiritually deep. For this reason and others, people are spiritually hungrier today than in any time in recent history. This is true not just in the United States but worldwide. Religious movements from Christian Pentecostalism and fundamentalist Islam to Mormonism are spreading at blinding speed throughout Africa, South America, and Asia.

Unfortunately, the spiritually hungry of North America live in a rapid, fast-food culture that desperately tries to satisfy spiritual hunger with fast-food answers: "Buy this book, buy this program, buy this crystal, buy this soap—it will make you spiritual!" People search and search, clinging to whatever offers the quickest, most painless route to spiritual fulfillment. They have little patience for processes that take time, and spiritual growth takes time. There are no quick, sound-bite ways to grow spiritually. Leaders who want to lead their churches into blessedness must be aware that leading their congregations to spiritual depth means calling people to a life of commitment—commitment to prayer, faith, love, and God—and to the transformation that comes with this kind of commitment.

Leading a church to blessedness also requires integrating two seemingly distinct devotions. On the one hand, leaders must be willing to make themselves their own spiritual projects. They must be willing to nurture the deep dispositions of the spiritual life discussed in chapter 6: being faithful, hopeful, loving, discerning, prayerful, humble, and serving. Nurturing these dispositions takes time. In fact, it takes a lifetime. It also requires that a person focus his attention on himself and his internal life, often spending long hours in solitude and study. Thus, forming leadership dispositions means spending time in continual self-reflection on how my sin impedes my service to God, God's call for my life, how to humble myself before God, and other issues that are part of the spiritual life.

On the other hand, leading a church to blessedness depends on possessing a certain set of leadership qualities—being trusting, encouraging, compassionate, visionary, able to articulate a vision, sacrificially selfless, and committed to outreach—that lead us to focus our attention away from ourselves and toward others, and that motivate people to grow. The inherent paradox of being a spiritual leader is that I must become self focused and other focused at the same time, committing time in my life to prayerful self-reflection that moves me onto God's agenda, while also committing time to learning leadership skills that move others onto God's agenda.

Many pastors and leaders focus on forming spiritual depth in themselves and others but become discouraged when they and their ideas are resisted by the members of their church. They desperately want their members to dive into the deep end with God. Answers to life's mysteries may not always be found in this "deep end," but a personal experience of the mysterious God will be. Unfortunately, pastors often have difficulty overcoming members' desire to stay in the safety of the shallow end of faith, where simplistic and false answers to life's mysteries are found—but not the mysterious God. Eventually, they can become so frustrated by the members' failure to take seriously the search for God that they leave their church and the ministry. In other situations, pastors and church leaders give up trying to lead people to spiritual maturity, settling for a ministry of leading their churches to become active, even frenetic, but still shallow places. They offer energetic worship and a multitude of programs, and move people into all sorts of activities, but they never ask members to move any deeper than the baby pool. They coddle members and make them feel safe, even communicating that just by being part of this particular church, they are saved and have eternal life. They also offer another implicit message: "If you become just like us, you too can wear nice clothes and sparkling jewelry, and look pretty." These churches grow broad but remain shallow. These are the main questions confronting us: Can their churches grow deep *and* broad? Will an emphasis on spiritual growth lead to nothing more than frustration? Can a church grow spiritually *and* numerically?

When we integrate spiritual dispositions with dynamic leadership qualities, blessedness begins to permeate the life of the church. I am not talking about creating a utopia. There is no such thing. No matter how blessed the church, it will experience difficult times and some dysfunction. These churches rise above their times of difficulty and dysfunction seemingly because they have blessed leaders who integrate their dispositions and leadership qualities in a way that moves people to spiritual maturity as individuals and as a community, so that the dysfunction cannot destroy the body of Christ.

The integration of dispositions with leadership qualities occurs in many of today's more dynamic churches. These churches span the theological horizon: Pentecostal, evangelical, conservative, moderate, liberal, and progressive. This chapter is an attempt to integrate dispositions and skills. Let's look at how we can integrate leadership dispositions with qualities to lead the church to become a place of blessing for members and leaders.

The figure on the following page charts the focus of this chapter (the integration of leadership dispositions and skills). Looking at the chart, you can see that each disposition naturally integrates with a corresponding skill, and that the integration of particular dispositions and skills builds upon previous ones. The arrow shows a progression of growth in grace from the first integration, *laying a foundation,* to the last one, *cultivating grace-filled ministry and mission.* The growth is a by-product of an increasing openness to God by grace. This chart is designed to help you quickly evaluate your ministry and leadership. By gaining a sense of where your church and leadership are on the chart, you can also gain a sense of the leadership challenges you face. For instance, if you are new to a church, you will want to focus especially on the first integration for a time. If you are mired in a time of struggle, by looking at the chart you can assess what integrations have been neglected and decide how to strengthen them. The chart also helps you clarify the potential challenges you face as your church grows.

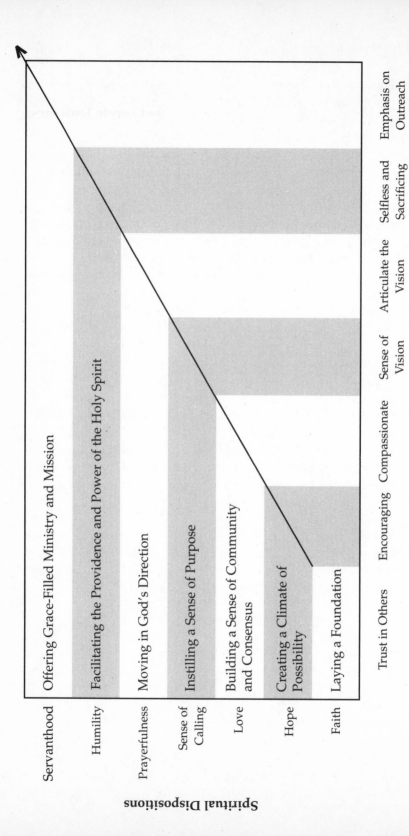

1. Laying a Solid Foundation

In one of the most subtly powerful parables in the Gospels, Jesus says:

> Everyone then who hears these words of mine and acts on them is like a wise man who built his house on rock. The rain came down, the streams rose, and the winds blew and beat against that house. The rain fell, the floods came, and the winds blew and beat on that house, but it did not fall, because it had been founded on rock. And everyone who hears these words of mine and does not act on them will be like a foolish man who built his house on sand. The rain fell, and the floods came and the winds blew and beat against that house, and it fell—great was its fall!
>
> Matthew 7:24-27

The parable's power is in challenging us to ask a fundamental question: What is my foundation? Whether we are talking about the construction of a house, a life, or a congregation, unless we lay a solid foundation upon rock, it will crumble, no matter how strong, beautiful, creative, or majestic it may appear. *Laying a solid foundation* is everything because a solid foundation gives the structure strength and constancy. In the case of congregations, that foundation is the linking of a faith in God and trust in others. Combining the two allows a creative, purposeful, and powerful ministry to be built.

Unfortunately, far too many modern, mainline churches have cracks in their foundations because they have paid too much attention to issues that stress and stretch their foundations. For example, they get so focused on maintaining their sanctuary, style of communion, form of worship, or emphasis on particular theological and social issues, that they turn these issues into false idols. When this happens, their foundations (perhaps poorly laid years before, or neglected over the years) begin to shift and crack. They start to care far more about one aspect of the church than about Christ upon whom the church must be built.

It's not just old, traditional churches that have foundation problems. So do many newer churches. I have seen churches start with a flourish of excitement, only to fall apart several years later. They fall apart because, even though they offer such flourishes as contemporary music, multimedia presentations, and gourmet coffee between services, their foundation is weak. They build their church on splashiness and the charisma of the pastor, not on faith and trust. Then, when the pastor has an affair with a secretary, absconds with funds, abuses his position, or just leaves, the church crumbles. The foundation of a healthy church is laid only when the leaders integrate a *disposition of faith* with a *trust of the members* that leads to a trust of the leaders. This foundation allows the church to prepare for spiritual growth. In healthy churches, leaders make nurturing their own faith in God a priority. This faith is more than mere belief. It is an abandoning trust in God that allows God to work through them. When this trust and abandonment to God are strong enough, they lay a powerful foundation on which to build one's trust in the congregation. This foundation enables the whole church to connect with God, while also empowering the members to grow into a transforming faith. It creates a dynamic energy within a congregation that is palpable. People can sense it just by walking into the church, although they can't always identify the source of the energy.

What does this foundation of faith and trust do? It connects people to God's purpose, presence, and power, and with one another. It does so through the leaders' faith, especially the pastoral leaders' faith. When pastors exhibit a strong faith in God and in the people of the church—a faith that enables the pastors to discover God's purpose, presence, and power for themselves, it communicates to people that they also can experience God's purpose, presence, and power in their lives and in the church. As people increasingly experience God for themselves and tell their stories, others begin to experience God, too, and the church becomes a place where God is found. Faith and trust, by their very nature, open people at the deepest levels to this encounter with God. Think about the people you trust most. You are able to say things to them that you cannot say to others. You can be yourself in ways you can't with the rest of the world. As a result, you experience a bonding with them that is transforming. When a whole church manifests at least an aspect of this kind of trust, God's power and providence can flow more freely in the members' midst. This becomes a foundation upon which relationships, ministry, and mission can be built.

Faith and trust lay a foundation for us to return to and solidify whenever our ministry falters. Whenever we struggle in the church, when we are lost and uncertain about what to do, and when we experience conflict, the first step for leaders is to spend time in prayer and solitude, reflecting upon and rebuilding their faith in God. At the same time, they need to focus on how to rebuild trust among members of the congregation. Why? Because times of turmoil deplete our faith, our relationship with God, and our trust, the basis for our relationships with one another—and church is always relational. Often tumult and dysfunction result when leaders and congregations lose sight of how foundational faith and trust are, and overemphasize the creation of programs over people, and the establishment of righteousness over relationships. They become overfocused on pursuing a particular vision and accommodating the needs of all sorts of people. In the process they neglect their relationships with God and each other.

I've seen far too many situations in which pastors, desperate to inject life into their congregations, try this program or that, only to become frustrated by the unwillingness of the members to participate. The problem is that they have neglected their faith as well as the trusting relationship between them and the congregation. I believe that there is a strong connection between a leader's faith and the faith of the followers. When a leader has a strong faith, and applies that faith in God by trusting others (faith in God generally results in a trust that God will work through others, thereby sharpening the leaders' ability to trust the members), the result is a stronger faith among the followers. The faith of the leader, in effect, flows into the followers through trust. In the same way, when the leaders have a weak faith and distrust the members, their weakness has the power to impede the faith of the members. Unfortunately, too many members of faltering mainline churches don't trust God, pastors, or each other. The more troubled a church's recent history, the more such distrust is present. There is no quick way to rebuild trust or faith; they accrue over time. They are built through experiences of increased faith and trust leading to a feeling of blessedness among leaders and members.

When immersed in tumultuous times, how do we return to strengthening and rebuilding a foundation of faith and trust? As leaders, we begin the process by spending more time in retreat, prayer, and study, grounding ourselves more in God. In my own ministry I have found that as I spend more time in retreat and prayer, I not only become calmer about my ministry, but I also gain clarity about what matters. I remember one period of my ministry five years ago when I felt overwhelmed by all the activities and challenges in our church. I was becoming burned out trying to meet all the demands. What made the period even more difficult was that our twin girls were infants, and I had decided to be closely involved in their care—to the point of sharing the nighttime feedings with my wife. For more than nine months, both of us were getting little more than five to six hours of sleep a night. During this period I decided to make my faith a priority. I spent 30 minutes to an hour each morning in prayer and spiritual reading. Once a month, I took a daylong personal retreat at a retreat center, praying, reading devotional material, and reflecting. I noticed immediately that these spiritual disciplines were having an impact on my ministry. Without my even focusing on it, the church seemed to grow more peaceful and caring.

At the same time I was focusing on my faith, I also decided to re-emphasize the building of relationships. I don't mean that I set out to visit every member of the church. I simply decided that in our ministry and the life of the church we would emphasize relationships more. During committee meetings I subtly encouraged sharing, telling stories, and laughing—by sharing, telling stories, and laughing myself. We did the same thing in our session meetings. We spent 30 or more minutes at the beginning of meetings relating what was going on in our lives, and I would often tell jokes or stories during our discussions.

Finally, I reemphasized delegating authority to members. I worried less about efficiency and completion of projects, and more about empowerment of people to do the ministry of the church. I don't want to give the impression that I was doing *everything* up until that point, but we were at a stage of transition from being a pastoral-size church to becoming a program-size church, and I realized that I needed to do less while empowering the members to do more. I decided to focus on teaching the members how to do ministry, rather than on doing the ministry myself.

What does it mean to reemphasize faith and trust? It means that as leaders we need to spend time in personal prayer and retreat. In our ministries, we need to delegate more authority to members, share ministry with the members, and spend time listening to their troubles and struggles, so that they learn that we can be trusted. And we need to spend time with them laughing and enjoying life. We need always to make sure that this foundation is solid, because when it cracks, and trust and faith are breached, it becomes difficult to fix the foundation without tearing down much of what has been built.

A great example of this kind of faith and trust outside the church is seen in the film *Seabiscuit*, based on the book of the same name by Laura Hillenbrand. *Seabisbuit* is the true story of a horse that captured the nation's imagination in the late 1930s and early 1940s. The story begins with a man named Charles Howard, who made a fortune in northern California selling cars. He had a wonderful life until his young son died in a tragic accident. The grief crushed him. His marriage crumbled, and he became a heartbroken man. Still, he was a leader of faith and trust, and he never let his brokenness rob him of these.

During the early years of the Great Depression, he met the woman who would become his wife, and the two of them took an interest in horse racing. They decided to buy a horse but went about it in a strange way. Howard, being a broken man, was exquisitely sensitive to the brokenness in others. He began his foray into horse racing by hiring a man named Tom Smith—also a broken man. A cowboy, Smith loved the life of the old West he had been reared in, but that wild world was fading with the taming of the West. Smith loved horses more than people and intuitively saw qualities in horses that others missed. With Smith's help, Howard sought out a racehorse. What they found was Seabiscuit.

Seabiscuit was also broken. He had been sired in the bloodlines of the great Man-o'-War and was born with promise, but his trainers failed to bring that promise out. They ended up abusing Seabiscuit, and in the process they turned a happy horse into a bitter, cantankerous animal that was no good at racing. Smith and Howard saw something special in Seabiscuit that others missed, though. They saw the heart of a champion, buried beneath years of mistreatment. They went about hiring a jockey who could bring out this heart.

The person they found, Red Pollard, was also a broken man. He was blind in one eye, having been in one too many fights. Cynical and jaded, he was a gifted jockey who could never win the big race, and he often squandered the little races in his propensity for fighting and losing sight of his goals.

Howard's ultimate gift was his faith and trust in people, and with this gift, he approached this odd collection of broken people and a horse. Howard trusted Smith's perceptions and training. He trusted Seabiscuit's innate abilities. He trusted Pollard's grit and determination. It didn't matter how often the four of them failed. Howard had faith in them and trusted them. And it was the combination of faith and trust that eventually laid the foundation for winning.

They grew together, each at his own pace. Slowly, Seabiscuit began to win races. As he beat better and better horses in all sorts of races, he gained the attention of the media and the public. Eventually, the men managed to set up a one-on-one race with Triple Crown winner War Admiral, the greatest horse of the day. Seabiscuit soundly beat him. A horse that had been considered a failure became one of the greatest horses ever to race. But success would not have been possible without the foundation of faith and trust that Charles Howard laid. This account reveals how powerful human trust can be. When we add faith in God to the mix, it exponentially strengthens the foundation and blessings within a church. If Howard's trust in two men and a horse could lead to such an astounding effort, imagine what miracles faith in God can bring.

2. Creating a Climate of Possibility

Another malaise that afflicts churches is a sense that "nothing good is possible in this church" anymore. I had lunch recently with a pastor who said something of this sort about his own church. He had been there for four years but was a bit frustrated over the general pessimism of his church. The members (and now he) just didn't believe that their efforts could lead to anything truly good and lasting. The pastor said that he couldn't convince members otherwise. Another pastor sitting nearby told me how a previous church he had led took this despair one step further. This church was a joint United Methodist and Presbyterian congregation. He said that in many ways they manifested the worst of both traditions. From the Presbyterians they had formed an attitude of Calvinistic fatalism, believing that it was their destiny that nothing good could ever happen in their church. From the Methodist tradition they had taken the idea that they had to be small, and that to grow would amount to selling out. Eventually, the pastor left in frustration over the cynicism and pessimism.

It's easy for churches to succumb to the kind of fatalistic despair shown by these congregations. This is especially true for small rural or urban churches that face diminishing membership, resources, and spirit. The longer a church experiences this kind of decline and dysfunction, the more it is poisoned by a climate of pessimistic inevitability, believing that nothing good can ever happen. Many pastors, leaders, and churches are caught in the grips of such pessimism, but there is another way. Overcoming pessimism requires leadership that is personally *hopeful* and that *encourages others* in hope.

I've experienced the power of hope and encouragement in my own church, and I've seen it in others. Frank Harrington, who, until his death several years ago, was the pastor of Peachtree Presbyterian Church in Atlanta, Georgia, the largest church in the Presbyterian Church (U.S.A.), spoke fervently about this kind of hope. I heard him speak 10 years ago, and he told a powerful story of an experience he had with a church and its pastor. He had been invited by a young pastor to come to Oklahoma to speak to his church. The pastor came to the airport to pick up Harrington. On the way to the church, he told Harrington all about his church, how wonderful it was, how great the members were, how they would do anything for anyone, and how they were on the verge of a great growth explosion. As they passed through the suburbs of Oklahoma City, Harrington expected to stop at one of the large churches they were passing, but the pastor kept on driving and talking. They passed by large towns. Certainly the church must be in one of those towns—but the pastor kept driving and talking. Several hours passed as they drove on through rural Oklahoma. From everything the young pastor had told him, Harrington expected eventually to arrive at a large, thriving church, so he was astonished when they pulled up to a tiny church way out in the country. The young pastor said to Harrington, "I know it doesn't look like much compared to your church, but I know your talk will be just the thing to cause amazing things to happen. I can feel it. This is such a wonderful church!"

Harrington said that he came away from the small church amazed at what hope can do. He kept tabs on that church from time to time, and it had grown. It was marked by a dynamic energy—due, said Harrington, to one factor. The pastor had such a belief in the members' potential, and such a hope and belief that God was going to do something wonderful in that location, that anything was possible. The pastor believed that his little church was the best little church in the world, and so it became that. I have taken that message with me into my congregation. When I came to Calvin Church, I was convinced that it was the best church in the world, and I've never been disappointed. I have learned from Harrington and the Oklahoma pastor that when we link hope in God with an infectious encouragement of others, the combination *creates a climate of possibility.* As Jesus said, "With God all things are possible" (Matt. 19:26).

Leadership that combines a strong spiritual disposition of hope with an encouraging leadership style taps into the power of *self-fulfilling prophecies.* "Self-fulfilling prophecy" is a psychological term referring to the tendency of people to *make* their expectations happen, even if such an outcome wouldn't come to fruition on its own. For instance, I might so strongly expect that I will catch the flu this winter that I will compromise my immune system, making me more susceptible to illness—and I will get sick. Self-fulfilling prophecies can interfere with almost every area of life. A friend of mine, a counselor, told me about a client who was so convinced that people would always reject her that she created conditions in which everyone eventually did reject her. She became so clingy, unstable, and pessimistic that people didn't want to spend time with her. She thus fulfilled her own prophecy of rejection.

The same dynamic exists in churches. If they believe they are doomed to failure, they will fail. If they believe they are called to succeed, they will succeed. To lead a church out of despair and pessimism requires leadership that can prophesy in a new, hopeful, and encouraging way. Moving a church from despair to possibility takes leadership that can persuade people that they can accomplish wonderful things.

I saw this kind of movement as one of my first tasks when I came to Calvin Church, which was in a slow, steady state of physical decline. When I arrived, I was almost instantly inundated by people suggesting that we recarpet the sanctuary, replace the wallpaper in the library, improve the lighting, and so on. I thought the only way we could do everything suggested was to start a capital campaign and do it all at once. The only problem was that some of the leaders at the time were doubtful that we could raise the funds we sought, $250,000, although other leaders believed we could. My role, after spending much time in prayer asking whether God was calling us to embark on a capital campaign, was to be hopeful and encourage the leaders and congregation. We slowly worked toward defining what we wanted to do and laid the groundwork for the campaign. There was a mild but not overwhelming pessimism that we wouldn't be able to do what we set out to do. My whole mode of leadership for that winter was to encourage the members while maintaining a fervent hope. Over the course of three years we raised not $250,000 but $330,000. In the process, we renovated the sanctuary, improved much of the building, started an endowment fund, gave $33,000 to a mission project, and, combining money raised with other assets, bought two adjoining houses. Now, our congregation believes it can do almost anything. We have a climate of possibility that came about because the leaders of our congregation combined an ardent hope with encouragement of the members.

At the same time, we need to temper possibility with patience. We can't be in a hurry, because hurry kills hope and breeds discouragement and frustration. Transformation of attitudes and perceptions takes time and experience—the experience of God's power working through us to make possible happenings we didn't expect. When I came to Calvin Church, it was moderately optimistic, and still it took four years, a major capital campaign, and lots of hope and encouragement on our leaders' part to transform it into a determinedly hopeful and optimistic place. For churches that have wallowed in dysfunction and despair, the transformation to a belief in possibility can take much longer.

Leaders need to assess the level of spiritual maturity in the congregation and lead accordingly. For instance, if the congregation is relatively immature spiritually, the church may not be able to take large steps toward a spiritual deepening. The leaders may have to guide it through a series of baby steps. For example, embarking on a capital campaign may be too big a step, so finding ways to forge small successes may be necessary—successes such as starting a mission project, upgrading the adult education courses, or hosting a concert. Like nurturing a baby to crawl, stand, and walk, we have to start slowly, hopefully, and with lots of encouragement. We have to let a congregation grow at its pace, not ours.

That can be agonizing for pastors, because they have a vision they want to accomplish *now*. They are in a hurry because they are inundated with stories about churches that grew from nothing to 3,000 members in three years. They think that explosive growth is the only proof of success. We have to remember that blessedness is not about numerical growth but spiritual growth. In healthy churches, numerical growth comes out of spiritual growth. Visitors start coming because they want to be around these spiritually deep and loving people. Like loving parents, we nurture and encourage our congregations to grow at their own pace until that day when they are ready to start taking bigger steps and finally leaps of faith and growth. But we have to accommodate ourselves to the congregation's pace of growth. Forcing members to grow at our pace leads to nothing but discouragement and despair as people fail over and over again to meet the expectations of impatient leaders.

One final note: being hopeful and encouraging does not mean that we become doormats for those we are encouraging. There are times that leaders need to set limits, lovingly challenge the congregation, and set standards for behavior and relationships. The key is doing these things in a way that does not destroy hope and encouragement. Setting limits and boundaries does not have to be harsh but can be done gently and respectfully. For example, I can suggest to a member that even a great idea might not be appropriate for us at this time. I can do it in a way that praises her for the idea, while encouraging her to wait until a more advantageous time.

3. Building a Sense of Community and Communion

If you survey the landscape of mainline churches across North America, you will find many places where a sense of community and communion is scarce and conflict reigns. Conflict management in churches is a growth business in all mainline denominations. Denominational executives are expected to have training and experience in conflict resolution. Church-conflict consultants are cropping up all over the map, offering this and that program to manage conflict. Among mainline Christian publishers, books on church conflict abound. While speaking at a recent conference for pastors of another denomination, I was introduced to several members of their conflict-resolution team, which they called the SWAT Team. As I reflected on the name, I had an image of a bunch of Christians dressed in black, with bulletproof vests and M-16 rifles, storming into a church to rescue the good and faithful members who were being held hostage by deranged and dysfunctional church deacons.

I don't want to belittle in any way the work of these denominational leaders, consultants, and conflict-resolution teams, because they are called to an important and emotionally dangerous ministry. Too many churches caught in the quicksand of conflict cannot escape, even with the help of these teams. Most conflict has a fairly simple origin. It stems from the failure of church leaders, both pastors and laity, to center their own lives on loving God and to serve as compassionate people who lead with love. By and large, those engaged in conflict are trapped in a cycle of scorn, derision, and denigration of others. I've seen it from the outside in churches where the pastor has contempt for the members and freely calls parishioners who see things differently "troublemakers" and "subversives." Such pastors never take responsibility for the church's failures that are rooted in their inability to treat those around them with compassion. The members begin to hate the pastors, and the pastors hate them back. The pastors regard the members as unlovable, creating a self-fulfilling prophecy in which the members act in unlovable ways.

I've also seen members of a church chew up one pastor after another. Whether the malcontents are "official" leaders serving on a board, or are "backroom" leaders taking potshots from the shadows, they stir up anger and hatred, while chasing away love. I know of one large church that has chewed up pretty much every senior pastor, including its founding pastor, for the past 50 years. I met one of its previous pastors, who has gone on to do dynamic things in a church elsewhere. Reflecting on his ministry with that congregation, he commented, "The best thing I can say about my ministry in that church is that I'm the only pastor in its history who didn't get pushed out the door. I left before they could open the door." When love and compassion are forgotten in a church, it is extremely difficult to recapture.

What is the reason for this loss of love for God and each other? Probably the most common reason is pastoral and lay leaders' self-focused, agenda-driven ministry that emphasizes program over people and numerical growth over spiritual and relational growth. For instance, the pastors may be dynamic preachers and have a charming presence in public, but on a private level they may care little for the struggles of people in daily life. They don't want to deal with the nitty-gritty realities of members' lives. They just want the church members to be present in the pews on Sunday mornings or Saturday nights all for the glory of themselves.

Another reason love is lost in a church is when overcontrolling pastors and leaders care more about maintaining order than about building relationships. They tightly centralize the ministry of the church, so that no one can take initiative or exercise creativity. They maintain control through a violent temper or sharp belittlement that crushes dissent. The members of the church are seen as potential enemies who, if left to their own designs, will sabotage everything.

Other pastors and lay leaders are guilty of emphasizing rightness and righteousness over relationships. They demand theological, doctrinal, and moral perfection from their parishioners, holding themselves up as exemplars. No one measures up to their standards, and through the sheer force of their self-declared holiness, they intimidate everyone in their presence, thus crushing growth, light, and love. Once love and compassion are lost in a church because of selfish, controlling, and self-righteous leadership, SWAT teams have to swarm in. Unfortunately, by then the climate of death and destruction has already set in, and salvation becomes difficult to achieve.

Blessed spiritual leaders acknowledge how important *building a sense of community and communion* in a congregation is by integrating the leaders' *love of God* with a deep *compassion for members*. Community and communion are different. Community is the sense of unity and connection among a church's members as they become friends and companions. Communion is deeper. It is a sense of spiritual union between God and God's children that arises in loving and compassionate churches. It arises as the members begin to love God in a way that allows love to permeate the life of the church. Community and communion grow in churches when the leaders fall in love with God and lead from the power of love. They love God so much that they love the members of the church no matter what. Even when disappointed with members, they respond with a sense of compassion, recognizing how frail and weak we all are. They recognize in members the same kind of sinfulness that afflicts us all. They see in the failures of others the same kinds of failures that are in them, and they are thereby led to love even more deeply—to say with Christ, "Forgive them, Father, for they do not know what they are doing." They also see the members of the church as companions on the road, all stumbling and fumbling together as they all seek God, God's way, and God's love.

A pastor once told me how he became aware of his own failure to love God and others in his church, and how it had inhibited the life of the church. He had been a pastor for 25 years, but it was only in the previous two years that he had really enjoyed his ministry. Before then, he hated it. He spent 23 years trapped in an anxious, defensive, self-protective ministry. Eventually, he sought counseling, because his hatred of his own ministry and the church was beginning to affect his marriage and his soul. After several months, the counselor asked him a pointed question: "How would you describe your ministry?" He thought for a while and responded, "It's like I am the warden of a big prison, and the members are the inmates. I'm responsible for making sure they get let out for exercise and then locked back up so that they can't cause any mischief." As soon as he said this, he was struck with horror. Had God really called him to be a warden?

After a week of reflection he made a choice. He decided to open up the prison doors, release the prisoners, and become one of them. He spent time with them, laughed with them, shared his own pains and troubles. An amazing thing happened. He discovered that he loved them. His ministry changed. His life changed. He began to grow spiritually himself and fall in love with God. He treated those around him with compassion. Slowly his church became a place of community and communion.

As we prepare to move on to the next four progressions of leading a church to blessedness, it is important to stress that the first three are the most vital in becoming a blessed church. When leadership emphasizes these three, real growth occurs. When a foundation is laid, a climate of possibility is created, and a sense of community and communion is instilled, the church becomes healthy. The integration of these three creates conditions that allow a church to become dynamic, creative, grounded, and deep. When problems develop, the solution is to return to an emphasis on laying a foundation of faith and trust, creating a climate of possibility through hope and encouragement, and building a sense of community and communion through love and compassion. We have to return to these three even if doing so means jettisoning plans and programs, as well as our expectations and desires for the church. If these three are lost, everything else will crumble. Once we have established this foundational triad, we can lead our church to blessedness by focusing our attention on the next four progressions, which are instilling a sense of purpose, moving in God's direction, embracing the providence and power of the Holy Spirit, and cultivating grace-filled ministry and mission.

4. Instilling a Sense of Purpose

The reality is that many church pastors and leaders guiding healthy churches are generally unclear about the specifics of their own calling and have little vision for their churches. While the church may be healthy, the lack of vision can inhibit dynamic growth in blessedness. When church leaders lead without having spent time *discerning their own call* nor having developed *a vision for the church,* the church they lead will lack a sense of purpose. The congregation may be a wonderful community of faith, hope, and love, but it probably won't have much more than minimal growth, a basic level of program, and a somewhat anemic approach to outreach. The church may garner a reputation as a social church. Still, given a choice, I would rather be a member of a social church filled with faith, hope, and love than of one of the many mainline churches that don't have even this love.

When a church is filled with a sense of purpose because its leaders integrate a sense of personal calling with a dynamic vision for the church, then almost magical things can take place. The most dynamic churches always have a sense of purpose that motivates and energizes their members, who take this purpose into their own lives. If the purpose is to reach out to those on the margin, these people become more caring to coworkers, family members, and strangers. If the purpose is to help others grow spiritually, the members become growing, if imperfect, beacons of spiritual light in their workplaces, homes, and everywhere else. A sense of purpose can galvanize people so that they discover a greater sense of call in their own lives, even if they can't always articulate what that calling is.

This sense of purpose emerges as leaders spend time prayerfully discerning both their own calling and the church's calling. Each leader becomes more aware that God has created him or her according to a plan, a plan grounded in God's overall plan for the universe, of which serving as a church leader is a part. Gaining a sense of purpose is not the same as articulating the purpose. We can discern a purpose and act on it without being able to explain what it is. Most of us do this much of the time. We act with purpose and intent without ever being clear what that purpose is. We have a marital, relational, budgetary, or business philosophy that guides what we do, although we may not always be able to articulate it to others, but that doesn't stop us from acting with purpose. Likewise in churches, developing a sense of purpose always precedes articulating it. We can act according to a discerned purpose for a long time before ever being able to explain it, and healthy churches often do this. I think that at Calvin Church, only in the past few years have we become more aware of and able to articulate our vision: doing only what God calls us to do and surrendering to God in everything. We did it before we knew it, but we have put it into words more clearly over the past few years. As this sense of purpose has grown, I see it reflected in more and more members as they tell me that they are increasingly seeking God's call and purpose for them in their careers, families, and lives. This sense of purpose is permeating our community.

Basically, we instill a sense of purpose when we lead with purpose. It is important for leaders to connect their own personal call with the vision God has for the church. The more we are willing to do this both as pastors and lay leaders, the more the church will have instilled in its core a sense of purpose that guides everything it does.

5. Moving in God's Direction

True purpose for a church or an individual emerges from deep within us, where God has planted it. It takes time to sprout, root, and grow. If the conditions of our lives aren't right—if we haven't nourished this purpose through prayer, reflection, and response to God—the seed of our potential can lie dormant like seed scattered on hard ground waiting for the spring rains. Even when our potential becomes slowly realized as we follow our purpose, it may take us years to recognize and describe what fruit following our purpose may bear.

For instance, I didn't recognize my own calling to become a pastor for a long time, even though I could sense the call as a young child. Even as a child I felt something deep within that called me to be a pastor, but I only barely recognized it. I could never think of anything I would dislike more than becoming a pastor, and so I never nourished the seed of that call. I first allowed myself to think about it just a bit in 1983. I was going through a bad time. I had recently broken up with my girlfriend. I was working as a counselor with adolescents and children in a psychiatric hospital that had little regard for its workers. The schedule was demanding as I continually followed an evening shift with a morning shift, or an evening shift with a night shift. Moreover, we had a particularly violent group of kids. Some of them threatened me with bodily harm as they stalked the halls hoping to catch me alone. At one point, a riot started during a teenage dance, and I ran around a corner to help, only to be met with a patient's fist in my face.

I became discouraged, despairing in my condition of burnout. I had a teary and woeful conversation with my father at the time, and he told me about a program through which I could earn a master of social work (a counseling degree) and a master of divinity (a ministry degree) at the same time. He prefaced this by saying "Don't laugh at me, but. . . ." My response was to laugh at him and say, "Dad, could you ever imagine me as a pastor?" He said, "Yes, I've always seen you as a pastor." I knew deep down he was right, even though I had walked away from the church nine years before and hadn't been inside any church in almost two years. Sixteen months later, I was attending seminary in this joint program. I had a deep sense that this had been my purpose all along, but it wasn't until after I followed this call that I was able to even begin putting it into words. As I more clearly articulated this calling, this purpose, it began to shape my life.

The same principle holds in the life of a church. All churches have a purpose, a calling. They act on that purpose whether they can articulate it or not, but when it is articulated clearly, continually, and persistently by the leaders of a congregation, it allows the church to *move dynamically in God's direction*. One can see this happening in the most vibrant churches in North America, such as Community Church of Joy in Arizona, Saddleback Community Church in California, and Willow Creek Church in a suburb of Chicago. These are among the most visible examples of churches that act out of an articulated purpose, but many others around the country and world can be found that that are less well known, more traditional, and less program oriented. The churches described above are evangelical churches, but the principle applies equally to moderate and progressive churches as well. The more a church senses and articulates its God-endowed purpose, the more it moves in God's direction— in the direction of blessedness.

What does it take to lead people to move in God's direction? It takes leaders who *ground their lives in prayer* and *articulate clearly and compellingly the vision* they have discerned in prayer for themselves and the congregation. Moving in God's direction is not a one-time act, but an engagement in constant prayer, discerning clarification, and continual communication. Blessed leaders move people in God's direction by communicating God's purpose in the activities of the youth groups, board meetings, committee meetings, newsletter articles, sermons, and one-on-one interactions.

At Calvin Church, moving in God's direction has meant that our lay leaders and I have all been responsible for continually reminding the session, committees, and members to do the best we can to seek God's call in everything we do. I talk about this topic constantly in sermons, not only motivating people to seek God's call, but teaching them how to do so. I also keep this purpose in the forefront through articles in our newsletter. I use these articles to teach, and much of what I write about is teaching people how to discern and respond to God's call in their private lives. Our youth director communicates this word to the youth through Bible studies and programs. We look for opportunities to communicate the church's purpose. The more we are able to communicate our prayerfully discerned purpose, the more it will move people in God's direction throughout the life of the church, whether in our public and communal ministries or in the personal and private ministries of our members as they quietly serve God in their own lives—their own mission fields.

It is amazing to watch a church move in God's direction, because when it does, *stuff just happens!* When a church and its members are led to move in God's direction, the movement creates the conditions for the move into the next progression, where amazing coincidences and providences begin to occur naturally as God's Spirit blows through the ministry, mission, and life of the church.

6. Embracing the Power of the Holy Spirit

The next step in leading a church to blessedness is a counterintuitive one. Most people tend to believe that once a purpose is ascertained and articulated, the next step is to engage in all sorts of frenetic, zealous activity to make this purpose become a reality. That's the way most leadership and development models work, right? According to this view, once we establish a vision and articulate it, we need to go about making the vision a reality as we create programs and activities that incarnate the purpose. From a functional perspective, this approach makes sense. As leaders, we are responsible for making sure the vision, the purpose, is acted upon. The problem is that from a spiritual and trinitarian perspective, launching into frenzied activity cuts out God. Remember that the goal of leading a church to blessedness is to guide it to become the body of Christ that serves God and is open to God's blessings. The goal is not to take what we have discerned from God and then say, "OK, God, you've done a nice job helping us develop this plan. We'll take it from here. You just relax on your throne, and we'll call you when we run into problems." The point of leading a church to blessedness is to put it in a position of opening the whole community to the work of the Holy Spirit.

The next step in leading a church to blessedness is for leaders humbly to guide the members to a greater sense of sacrifice. While their personal spiritual growth has led them to a sense of *humility*, they still lead by *emphasizing selflessness and sacrifice*. The combination leads the church truly to *embrace the providence and power of the Holy Spirit*. Ultimately, blessed leaders want to help the church get to the point at which the Holy Spirit can work in its midst. To do this, blessed leaders lay a foundation of faith and trust that gives the Spirit somewhere to stand. They create a climate of possibility in the church, so that people actually believe the Holy Spirit can affect their congregational life. They build a sense of community and communion that binds people to God and each other. They instill a sense of God's purpose in the life of the church and move the church in God's direction through articulation of the purpose so that God's purpose enters the heart of the community. Now the role of leaders is to do whatever they can to allow the Holy Spirit to "do its thing" in blessing the church. This is the point at which ministry and mission begin to grow dynamically and exponentially.

You can see the effects of embracing the Holy Spirit in churches that emphasize team ministry and the creation of task forces to deal with the works of the church. Instead of creating programs, the leaders encourage members to listen for what God is calling them to do in the church and to create the conditions for these calls to become realities. If someone feels called to organize a group for separated and divorced people, the leaders don't necessarily tell the person to write up a proposal to be submitted to the appropriate committee and then the board. The leaders say, "Go ahead. Do what you are called to do. We will find space, money, and whatever else you need to help you." If someone feels called to start a ministry to the unemployed, the leaders give her permission to go ahead and do it.

There are limits, though, to their permission giving. They must maintain a sense of prayerful wisdom, not just letting anyone do anything. That to which they give permission must maintain fidelity to the church's calling. The idea of this style of permission giving is that the leaders quit acting as a clearinghouse for all ideas and instead become a force that gives people the freedom to do what the Spirit wants. This does not mean that the leaders abdicate responsibility for oversight and accountability. They still monitor these ministries but step in only when problems surface. Otherwise, they give guidance and direction when needed, support and encouragement on occasion, and prayers of blessing always. Eventually the whole church community forms an encouraging culture, which allows ministry to grow naturally at its own pace.

The whole point of this kind of leadership is to seek the winds of the Holy Spirit and to hoist the church's sails up to catch them. When leaders are too proud and controlling to put up sails, the church stagnates. When leaders become sensitive to the blowing of these winds in the church's ministry, they learn to get the right sails in the right places, so that the ship of Christ can flow easily and effortlessly across the seas. They don't have to paddle or row as often. The wind provides a natural energy that allows ministry to become more of a breeze. All that is required of the leaders is to move the rudders at times to make sure that the ship is sailing in God's direction.

When leaders embrace the providence and power of the Holy Spirit, wonderful things happen. I'm not saying that the power of the Holy Spirit will cause a 200-member church suddenly to become a 1,000-member church. Such a thing has happened, but that phenomenon is the exception, not the rule—an exception far too often glamorized in books and magazine articles, and one that becomes the standard for success. Church growth is not the only measure of the Spirit's power working among us. More often the Spirit works in other ways by causing wonderful coincidences, or better yet, "providences" to occur. Adrian van Kaam once said to me, "There are no coincidences, only providences." This statement captures what happens when we embrace the power of the Holy Spirit. We find that all sorts of providential coincidences occur in the church.

When we open our churches to the power of the Holy Spirit, providences happen constantly. I've learned to rely on them. For example, when we needed someone to develop a Web site, suddenly a new member told us that she wasn't working for the first time in 20 years and would love to develop a Web site. When we needed more room to expand our church program, suddenly a house next door to the church became available, and because we were already involved in a capital campaign, we were able to buy it without going into debt. When we needed to hire an extra staff member to help with pastoral care, but didn't have the necessary funds, a visitor who had no idea of our plans made a substantial donation to be used at our discretion. The donation was large enough to cover most of the associate pastor's salary for a year. Many people have told me over the years of occasions when they came to worship struggling with a crushing problem, and providentially found the exact answer they were looking for in the sermon. Some have said that it was almost as if I or another preacher were in their head. In a sense we were, because we were listening to God as we prepared the sermon, and God was in the worshiper's head. These are the kinds of things that happen in a church where the providence and power of the Holy Spirit are supported and welcomed.

What happens is what I would call *natural ministry.* The church, which is an organism and a body, grows naturally. Like a plant that has been nourished, watered, and cultivated under the sun, the church flourishes in the way it was intended to. Sometimes this flourishing results in the development of a large church. For many other churches it means staying relatively small and dynamic, with the focus on growing in the ways that the Spirit leads it. If that means growth in numbers, fine. If that means growth in mission, fine. If that means growth in care, fine.

However the church is called to grow becomes the focus, and the ministry of the church becomes natural, easy, and fun.

7. Cultivating Grace-Filled Ministry and Mission

The final progression in leading a church to blessedness is for leaders to integrate their *personal sense of servanthood* with an *emphasis on outreach*. This integration leads to *the cultivation of grace-filled ministry and mission*. I wish I could say that Calvin Presbyterian Church is this beacon of ministry and mission, but in truth we are only beginning slowly to enter this phase, and in fact we may be many years away from truly reaching our potential in this area. Perhaps the slow pace has to do with my own limitations as a leader, or with the fact that the fruit we are to bear is only now beginning to bud. Whatever the reason, I think we are moving in the right direction. Even more powerfully, I can see this kind of grace-filled ministry and mission growing in many other churches—some well known, some not.

The churches that offer grace-filled ministry are the ones that excel at ministry and mission to the divorced, singles, the mentally ill, the illiterate, the poor, the hungry, the homeless, the disabled, and especially the spiritually hungry. They are churches that cultivate and bear fruit of the Spirit. I don't want to give the impression that such churches are able to address every need. It is rare to find churches that address every hardship that confronts them. What grace-filled churches do is to create unique ministry and mission responses that connect the community's need and the church's calling. For instance, it would not make sense for our church to build a homeless shelter, because we are not in an area with a large number of homeless people. Often our role is to give support to the homeless who pass through town. It does make sense for a church in an urban area to build or to support a homeless shelter. Grace-filled churches nurture mission and ministry that matches their calling and the community's need, and when they do, their ministry and mission is filled with God's grace and blessings.

Cultivating grace-filled ministry and mission is the most natural of all phases of becoming a blessed church, for this is a cultivation of God's seed planted in the soil of faith, hope, and love. When a church enters this period of cultivation, ministry just flows. The church grows in God's direction and bears God's fruit in ways that are truly God filled. The church is grounded fully in God's purpose, alive to God's presence, and both open to and manifesting God's power. Wonderful things happen.

Final Strategies

In closing I offer some final thoughts and comments that will help you as you devise strategies to lead a church to blessedness. Above all, let me stress that while I have just presented seven progressions to leading a church to blessedness, don't assume that they are strictly sequential and that you must complete one to move on to the next. They all grow together. The point of this model is to show how the progressions can build on each other. When you work on laying a foundation, you still need to emphasize ministry and mission. In many ways these progressions are cyclical. In other words, as we move through each progression, the movement naturally leads us to reemphasize the previous progressions. The church that cultivates grace-filled ministry and mission ends up returning to the other progressions to strengthen this most recent progression These progressions are also integrative. As you work on one, you work on the others; and as you accomplish one, you accomplish the others.

It is important to understand that if your church is struggling, this model can be used to help you discern what to do. My belief is that any time a church struggles, and especially when conflicts begin to develop, it is important to return to an emphasis on the first three phases, and especially the first by working on the foundation. Conflict is often rooted in a lack of trust and faith, pessimism and cynicism, and lack of love and compassion. So it makes sense to work on rebuilding these.

Next, it is important for blessed leaders always to lead with patience. Most mistakes leaders make result from their haste to get where God is leading. Take a lesson from Scripture, and especially the exodus of the Israelites from Egypt to the Promised Land. They were in a hurry, but they weren't ready. God put them on a 40-year program of preparation. You cannot lead a church directly from foundation to grace-filled ministry and mission. It takes time—God's time. So be patient and let God dictate the pace. If, as a leader, you find yourself becoming impatient with your church, go off and spend some time in prayer. Go on a retreat, because your ministry is becoming too much your own, not God's. The point is to serve God at God's pace, to let the church grow at its own pace. This is especially crucial if the church is coming out of a period of dysfunction.

Remember that the transformation of a church is rooted more in spiritual dispositions than in leadership qualities. Whenever you are in doubt or struggle, go back and work on your relationship with God. That is the key. Then you can work on your leadership.

Implicit in the idea of always rooting transformation of the church in our own relationship with God is the recognition that spiritual leadership always emerges from the spiritual. God is the one who leads us to become leaders. All the seminars on leadership cannot help us become spiritual leaders without the leadership of the Spirit in our lives. God transforms us so that we can become leaders of transformation in our churches. Ultimately, true blessedness arises out of our personal surrender to God as leaders. Whenever there is a problem in the church, begin by asking whether you need to change. Surrender to God and let God be in charge. A wise man once said to me, "God never sets you up to fail." I have always taken this declaration to heart, and I've never been disappointed. When we surrender our lives to God in faith, we can discover God responding to us by blessing us in so many ways.

Reflection Questions

1. To what extent do you sense that your church's leaders have laid a foundation? Created a climate of possibility? Built a sense of community and communion? Instilled a sense of purpose? Moved people in God's direction? Facilitated the providence and power of the Holy Spirit? Cultivated a grace-filled ministry and mission?
2. What concrete things can your leaders do to lay a foundation of faith and trust? Create a climate of possibility? Build a sense of community and communion? Instill a sense of purpose? Move people in God's direction? Facilitate the providence and power of the Holy Spirit? Cultivate grace-filled ministry and mission?

Appendices

Appendix A

Assessing the Church's Spiritual Openness

Suggested Use
1. Invite the leaders of the church to take this assessment home with them and to spend time prayerfully reflecting on the questions and answering them on a separate sheet of paper.
2. Gather the leaders together on a Saturday morning or weekday evening to discuss what they have discerned individually in prayer. You are encouraged to add a short time of worship and/or a short Bible study based on Proverbs 3:5-6 (focusing on what that passage is saying about what the emphasis of leadership in the church should be).
   - Form discussion triads and set appropriate time for leaders to discuss their answers honestly and humbly. Invite them to formulate new answers to the same questions on a separate sheet of paper.
   - Gather the triads together and set an appropriate time for a large-group discussion of their discernings. Have each group present its assessment of the church.
   - Invite the whole group to answer the questions again together, and to craft an overall assessment of the state of the church.
3. Follow up with another Saturday session to discuss concrete ways to increase prayerfulness, discernment, spiritual vibrancy in the church, and faith.

Discussion Questions

Prayerfulness
   - To what extent are people in the church comfortable with prayer? Do they generally make public and private prayer a priority in their lives?

- How comfortable are the lay leaders with prayer, especially in making prayer a priority in their lives during times of confusion and crisis?
- How comfortable is the pastor with prayer, especially in making prayer a priority in her or his ministry?

Discernment
- To what extent do members seem to give priority to seeking God's guidance through prayer and Scripture?
- To what extent do the leaders, pastoral and lay, give priority to seeking God's guidance through prayer and Scripture in their lives and ministries?
- To what extent do the leaders of the church board and committees encourage the board and committees to spend time in prayer seeking what God wants, instead of simply going with majority rule?

Faith
- To what extent would you say that the members of your church have a strong faith in that they are willing to trust God in all situations and circumstances, especially in times of crisis and turmoil?
- To what extent would you say that the leaders of the church act in faith during times of crisis and trouble, and to what extent do they trust mainly in their own powers and abilities?

Spiritual Vibrancy and Integration
- To what extent would you say that your church seems spiritually vibrant?
- To what extent do you believe people sense God's purpose, presence, and power working in their lives?
- How strong is the spiritual dimension in the church; that is, to what extent do spiritual concerns lie at the center of all decisions and determinations of the church and the leadership?

Appendix B

Session Agenda

Calvin Presbyterian Church
Zelienople, Pennsylvania
Session Agenda for February 17, 2004

Gather in God's Name

Lighting of the Candle and Time of Centering

Prayer of Blessing

> Holy God, bless us this evening so that in everything we do we will be
> doing your will. Help us to put aside our pride and ego that tells us to
> seek what we want, so that we can be filled with your Spirit that seeks
> only what you want. Hear us in silence as we center ourselves in you
> and ask you to guide us this evening . . .

Gathering Chant

Prayer of Praise

> Eternal God—Father, Son, and Holy Spirit:
> You have called us to be spiritual leaders of your body, this church
> Help us to surrender our hearts and minds to you;
> To humbly seek your voice;
> To boldly do your will;
> To compassionately share your love;
> To faithfully be your servants;
> And to reverently lead your people.
> Bless all that we do,
> So that we can do what you bless.
> In Christ's name we pray. Amen.

Time of Sharing

Time of Prayer

Concerns, Receptions, and Approvals

- Clerk Concerns
- Committee Concerns
- Staff and Pastoral Concerns
- Votes of reception and approval:
  - That session approve minutes from the regular January session meeting.
  - That session receive the Financial Report for January 2004.
  - That session approve the baptism of [name].
  - That the following Special Mission Project funds be approved:
    - That $100 be donated to a Dollar Bank trust fund for a person who has RSDS.

Prayerful Consideration of Session Matters

Long Range P C:	no recommendation
Phase II Committee:	no recommendation
Building and Property:	• *That renovations of the upstairs bathroom and the sacristy be funded by the memorial fund.*
Worship and Arts:	no recommendation
Personnel and Finance:	• *To approve salary increase for the church secretary to $12,000 from $10,806*
	• *For Calvin Church to support [name] as she enters the candidacy phase of her preparation for ministry.*
Youth Formation:	no recommendation
Spiritual Nurture:	no recommendation
Mission:	no recommendation
Nominations:	no recommendation
Clerk and Staff:	no recommendation
Other actions	• *That the session observe a Lenten meeting fast during the month of March.*

A Time of Prayer
- Prayers for the church, members, session, and personal concerns
- The Lord's Prayer

Doxology

Blessing and Benediction

Next Session Meeting:
  • Regular session meeting, April 20 at 7:30 p.m.

Appendix C

Discerning God's Purpose for the Church

The following is a guide to be used by the church board and invited members to discern and articulate what God's purpose and overall calling are for the church. The meeting should be held on a day when there is ample time to discern and discuss. It can also be split up and be held over several days in a row, or on specific days over the course of several weeks. Things to consider in preparing for the meeting:

- Invite members of the governing board to be a part of the discernment process
- Invite from outside the church board only those who seem to be respected leaders *and* who have a sense of spiritual maturity
- Let this process be fluid, allowing for as much time to be spent as needed—some groups are quicker, others may be slower

Meeting Agenda

1. Begin with a time of worship and prayer.

2. Invite the members into a time of Bible study focusing on discerning God's call. Suggested passages are provided below. Depending on the size of the group, three smaller groups can be created, each to discuss a different passage. The group(s) should be asked to discuss what the passage says about the nature of God's call and our discerning God's call as individuals and a church.

   - 1 Kings 16:1-13
   - Proverbs 3:5-6
   - Ephesians 4:1-16

3. In a large group, have members share what they have heard in their small-group discussions. Specifically, have them address the following questions:

  - What do these passages say about God's call to us and how we hear it?
  - What guidance do they give us as we seek God's calling here in our church?

4. *Small-Group discernment*

  - Divide the group into smaller groups.
  - Give each group several newsprint sheets, large enough to draw a large picture on, along with colored markers.
  - Give the following directions: You are responsible for building this church. Each church must have a foundation upon which it is built, as well as pillars that support the ministry of the church. Basing your discussion and final drawing on the earlier Scripture passages we discussed, discussions we have had so far, and what you know of the ministry of this church, draw two elements for this church:
    - A foundation that articulates what you sense is God's foundational call and purpose;
    - The pillars, which are anchored in this foundational purpose and that support the ministry of the church.

5. *Large-Group Discussion*. Have the participants gather in a large group. Invite each group to present its drawing, presenting what its members sensed the foundational purpose of the church is, along with the pillars that support the ministry grounded in this purpose.

6. *Integration of Discernments*. Engage all participants in a process of integrating the various drawings into a single cohesive drawing. This may mean jettisoning some aspects while rearticulating and emphasizing others. New insights may also lead to articulating a clearer foundation and pillars.

7. *Formation of a purpose statement*. Form a short, one-sentence statement that captures the essence of the one drawing created by the large group.

8. *Refining of the purpose statement.* After closing the session with prayer and worship, give the members several weeks to sit with the formulated statement, and invite them back in a few weeks to a month to reflect on the statement and refine it if necessary.

Appendix D

Discerning Direction for a Particular Issue

The following is a simple guide to discerning God's voice when seeking God's call in a particular situation. It is most valuable when a church board or committee is stuck on an issue.

1. Identify the issue to be discussed.

2. Offer a Bible study and a time of prayerful reflection as preparation for discussion:

   • Choose a Bible passage or a passage from a book or article that pertains to the issue being discussed.
   • Have the members identify specific aspects of the Scripture that seem to speak to the issue.

3. Spend a short time in prayer seeking God's guidance.

4. Have a time for open discussion and clarification.

5. Before voting on an issue, take time for centering prayer.

   • Invite participants to spend time in quiet prayer, specifically asking then to put aside their egos to gain a sense of what God wants.

6. Re-engage in brief discussion, asking people to share what they sense God may want.

7. Vote on the issue. Have the presiding officer call for the vote using these words: "All who sense this may be God's will, say aye. All

who don't, say no." These words invite members to seek God's will rather than their own.

8. Afterward, if the members have not come to a sense of agreement over what God is calling them to do, and they remain divided, invite them to lay aside the vote willingly and to postpone the matter. The point of this action is to emphasize seeking unity (a willingness to act as one body, even if not all have sensed the same directives from God), even if unanimity is not possible. A lack of unanimity suggests that various members may have sensed conflicting guidance from God. Postponing for prayer allows more time to be devoted to discernment. When members are willing to lay aside a decision to better seek God's will, they create an environment for discernment.

9. When necessary, because a matter has been postponed for prayer, return the following month and prayerfully revisit the issue. If unanimity is not possible, then the board should seek to go forward in unity—meaning that all members, even dissenting members, prayerfully agree that it is God's will that the board move forward together despite disagreements.

Note: This process does not have to become lengthy. For instance, if the division is not great, the Bible study may be unnecessary, and the group can move directly to the short prayer. If the process gets bogged down, then postpone the decision and take time for prayer. On occasion the leadership board must move forward even though it is divided. Moving forward in disunity should be done only when absolutely critical—a rare occurrence.

Appendix E

A Prayerful Process for Discerning Committee Budgets

The following is a guide for committees to use in seeking God's will as they prepare their budget for the coming year. A copy of this guide can be handed out to all committee members.

1. Begin by opening the meeting with a short time of prayer, asking God to guide you during your meeting.

2. Read Proverbs 3:5-6.

    > Trust in the Lord with all your heart, and do not rely on your own insight.
    > In all your ways acknowledge him, and he will make straight your paths.

3. Take 15 minutes to discuss the passage and how it relates to the committee's ministry and budgeting for the church.

    - What does this passage say about what our goal should be as a committee?
    - What does this passage say about what our goal should be as a church?
    - What should our focus be as we determine our budget for the coming year?

4. Spend a short time in prayer, asking members to center their hearts in God so that they can hear God. Then gather suggestions from the members about what God may be calling your committee to do for the coming year. Don't worry about the cost yet.

5. Ask people to take a minute in silent prayer to put aside their egos and what they want, so that they can ask in prayer what God wants for this committee.

6. Have the members discuss the committee priorities they sense God wants for the coming year. Remember that God speaks through hearts, and it is impossible to know with certainty what God wants. The focus is seeking to do God's will, not necessarily doing it with perfection. Try to avoid setting priorities based on beliefs that:

   - We *should* do this because it is what we've been doing.
   - We *should* do this because it would be good to do it.
   - We *should* do this because we haven't done it before.
   - We *should* do this because we said in years past that we would.

   The focus should be solely on what we sense God is calling us to do in the coming year.

7. After setting the priorities you sense God wants, spend time determining what it may cost to accomplish these priorities.

8. Set a committee budget to be shared at an all-committee budgeting meeting. Invite all your committee members to attend that meeting.

Appendix F

All-Committee Budgeting Process

Invite all members of the church board and committees to this meeting. This meeting serves to guide the board and those involved in setting the budget as to what God is calling the church to do. The results should not be binding but should be taken seriously as God's will. As the finance committee and board consider setting the budget for the coming year, they should do so prayerfully, basing their action on the results of this meeting. Hand this sheet out to all present.

Opening Hymn

"Be Thou My Vision"

Prayer

Holy and gracious God, help us to come before you with humble minds and hearts that are ready to listen for your voice and do what you will. Let this be a time of discerning your will so that our leadership and church may be filled with your blessings. Through Jesus Christ our Lord. *Amen.*

Scripture and Short Discussion

Proverbs 3:5-6:

Trust in the Lord with all your heart, and do not rely on your own insight.
In all your ways acknowledge him, and he will make straight your paths.

1. What does this passage say about what our goal should be as leaders of this church?
2. What does this passage say about where our focus should be as we discuss the budget for the coming year?

Centering Prayer

- Ask the members to spend a minute in silence, centering their hearts in God's will.

Presentation of Committee Budget Requests:

- One at a time, a representative of each committee presents that committee's budget request, explaining the discerned reason for each request.
- After the presentation, offer a time for questions and discussion.
- Afterward, ask someone to offer prayer for each committee.
- During this process, if discussion becomes divisive, stop and ask the group to spend time in prayer, seeking God's unity.

Centering Prayer

General Discussion

Engage members in a general discussion about overall budget priorities. Remind the members that during this discussion, their focus should be on what God is calling them to do for the *whole* church, and not just for their committee. Guide members to set priorities for the whole church budget by asking them to reflect on the overall budget, and then sum up what general budget priorities God has revealed through the budgeting process.

Closing Hymn

"Breathe on Me, Breath of God"

Appendix G

Guiding Members to Give

The following is a step-by-step yearly stewardship program guide for finance committees and pastors that encourages members to root their giving in prayerful discernment.

1. *Stewardship Sermons.* Encourage pastors and finance committee to talk about prayerful stewardship throughout the year. Instead of speaking of giving only during the yearly stewardship drive, pastors and other preachers should sprinkle into their sermons throughout the year short discussions and stories on the importance of giving. Then people hear an ongoing, cumulative message of the importance of giving and its connection to spiritual maturity.

2. *Scheduling a Stewardship Campaign.* Time the stewardship program so that it begins after the committee and all-committee budgeting processes have concluded, allowing the finance committee to summarize and communicate to the congregation the prayerful processes they have engaged in, along with the priorities that have been discerned by the committees and church board.

3. *Conducting the Stewardship Campaign.* Allow four weeks for the campaign.

   - *Week 1.* Send a stewardship letter along with a one- to two-page "stewardship campaign circular." The circular describes changes or additions to the budget in the coming year.

     a. The letter should discuss how important member giving is to God's work in the church. It should also invite people to spend time in prayer, seeking what God is calling them to

give, while offering them specific Scripture passages to reflect on. (See appendix H, "First Sample Stewardship Letter.")

   b. The Sample Campaign Circular should explain the discernment process the committees and board have engaged in, and
tell the congregation what changes they prayerfully sensed
God is calling them to make in the budget for the coming
year. (See appendix H, "Sample Stewardship Campaign Circular.") It should also encourage them to read the Scripture
passages cited in the first stewardship letter, as well as encouraging them to begin the process of seeking God's will,
especially suggesting that they give only what God is calling
them to give, even if that means giving less.

- *Week 2.* Offer a brief time in worship and include a sentence in
the bulletin to remind people that the church is in the midst of
the stewardship campaign, inviting them to use the resources that
have been sent to them to ask prayerfully what God is calling
them to give in the upcoming year.

- *Week 3.* Send another stewardship letter with a pledge card en-
closed. This letter should again summarize what was said in the
first letter and document, and then offer members a process on
the back of the letter for praying about what they are called to
give. (See appendix H, "Second Sample Stewardship Letter.")

- *Week 4.* Have the members bring their filled-out pledge cards to
worship and dedicate the pledges during worship.

After this process, the finance committee and church board should match
member giving with the discerned priorities, and once again engage in
a discernment process, asking what budget God wants them to set.

Appendix H

Sample Stewardship Materials

First Sample Stewardship Letter

October 3, 2003

Dear Calvin Church Members:

We know that you appreciate what a special place Calvin Church is. It is a church of care and compassion for so many, as a well as a place where people from the very young to the very old truly experience God in their lives. Your support and involvement in the church is a big part of the whole ministry of Calvin Church. You don't even realize the impact you make through your support of the ministry of Calvin Church.

A large part of that support is your financial giving to the church. Through your financial support you share in the whole ministry of Calvin Church. For instance, you help teach close to 80 children each Sunday morning. You help lead the youth groups for more than 50 teens each week. You help visit people in hospitals, at home, in prisons, and much more. You offer counseling to many who seek guidance from the pastors. You support through our mission work people in the area who are hungry, struggling financially, and facing all sorts of difficulties. You offer worship and music each Sunday, giving spiritual inspiration and guidance to approximately 260 people. What you give to the church does much to make God's love and presence real to so many people—many whom you may never meet.

To prepare a budget for 2004, the committees and session of the church have spent time in prayer asking what God wants us to do in 2004. This is a huge theme in Calvin Church, seeking God's will rather than our own. We are enclosing a description of what we sense we are called to do in 2004, as well as a guide to prayerfully discerning what you are called to give. We ask that you read the description, and afterward spend time in prayer over the next few weeks asking what God is calling you to give to support God's work in Calvin Church and beyond. To help you, we offer these Scripture passages for you to read as you reflect:

- Matthew 6:19-21
- 2 Corinthians 9:6-15

In a few weeks, you will receive a pledge card asking for your commitment. We hope that both now and then you will prayerfully consider how God is calling you to support the ministry and mission of Calvin Presbyterian Church.

Yours in Christ's Ministry,
The Personnel and Finance Committee
Calvin Presbyterian Church

Sample Stewardship Campaign Circular

> Each of you must give as you have made up your mind, not reluc-
> tantly or under compulsion, for God loves a cheerful giver. And God
> is able to provide you with every blessing in abundance, so that by
> always having enough of everything, you may share abundantly in
> every good work.
>
> > 2 Corinthians 9:7-8

What is Calvin Presbyterian Church's greatest strength? Its members?
Its programs? Its music or mission? Actually, Calvin Church's greatest
strength is you and your faith. Because of the faith of the people of this
church, we are able to do wonderful things for many people.

At the foundation of all we do is prayer. In everything we do we try
to listen for God's voice so that we can do God's will. God is deeply
present in everything we are doing. And that focus is due to the fact that
over the years we have prayerfully placed one question at the center of
our ministry and mission: "God, what are you calling us to do?" Much
of what we have accomplished over the years has been the result of
asking that question, and then acting in faith on what we have heard.

The committees and session of the church have earnestly and prayerfully asked what God is calling us to do in 2004. Each committee, and
then the session, has spent time in prayer seeking God's guidance. Here
are some of the things we have sensed that God is calling us to do in the
coming year:

Parish Associate for Pastoral Care
Last year we invited the Rev. Dr. Stephen Polley to join our staff as a
parish associate for pastoral care. Dr. Polley has brought wonderful things
to this church over the past year, not the least of which is his love for
people. Each week Dr. Polley visits people who are homebound, lonely,
or struggling with some sort of difficulty. He visits visitors and those
interested in Calvin Church. He also visits those who are doing well,
but just may need a shot of faith and love in their lives. With his work at
Calvin Church, he has also allowed Dr. Standish to focus on some of the
more serious problems that face some of the members of Calvin Church,
such as those struggling with difficult issues of divorce, addiction, legal
problems, and other personal and spiritual issues. It has also allowed
him to focus his attention on the growing program needs of the church.
This work is important since the church has doubled in size over eight

years and increased even more in the number of people seeking the care of the church.

We were able to hire Dr. Polley in 2003 in part because of a generous gift of $6,000 given by several long-time visitors to Calvin Church. This year we hope to fully fund Dr. Polley's position. Through your giving, you become a part of the pastoral ministry in this church.

Mission

One of the things that Calvin Presbyterian Church has valued over the years is mission. We have made it a priority to increase our mission giving each year as a proportion of our budget. In other words, even though we have continually increased our budget each year, we have also increased the proportion devoted to mission. Six years ago, 17 percent of our budget was devoted to mission. For the past two years it has been approximately 20 percent. This year we have sensed that God is calling us once again to keep the same level of support. The mission that goes on in this church often flies below the radar screen of most people, but through it we help so many. You are a crucial part of this help when you give.

Ministry

As the church continues to grow, we discover more ways that God is calling us to reach out to members and others through our various ministries. Here are some of the ways we sense God calling us to expand our ministry in 2004.

1. *Staff.* The staff of Calvin Church is among the most talented and accomplished you will find in any church. Staff members bring a high level of commitment and ability to everything they do. Recognizing the importance of the staff, we have had a policy of offering a 3 percent cost-of-living adjustment each year. Last year was the first in many years that we did not because of concerns over whether we could afford this increase. This coming year we are proposing a 6 percent increase, which would offer a 3 percent increase for this year and make up for the lack of a 3 percent increase last year. Through your support, you enable our church staff members to continue their dedicated and important work.

2. *Youth Program.* Our youth program continues to grow, and as it does we increasingly recognize that we are not only nurturing young Christians, but also future leaders. We have decided to hire two col-

lege-age interns each year to help us with our program and to form them in their future work with youth. Your support not only reaches out to the youth, but supports future youth work though our training of youth leaders.

3. *Adult Education.* We are committed to strengthening our Wednesday classes by bringing in more outside speakers. We also are hoping to offer more one-day retreats to help you grow in your faith.

4. *Building and Grounds.* The projects we are hoping to accomplish for 2004 include repaving the parking lot, expanding our parking into the new property we bought at 110 Division Street, and renovating our sacristy to create more room for our worship needs.

You

All of these efforts are not just what the leadership of the church is hoping to do. These efforts are what we feel called to do, and they are a part of how you make a difference in the world. By supporting the ministry of Calvin Church with your financial commitment for 2004, you make so much possible. As you consider your financial support of Calvin Church for 2004, we ask you to:

- Read Matthew 6:19-21 and 2 Corinthians 9:6-15.
- Reflect on what the passage is saying to you about giving, and what importance God places on our giving.
- Spend time in prayer asking what God is calling you to give for 2004. If you sense God calling you to give more, please increase your pledge. If you sense God calling you to give the same, please do so. If you sense God calling you to give less, please give less.
- The important thing is for you to join us in seeking God's voice and doing God's will.

Second Sample Stewardship Letter

October 20, 2003

Dear Calvin Church Members:

A few weeks ago we sent you a letter and a flyer talking about the Calvin Presbyterian Church 2004 Stewardship Campaign. In the flyer we told you how the church session and its committees had spent time in prayer seeking what God was calling us to do in 2004. We also told you how we are setting our budget for 2004 in response to this prayerful seeking.

Among what we feel called to do in 2004, in addition to the important ministries we already are doing, is hiring interns to help run our youth program and to be trained for their own future youth ministries; assuming full financial responsibility for Dr. Polley's position; adjusting the salaries of staff members to reflect what they give to us; and pursuing various mission and building projects, including hiring new, part-time custodians. These are significant additions to our budget. In all, we estimate that these will require an increase in the budget of about $30,000, an increase of 10 percent.

We do not embark on these projects lightly, but do so in response to the growth of Calvin Presbyterian Church, and the needs and demands that come with a growing church. Did you know that since January 2001 we have grown from 299 to 385 members? Our worship attendance has grown as much, from an average of 200 to 250 every Sunday. These figures represent tremendous growth, and while growth is a blessing, it also puts strains on the workings of the church. By embarking on these projects and ministries for 2004, we hope to ensure Calvin Church's health and spiritual growth for years to come.

You are such a blessing to Calvin Presbyterian Church. Now we are asking you to join us in prayerfully seeking and doing God's will. We ask you to spend time in prayer asking what God is calling you to give for 2004. If you sense God calling you to increase your pledge, please do so. If you sense God calling you to give the same, we hope you will do so. And if you sense God calling you to give less, we hope you will do so. The key is that you seek what God wants from you and for the church.

To help you seek God's will, we have placed a guide to prayerful listening on the back of this letter. We have also included a pledge card for you to use. We ask you to take the next two weeks to ask in prayer about what God is calling you to give, and then to bring the card with you on Sunday, November 2, to either worship service. That Sunday is Commitment Sunday, and we will be accepting your commitment then. Thank you for your prayers and support.

> In Christ,
> The Personnel and Finance Committee
> Calvin Presbyterian Church

A Guide to Prayerfully Seeking God's Will

The following will help you as you seek what God is calling you to give to Calvin Presbyterian Church in 2004:

1. Take time with your spouse or alone in prayer. Find a quiet place away from distractions. In your time alone, use a Bible and any kind of financial information that might be helpful.

2. Take time in silent prayer to ask God to guide you in your giving.

3. Read the following Scripture passages. After reading each, try to listen to what God is saying to you about giving.

   - Matthew 6:19-21
   - 2 Corinthians 9:6-15

4. Don't make any decisions at this time, but instead ask God to guide you over the next few days on what you should give.

5. Continue to return to God in prayer to ask what you should give. God will speak to you in some way. When you sense an answer, fill in your pledge card and offer it to God on Sunday, November 2.

Appendix I

A Guide to Healing Prayer

There is healing power available from God, if you are willing to believe and trust. Jesus came not only to preach and teach, but also to heal. Almost one-fifth of the stories in the Gospels are about Jesus healing all kinds of illness: physical, mental, and spiritual. After Jesus died, the apostles continued the ministry of healing, as did their followers. Belief in healing has always been at the core of Christianity, whether all churches have practiced it or not.

How can you receive God's healing? It begins with *faith* and *surrender*. Recognize your doubts and put them aside so you can open yourself to God's healing power. If you have difficulty doing this, tell God that you have trouble giving up your doubts. Ask God to have faith for you. Healing also includes surrender—giving God everything, including the power to choose what kind of healing to give you. To truly let God heal you, you must let God decide what kind of healing is best, even if it is different from what you want. God is not a genie who obeys our commands. God is the loving healer who will do what's best for us. Trust in that.

God wants to heal you, but not necessarily according to the plan you may have for your own healing. Most of us want to be healed on the outside. We want to be healed of physical or mental disease, but God is interested most in healing from the inside out—from the soul outward. The more open you are to God, the more God can heal you spiritually and then let that spiritual healing turn into mental and physical healing.

The most important things are to try your best to trust in God to heal you, and to trust that God is healing you, even if you can't feel anything happening. Like seeds planted in the soil, growth cannot always be seen until it sprouts. You need to be patient and let God work. Healing, like anything lasting, takes time to grow.

The following, then, are suggestions to you as you begin healing prayer for yourself or someone else:

1. *Lay aside your doubts, worries, and cares.* Psalm 46:10 says, "Be still, and know that I am God." As you begin your prayer, be as still and calm as possible. If you can't let go of your concerns, don't worry. God will accept you as you are. Just trust that God will act.

2. *Open yourself to Christ.* Just as we need to plug a lamp into an electrical outlet to receive light, we need to plug into God to receive healing power. Try taking a minute to silently recite to yourself, "Bless the Lord, O my soul." When you feel more open to Christ, ask him to enter you and grow within you.

3. *Pray.* Pray for your healing. Be specific. Imagine what you want Christ to do and ask for it. Ask with confidence. A suggested prayer: "Lord, I know that it is your will for me to be whole and holy. Let your power enter me and heal me. Heal me by . . . [name your specific request]. Thank you for healing me."

4. *Trust and believe that God's power is entering into you.* When the Holy Spirit works, we usually *don't* see, sense, or feel it. Sometimes healing is immediate. More often it is slow and gradual. This is especially true of pervasive physical diseases like cancer or degenerative diseases and mental illness. Don't spend time analyzing whether you are being healed or not. Just trust and believe.

5. *Thank God for healing you.* When we thank God, we are appreciating God, and the more we appreciate God, the more we allow God into our lives. After you've prayed for healing, thank God for being with you.

6. *Set up a prayer discipline.* Too often people pray once, and when nothing happens, quit praying. God wants us not only to pray, but to pray constantly. It is through our constant prayer that God increases in our lives. Make regular times for healing prayer. Do it two or three times a day. Keep it down-to-earth and direct. The best prayers are simple: "God, I know you love me and are with me. You know my struggles and pain. In the power of Christ, fill me with your spirit and heal me."

As you begin to pray for healing, try this simple prayer:

God, I give you my life to do with as you will. I know that you can heal me, yet my faith is weak. Give me the faith to trust in you. Let your healing Spirit enter me and heal me by *[name your specific need]*. I thank you, God, for you presence. Let your grace shine in me and through me.

Follow the Guidance of Scripture

One of the best ways to increase the Spirit's power in your life is to follow the guidance of 1 Thessalonians 5:16-18: "Rejoice always, pray without ceasing, give thanks in all circumstances; for this is the will of God in Christ Jesus for you." Rejoicing, praying without ceasing, and giving thanks increases the Spirit's power in your life by opening your mind, heart, and soul to the Holy Spirit's healing power. It creates the confidence we have in God's willingness and power to heal us.

- *Rejoice always*. It is easy to slip into a dark, pessimistic, doubting, and cynical spirit. This is especially true when one is suffering from the depression that so often afflicts us because of either physical or mental illness. Look around and appreciate God's presence. You might notice the love of family, the movements of nature, or anything else that reveals Christ's work in the world. Try to find ways to rejoice, even if is difficult and you see no joy in life. Rejoicing increases God's presence.
- *Pray without ceasing*. Turn your life into prayer. You don't have to pray in a formal way. Talk to God all throughout the day. Give Christ your burdens. Let the Holy Spirit be a constant companion by constantly speaking and listening to God throughout your day.
- *Give thanks in all circumstances*. The more we thank God, even when we don't sense God's presence, the more we create openings for the Holy Spirit to enter our lives. Think about this. Have you noticed that when you are thankful, others tend to be giving and caring toward you? And the opposite is true: the more ungrateful and grudging we are in life, the less positively people respond. Our attitude can either open or close us to others, and it can open or close us to God. Look for reasons to thank God.

Appendix J

Nominating Committee Members

Guidelines

As a member of the nominating committee, you are serving this church in an important ministry. Through your work, you are having a direct impact on the future of the church by nominating future church leaders who will guide our future direction. How you make your decisions will determine the extent to which this church becomes a place that listens to and serves Christ. For that reason, it is important to keep several principles in mind as you go about the process of choosing nominees.

1. *Remember that you are Christ's eyes, hands, and voice.* God is working through you to call new leaders to the ministry of this church. So, as a way of being God's eyes, hands, and voice, you are being asked to:
   - Seek God's will in prayer, asking God the question, "God, who are you calling to be a leader of this church?" Take this process seriously, because it is the foundation of everything you do.
   - Prayerfully seek people of faith and commitment whom you sense will act with faith, hope, and love—not fear, cynicism, and selfishness—in their leadership.
   - Avoid choosing people based upon conventional thoughts such as:
     - Let's get someone who will say yes.
     - Let's get someone who has experience.
     - Let's get someone I want, the pastor wants, or the leader of the nominating committee wants.
     - Let's get someone who has been serving on a committee.

2. *Choose leaders who you sense will be spiritual leaders for the church.* Church board leaders are called to be spiritual leaders of the church. The people you nominate should be people who are willing to struggle

with the process of listening to God's gentle calling for themselves and the church. They do not have to be perfect (who is?), but they are people who you believe take their faith seriously and will bring their faith into their service to the church.

3. *Give people time to sense whether this is or isn't a calling for them.* When you extend an offer to someone to become a board member:
   • Visit prospective leaders at home or in a private place where questions can be asked and answered in an unhurried environment.
   • Give prospective leaders the sheet explaining the position and expectations.
   • Explain to them why you sense that they may be good candidates for the position.
   • Give them time and encourage them to consider the position prayerfully. This process does take a commitment of time, but remember that the point is to get good people, not to hurriedly get warm bodies to fill the positions. It is better to operate shorthanded with a few excellent people than to operate with a full slate of less-qualified people.

4. *Try your best to avoid these pitfalls:*
   • Don't choose only people you know, but seek out also those you don't know. It is easy to keep choosing the same people again and again, but when we do this, we end up weakening the leadership base of the church.
   • Don't avoid choosing people who have served in the past. Often, certain people possess wisdom, faith, and skills that have been proved over time. Seek to balance diversity with consistency.
   • Don't choose only those people who are successful in the secular realm. Often people who are strong secular leaders have strong egos that inhibit their ability to seek God's will over their own. Faith, humility, and love for others are more important qualities. Still, you do need to assess whether people have the skills necessary to lead a committee.
   • Don't make serving on a committee a precondition for serving on the church board. When we impose such a requirement, we end up serving a custom, not God. Sometimes excellent people have not been asked to serve before. At the same time, don't ignore previous service on a committee.
   • Make sure that the people you nominate don't have an ax to grind. Sometimes people want to serve on the church board so that they

can move the church in a certain direction. It is important for leaders to have a vision, but when elders are more interested in serving their own causes rather than God, their personal drive becomes divisive. Make sure that the people you nominate are willing to ask what God wants first, and what they want second. People who are interested only in their own goals should be disqualified.

- Don't forget to pray, pray, and pray. Prayer is not just a ritual. When we pray, we are asking God to be present among us. So pray constantly that God will help you find the right people to lead this church and pray for it.

A Process for Nominating Committee Meetings
The focus of the agenda is to help members remain grounded in seeking and discerning God's will in calling candidates to the leadership positions of our church.

1. *Centering and prayer.* Begin the meeting with quiet centering for a minute, and then offer an opening prayer asking God to guide the committee.

2. *Grounding in God's Word.* Spend 15 minutes in Bible study to ground what you are doing in Scripture, and to open yourself to God's guidance in Scripture. Scripture should be chosen that is relevant to discerning God's will in prayer and faith. Suggested Scripture passages include Proverbs 3:5-8; 1 Corinthians 12:4-31; Ephesians 3:14-21; John 15:1-17; Ephesians 4:1-16; John 13:1-20; 2 Timothy 2:14-19; and James 4:1-10.

3. *Prayer discernment.* Take time in quiet prayer to gain a sense of whom God is calling to be leaders. Have members prayerfully focus for a time and then make a list of names. If the members don't sense much, encourage them just to spend the time in prayer asking God to lead them.

4. *Compare discernments.* Have members share their lists, and then begin to make a master list from their comments.

5. *Come to consensus.* Make sure that when you discern a candidate as suitable for a position, there is consensus among the members that this person is qualified. This step prevents one person from dominating the process and pushing a particular candidate. If there is division among nominating committee members about a candidate, there is a good chance that this person is not necessarily being called by God just now. If disagreement persists, then lead the committee back into prayer to ask God to cleanse members of their own agendas, so that they can be more open to God's will.

6. *Resist discouragement.* If the committee gets bogged down and has trouble getting people to say yes to a position, do not get discouraged or desperate. Such frustration can lead to seeking people just to fill a spot, instead of seeking God's will. When a time of confusion occurs, reground the committee in prayer and Scripture. Devote a whole meeting to prayer and Bible study, and then return to the process in the next meeting.

7. *Close in prayer.* Spend time praying for the work of the church and for God's continuing guidance.

Appendix K

Becoming an Elder at Calvin Presbyterian Church

We are grateful that you are considering the invitation to serve as an elder for Calvin Presbyterian Church. As you take time to make your decision, the following information may help you discern whether this is God's calling for you.

The Calling to Be an Elder

Being an elder is a calling. One of the convictions we take seriously at Calvin Presbyterian Church is that God cares deeply about what goes on in this congregation. The members of the nominating committee may ask you to serve as an elder, but it is really God who calls people to serve. The nominating committee members are merely acting as servants who try to sense God's call for the church. You have been asked to consider becoming an elder because the members of Calvin Church's nominating committee have sensed that God *may* be calling you. They have looked at your leadership abilities and skills, and they sense that you have made God central in your life. As a result, they believe that God may be calling you to serve as a leader of Calvin Presbyterian Church.

What Is an Elder?

Elders have been the church leaders since the earliest church was formed in Jerusalem on the Day of Pentecost. The following points may help you understand what an elder is:

- Elders are called to be spiritual leaders of the church, not political leaders. They are to "lead the congregation continually to discover what God is doing in the world and to plan for change, renewal, and reformation under the Word of God" (*Book of Order*, G-10.0102j).

- Elders' primary concern is trying to discern what God seeks for the church. They act as leaders by listening together for what God is calling all the members to do as a church, and then by creating opportunities to turn what they hear into action.
- Elders are expected to be people of faith, dedication, and good judgment who try to do their best to serve God.
- As the Presbyterian *Book of Order* states, "Together with the pastor, [elders] should encourage the people in the worship and service of God, equip and renew them for their tasks within the church and for their mission in the world, visit and comfort and care for the people, with special attention to the poor, the sick, the lonely, and those who are oppressed. . . . Those duties which all Christians are bound to perform by the law of love are especially incumbent upon elders because of their calling to office and are to be fulfilled by them as official responsibilities" (G-6.0304).

What Will Happen if I Say Yes?

If you agree to serve as an elder, you will become part of an important ministry in this church. You will serve a three-year term and in the process share in the administration of this church. That means serving on and possibly chairing a committee of the church. It means looking toward the future with other elders, and helping form a vision for Calvin Presbyterian Church. If you have more questions, please call Dr. Standish at the church office or talk to one of the present elders.

A Guide to Discerning Your Call

As you consider whether you are called by God to be an elder, the following guide may help you:

1. Take time in quiet prayer, away from others, to make your decision.
2. After quiet prayer, ask God whether you should serve as an elder.
3. Try to get a sense in your heart about what the answer may be. If you don't sense anything right away, don't worry. God will still be working to give you an answer.
4. Talk with your family members about their thoughts.
5. Look at your life and get a sense of whether you have the necessary time and personal commitment to the church to accept this important call.

6. Take several days to continue this process of asking in prayer what God's will is, listening to your heart, talking with your family, and assessing your life.

If it is God's will that you be an elder, you will discover three things happening:

1. You will get a sense in your heart that this is the "right" thing to do.
2. The idea of serving as an elder will make rational sense to you.
3. As you assess your life and talking with your family, everything will fall into place and make the way clear for you to serve as an elder.

Appendix L

A Guide to Holding Spiritually Grounded Meetings

One of the problems in making decisions as members of a church committee is that we often are not clear about the foundations of our decisions. For instance, do we just do what makes the most rational sense? Should we do something only if we think it can be achieved and implemented efficiently? Do we do something only if we have money on hand to pay for it? Do we stick with those proven ministries and efforts that have worked in the past?

The problem with all these questions is that they are founded upon common human concerns and ignore the greater spiritual concerns that are central to being a church community: What is Christ calling us to do?

What should the foundation of our decisions be? Scripture tells us that the wise person who hears Jesus builds a house on rock instead of sand (Matt. 7:24). While many of the concerns stated above are legitimate ones, they are still "sand," because they are not rooted in faith. When we make decisions in the church, we need to make them in the light of spiritual concerns. In short, our decisions need to be based more upon what we sense we are called to do, rather than on what we think is practical.

The spiritual focus of our decisions does not mean that we should ignore questions of practicality, efficiency, and finance, but these concerns should always be tempered by what we sense God wants us to do. For instance, if we feel genuinely called to some ministry or activity, then we should use our concerns about finances to help us create something that is financially responsible as well as spiritually faithful.

With these principles in mind, then, here is a guide to help your committee make decisions that are spiritually sound, as well as pragmatic and realistic. It will show you on how to be guided by God's Spirit in your work and ministry.

Spiritual Reflection

Spiritual reflection means using our hearts and intuition to determine whether something is what God wants for us. When we reflect spiritually, we ask whether or not God is guiding us in this or that particular direction. Spiritual reflection is like a thread that runs through all our other kinds of reflection. Here are five steps in reflecting spiritually:

1. *Always begin with prayer.* As you begin to talk about what makes sense, call upon God's Spirit to guide you, and *believe* that if you do this, God will lead you. For as Christ says, "Where two or three are gathered in my name, I am there among them" (Matt. 18:20). If you ask God to lead you, God will.

2. *Continually check your heart.* During discussions and as you come to conclusions, continually ask whether something feels spiritually "right." Ask whether this is something that we sense God does or does not want for us. Certain actions can make perfect sense, yet at the same time be wrong spiritually. Good decisions feel right spiritually.

3. *Continually take time for prayer and silence.* This is especially important if there is either continued confusion or disagreement. Often these two emerge when we become uncentered. By taking time to refocus on God through silence and prayer, our decisions will become more clear and focused. Trust in this knowledge.

4. *Try to reach a prayerful consensus.* While it is silly always to expect to reach unanimous agreement in all decisions, the best decisions are the ones that are so compelling spiritually that they make decisions easy. A seriously divided vote signifies either that the decision is not quite theologically and spiritually sound, or that some in the group are letting their egos get in the way and are not taking spiritual reflection seriously.

5. *Always bless your actions with prayer.* After making a decision, ask God to bless it, and believe that with this blessing, anything is possible. If you have seriously sought God's way and blessings, then your efforts will work. Have faith and trust.

Reflecting spiritually does not need to be formal. Instead, it should be as natural as possible. Do not be afraid to include spiritual reflection and prayer as part of your meetings. The more you pray, the better you will become at it.

A Suggested Format for Committee Meetings

One of the most important ways to make your meetings more spiritually alive is to structure your meetings around prayer. Like any new activity, grounding the meeting in prayer will be somewhat uncomfortable at first. With time, it will feel more natural. It will also help committee members become more accustomed to bringing prayer and reflection into all parts of their lives.

1. **Beginning the Meeting**

   Begin the meeting with 30 seconds of silence, and ask members to center their hearts upon God. Ask for a volunteer to monitor the meeting for anything that needs to be prayed about at the end of the meeting. Then the committee chair can say a prayer for the work that the committee is about to do and read a passage of Scripture.

2. **Sharing Time**

   Ask people at the committee meeting if they have anything that they would like to share with others about recent concerns or joys in their lives. Especially encourage people to share anything that could be prayed about as a group, such as illnesses, struggles, and difficulties in their or family's and friends' lives.

3. **Business**

   Discuss the business of the committee. As you conduct your business, keep two things in mind. If any matter comes up before the committee that is confusing or that you are uncertain about, take time then and there for silent prayer and reflection. Also, if any matter has caused disagreement, take time to pray about it in silence and together before voting. When taking a vote, instruct the group: "All who sense this may be God's will for us say yes. All who sense it may not be God's will for us say no."

4. **Prayer**

   At the meeting's end, clasp hands and form a circle. The chair begins, and when she is done, squeezes the hand of the person to the left. If that person wants to pray, he prays and then squeezes the next person's hand. If he doesn't want to pray, then he squeezes the next person's hand. This continues around the circle. The person who has been monitoring the committee for prayer should pray for the concerns of the committee.

   Close with the Lord's Prayer.

Appendix M

Four Principles of Discernment

Here are four simple principles to keep in mind whenever seeking to discern God's will as an individual or group.

1. Grounding in Scripture

Discernment always starts with Scripture. That doesn't mean that to discern, a person must immediately open the Bible and look for particular guidance. That works at times, but it isn't the best way. For effective and powerful discernment, it is best simply to become a person of Scripture. This means engaging in regular devotional reading of Scripture, becoming part of Bible studies, and listening to Scripture through sermons. Grounding our discernment in Scripture allows us to be formed by Scripture so that the words begin to guide us even when we are not aware of their influence.

2. Listening for Christ's Voice

God's voice is so much richer than ours, and God can speak to us through anything—a song, a poem, a leaf, a graduation ceremony, the lettering on a truck, the stray comment of a stranger—anything. Learn to become attuned to how God is speaking. At the same time, don't assume that everything you hear is from God. Be discriminating and somewhat skeptical. The true voice of God will resonate within. Your heart will leap at its sound.

3. Clarifying

Don't just assume because you have heard something that it has to be God's voice. Far too many false preachers, teachers, and prophets have been deceived by their own pride masquerading as God's voice. Have the humility to ask, "Is this really you, God?" Then talk with others, especially those who you believe are spiritually attuned. If God is speaking to you, they will sense it too. If the voice isn't God's, their doubts will help you go back and listen again. The important part of clarifying God's voice is recognizing that Christ is present and speaks to us throughout life, but that our egos, especially when they are immature and afraid of seeking Christ, can speak to us through a false voice that mimics Christ's voice. Discernment requires us to spend time clarifying, to whatever extent we can, whether the voice we hear is Christ's voice. If it is, then it will be affirmed by others who also are seeking to discern God's will.

4. Following in Faith

Following in faith is the thing that separates real ministry and mission from activities that are self serving. When we follow God in faith, we still have doubts, we still are a bit reluctant, we still have trepidations, but we act anyway. If Christ is really the one calling, something special will happen. The impossible will become possible—and sometimes the possible becomes impossible when our timing isn't God's. Generally, God will find a way to work through us to make what God wants happen. This is how God as Presence works. God as Purpose calls us to ministry and mission, and God as Presence makes it happen through us. To be a blessed church means acting in faith.

Appendix N

A Guide to Creating a Prayer Group

The purpose of prayer groups is to give members of the church the opportunity to engage in a ministry of prayer for the church, other members, specific concerns, and local and world events. These groups will further the mission of being a church that listens for and serves God in prayer. Prayer groups root the church in the purposes of the God the Creator, prepare the church for the presence of God in Jesus Christ, and open the church to the power and work of the Holy Spirit in the church.

How to Invite Others to Join
The best strategy for forming a prayer group is to identify eight to 10 members of the church who either already take prayer seriously in their lives or seem to have the potential to do so. (The latter may be people who do not have much experience in prayer but have expressed a desire to pray.) The more people initially invited, the larger the eventual group will be. Expect 20 to 40 percent of those invited to drop out of the group at some point. Invite them to a preliminary meeting to introduce them to the idea of a prayer group, explaining the process described below. Then invite them to make a six-week commitment to form a group and meet weekly at a designated time. Explain that you will ask them to assess whether they want to remain in the group at the end of the six-week period. During the assessment, invite those who want to remain to sign the covenant provided below and officially to become part of the prayer group.

Features of the Prayer Group
- Each group ideally consists of six to eight members. Whenever the group grows larger than this, the members should consider dividing it and creating a new group.

234

- Each group member should have a specific role and duty in the group (although this may mean that some share duties). Having a specific role or duty in the group encourages commitment to the group. The following are suggested roles and duties of the members, along with their responsibilities:

  - The *group coordinator* is responsible for opening the group and for ensuring that the group's agenda is followed.
  - The *assistant coordinator* helps the group coordinator and acts as coordinator whenever the leader is absent. Also, the assistant coordinator is responsible for offering prayers for special concerns that might arise. In addition, she or he would be responsible for dividing up the church directory, so that a certain number of members can be prayed for at each meeting.
  - The *church pray-er* would be aware of events in the church and offer prayers for the church, staff, committees, and special events.
  - The *concerns pray-er* would offer prayers for members and non-members who have special needs. These concerns would be gathered from Sunday bulletin prayer inserts and from people requesting prayer. The prayer group may need to set up a process for people in the church and community to request prayers, such as placing a prayer box somewhere in the church or a providing a contact link on the church's Web site.
  - The *local and world events pray-er* would keep abreast of events in the world and locally and offer prayers for these concerns.

These roles are all flexible, and each group can create and assign additional roles as seems appropriate. The pray-ers do not have to offer all the prayers for their particular area of concern, but can distribute them among the rest of the group. The group is confidential, and no personal matters prayed for in the group are to be discussed outside the group.

Particulars of the Prayer Group
- The group meets for an hour each week.
- The group follows a ten-week cycle (except during the initial six-week cycle).
- Every 10 weeks an invitation to new members is extended, either through the newsletter or through personal invitation, to those deemed by the prayer group as potential members.

- Two weeks after the beginning of a group, a covenant is drawn up. (A sample covenant is provided below.)
- A suggested agenda for the weekly meeting follows:
  - *Opening Prayer.* The coordinator opens with a short prayer, which might be the Lord's Prayer, another written prayer, or a personal, extemporaneous prayer.
  - *Sharing.* Members take time for sharing—10 or fewer minutes.
  - *Centering.* The assistant coordinator leads a one- to two-minute time of quiet centering, a time for members to let go of their concerns and to become more open to God's purpose, presence, and power.
  - *Offering of Prayer Concerns.* When the coordinator believes all are centered, she or he begins by offering a prayer for the group. Each member then offers prayers for his or her assigned area. Those who are not assigned a role, or who share a role and have not prayed, pray for whatever concerns they feel inspired by the Spirit to offer. Members also may offer prayers for any personal concerns brought up during the time of sharing.
  - *Closing.* When personal prayers are finished, members say the Lord's Prayer together.

Covenants

Every 10 weeks, members are encouraged to sign a covenant of commitment to the prayer group. Covenants should address the following issues:

- Who the members of the group are
- The group's purpose
- Where and when the group will meet
- Expectations of the members, such as:
  - Members should be committed to being at the group each week. When a member cannot attend, she or he should covenant to pray for the group and the concerns of the group at some point during the week.
  - All prayer concerns offered each week should be kept confidential.
  - The group should strive to avoid becoming a divisive agent in the church and seek to be a healing one. This aim is accomplished by focusing only on God and God's will in prayer. In other words, the members are not to pray against the ministries of particular staff people or members, against the work of

committees or board, or for a certain resolution other than what God wills regarding any issue.

* A sample covenant follows.

Prayer Group Covenant

A covenant is an agreement among people establishing a commitment between them and God. When we make a covenant with God and others, we trust that if we remain faithful to our part, God will be faithful to us and bless what we are doing. As members of this prayer group, we are committed to praying together once a week, trusting that God will listen and bless those for whom we pray.

> As for me, I am establishing my covenant with you and your descendants after you. This is the sign of the covenant that I make between me and you and every living creature that is with you, for all future generations: I have set my bow in the clouds, and it shall be a sign of the covenant between me and the earth.
>
> Genesis 9:9-13

Covenant

- We agree to be part of the Prayer Group.
- We agree to meet every _____ *(day)* from _____ to _____ *(times)*.
- We agree to make this activity a priority for our lives, and to do our best to put aside all other commitments during this time between the dates of _____ and _____.
- We agree to spend the time praying for:

  _____

  _____

  _____

- We agree to share and pray with each other; to be honest with one another; to keep the names of those for whom we pray and other matters discussed within the group confidential; to affirm each other and the church; and to refrain from criticizing the church, members, or others.
- We agree that the following people will have or share these specific roles:
  Group Coordinator: _____
  Assistant Coordinator: _____
  World and Local Events: _____
  Church Members: _____
  Church Committees and Events: _____
  Others: _____

  _____

  _____

- We agree to pray for each other throughout the week.

  Signed:

  _____   _____

  _____   _____

  _____   _____

Notes

Chapter 1, What Is a Blessed Church?

1. Christian A. Schwartz, *Natural Church Development: A Guide to Eight Essential Qualities of Healthy Churches* (St. Charles, Ill., Church SmartResources, 2000), 23.
2. Bill Easum, *Leadership on the Other Side: No Rules, Just Clues* (Nashville: Abingdon, 2000), 111.
3. Easum, *Leadership on the Other Side*, 113.
4. E. Stanley Ott, *Twelve Dynamic Shifts for Transforming Your Church* (Grand Rapids: Eerdmans, 2002) 14–22.
5. Rick Warren, *The Purpose-Driven Church: Growth without Compromising Your Message and Mission* (Grand Rapids: Zondervan, 1995), 16.
6. For a clearer understanding of the Trinity as Purpose, Presence, and Power, see N. Graham Standish, *Discovering the Narrow Path: A Guide to Spiritual Balance* (Louisville: Westminster John Knox, 2002), chapter 5.

Chapter 2, Setting a Spiritual Foundation

1. For more information on van Kaam's theories, especially as they relate to these four dimensions, see Adrian van Kaam, *Fundamental Formation: Formative Spirituality,* vol. I (New York: Crossroad Publishing, 1989); Ellen McCormack and N. Graham Standish, "Formative Spirituality: A Foundational and Integrative Approach to Spiritual Direction, Part I: Understanding the Individual," *Presence: The Journal of Spiritual Directors International,* vol. 7, no. 1 (Jan. 2001); 3–19; or Standish, *Discovering the Narrow Path,* chapter 3.
2. Danny E. Morris and Charles M. Olsen, *Discerning God's Will Together: A Spiritual Practice for the Church* (Bethesda: Alban Institute, 1997); Roy M. Oswald and Robert E. Friedrich, Jr.,

Discerning Your Congregation's Future: A Strategic and Spiritual Approach (Bethesda: Alban Institute, 1996).

Part II, Forming a Church of Purpose, Presence, and Power

1. See N. Graham Standish, *Paradoxes for Living: Cultivating Faith in Confusing Times* (Louisville: Westminster John Knox, 2000), 4.
2. If you would like to engage in a deeper discussion of God as Purpose, Presence, and Power, see Standish, *Discovering the Narrow Path*, chapter 4, where I explore the need to become more experiential, relational, and spiritual in our understanding of and approach to God as Trinity—as Purpose, Presence, and Power.

Chapter 3, Grounded in God's Purpose

1. Warren, *Purpose-Driven Church*, 86.
2. Easum, *Leadership on the Other Side*, 88.
3. Suzanne G. Farnham, Joseph P. Gill, R. Taylor McLean, and Susan Ward, *Listening Hearts: Discerning Call in Community* (Harrisburg, Pa.: Morehouse Publishing, 1991); and Oswald and Friedrich, *Discerning Your Congregation's Future.*
4. See "An Atmosphere of Discernment: Beyond Robert's Rules," in Kent Ira Groff, *The Soul of Tomorrow's Church* (Nashville: Upper Room Books, 2002), 73–82.
5. The difference between a context and a situation is that context has to do with particular geographical characteristics of the church, whether it is suburban or urban, high- or low- income, racially integrated or segmented; whereas situation has to do with more intangible factors such as prevailing conditions facing the church: Is it in transition or in a stable period? Has it had conflict or harmony? Has it had growth or decline?

Chapter 4, Alive to God's Presence

1. Neil Howe and William Strauss, *Millennials Rising: The Next Great Generation* (New York: Vintage Books, 2000), 236.
2. Thomas R. Kelly, *A Testament of Devotion* (San Francisco: HarperCollins, 1992), 54.
3. Kelly, *Testament of Devotion*, 56–57.
4. Ibid., 57.
5. Ben Campbell Johnson, *95 Theses for the Church: Finding Direction Today* (Decatur, Ga.: CTS Press, 1995), 28.

6. For a more thorough discussion of healing, see Standish, *Discovering the Narrow Path,* where I offer a much more detailed discussion.

7. Agnes Sanford, *The Healing Light* (New York: Ballantine Books, 1983); and John Wilkinson, *The Bible and Healing: A Medical and Theological Commentary* (Grand Rapids: Eerdmans, 1998).

8. Edwin H. Friedman, *Generation to Generation: Family Process in Church and Synagogue* (Guilford Press, 1985); and Edwin H. Friedman, "Family Process and Process Theology: Basic New Concepts," video (Washington, D.C.: Alban Institute, 1991).

Chapter 5, Open to God as Power

1. For a more detailed account of Müller's life, see Standish, *Discovering the Narrow Path.*

2. Warren, *Purpose-Driven Church,* chapter 1.

3. Eberhard Arnold, *God's Revolution: The Witness of Eberhard Arnold,* Hutterian Society of Brothers and John Howard Yoder, eds. (New York: Paulist Press, 1984), 56–57.

4. Arnold, *God's Revolution,* 57–58.

5. Rufus Jones, "Finding the Trail of Life," in *Quaker Spirituality: Selected Writings,* Douglas Steere, ed. (New York: Paulist Press, 1984), 266.

6. Walt Kallestad, *Turn Your Church Inside Out: Building a Community for Others* (Minneapolis: Augsburg Fortress, 2001), 51–52.

7. Kallestad, *Turn Your Church Inside Out,* 64–65.

Part III, Leading a Church to Blessedness

1. Henry T. Blackaby and Claude V. King, *Experiencing God: How to Live the Full Adventure of Knowing and Doing the Will of God* (Nashville: Broadman and Holman Publishers, 1994), x–xii.

2. Ibid., xii.

Chapter 6, Becoming a Blessed Leader

1. Annie Dillard, *Teaching a Stone to Talk: Expeditions and Encounters* (San Francisco: HarperPerennial, 1982), 36–38.

2. Henry and Richard Blackaby, *Spiritual Leadership: Moving People on to God's Agenda* (Nashville: Broadman and Holman, 2001), 20.

3. Ibid., 20–23.

4. Ibid., 128.

5. John Maxwell, *The 21 Irrefutable Laws of Leadership: Follow Them and People Will Follow You* (Nashville: Thomas Nelson, 1998), 89.

6. Blackaby and Blackaby, *Spiritual Leadership*,.134.

7. Ibid., 24.

8. Erwin Raphael McManus, *An Unstoppable Force: Daring to Become the Church God Had in Mind* (Loveland, Colo.: Group Publishing, 2001), 150.

9. For more on "appreciation," see Adrian van Kaam and Susan Annette Muto, *The Power of Appreciation: A New Approach to Personal and Relational Healing* (New York: Crossroad Publishing, 1993).

10. Steve Gottry, "The Church that Refused to Grow," Community Church of Joy Web site, *http://www.communityofjoy.org*, accessed September 2000.

11. Gottry, "The Church that Refused to Grow."

12. Corrie ten Boom with John and Elizabeth Sherrill, *The Hiding Place* (Carmel, N.Y.: Chosen Books, 1971), 237–238.

13. Evelyn Underhill, *Life as Prayer and Other Writings of Evelyn Underhill*, Lucy Menzies, ed. (Harrisburg, Pa.: Morehouse Publishing, 1991), 55.

14. Kallestad, *Turn Your Church Inside Out*, 69.

15. Richard Florida, *The Rise of the Creative Class: And How It's Transforming Work, Leisure, Community, and Everyday Life* (New York: Basic Books, 2002), 129–143.

16. Kelly, *Testament of Devotion*, 62.

Chapter 7, Leading the Blessed Church

1. Maxwell, *21 Irrefutable Laws of Leadership*, 147–149.

2. George Cladis, *Leading the Team-Based Church: How Pastors and Church Staffs Can Grow Together into a Powerful Fellowship of Leaders* (San Francisco: Jossey-Bass, 1999), 21.

3. Alan Briskin, *The Stirring of Soul in the Workplace* (San Francisco: Berrett-Koehler, 1998), 244–245.

4. Maxwell, *21 Irrefutable Laws of Leadership*, 183.